T0110336

PRAISE FOR

Grande

* EXPECTATIONS *

"A brisk narrative that seeks to answer the question of what really moves markets. Blumenthal deftly illuminates the psyches of investors. . . . Her fly-on-the-wall reporting brings [the stock market] to life." —*Condé Nast Portfolio*

"Stockland has rituals, if not an actual science, and Blumenthal proves to be an entertaining tour guide. . . . Skip four trips to Starbucks and invest in this book."

—*Advertising Age*

"A venti read . . . [Blumenthal] gives us a twofer with her informative, well-researched, and very readable book. She takes a look at the factors that move a blue-chip stock these days . . . while weaving in the fascinating history of a company that twenty years ago experts would have said couldn't exist."

—Forbes.com

"Chock-full of object lessons for anyone keen on growth-stock investing." —*Barrons*

"Introduces novices to [the world of the pros] and makes sense of it." —*USA Today*

A YEAR IN THE LIFE

Grande

★ EXPECTATIONS ★

OF STARBUCKS' STOCK

KAREN BLUMENTHAL

THREE RIVERS PRESS
NEW YORK

Published in the United States by Three Rivers Press,
an imprint of the Crown Publishing Group,
a division of Random House, Inc., New York.
www.crownpublishing.com

Three Rivers Press and the Tugboat design are registered
trademarks of Random House, Inc.

Originally published in hardcover in the United States in
slightly different form by Crown Business, an imprint
of the Crown Publishing Group, a division of Random House, Inc.,
New York, in 2007.

Library of Congress Cataloging-in-Publication Data
Blumenthal, Karen.
Grande expectations : a year in the life of Starbucks' stock /
Karen Blumenthal.—1st ed.
p.   cm.
Includes bibliographical references and index.
1. Stocks—United States.   2. Starbucks Coffee Company.
3. Corporations—Valuation—United States.   I. Title.
HG4910.B595   2007
332.63'22—dc22   2006034135

ISBN: 978-0-307-33972-0

DESIGN BY BARBARA STURMAN

First Paperback Edition

144782292

To Scott,

who exceeds all expectations

Contents

Preface

THE FIRST SEVERAL MONTHS of 2008 were tough ones for investors. The broader stock market ricocheted between rallies and 200-point slides as high oil prices and a credit crisis buffeted consumers and businesses alike.

Difficult as that time was, it was even worse for shareholders in Starbucks. After reaching an all-time high in 2006, the stock of long-time-market darling cratered as traffic at existing stores slowed and then fell for the first time. The company that keeps America caffeinated was now mired in the longest slump in its sixteen-year history as a publicly traded company.

It was ugly, no doubt about it. But these kinds of times, painful as they are, present wonderful opportunities for investors. Down-markets are the perfect time for reevaluation, for pruning the weeds and tending the flowers in your portfolio.

That's where this story comes in. Unlike so many other investing books, this book isn't about the benefits of mutual funds or another set of guidelines on how to diversify your portfolio; there are plenty of books already in those areas. Rather, this aims for a different target: how the game really works, who you're up against when you buy and sell, and who has what advantages and when.

That's why delving into a year in the life of a stock can be so valuable. By looking at the goings-on behind the scenes, tracking others as they make similar buy-and-sell bets, and watching how executives can manage expectations, you can see the whole playing field as the game evolves, much like sitting in the stands instead of watching on television.

Following anything for a specific time period is problematic. Before your printer ink is dry, something has already changed. In fact, by the time you read this, Starbucks may have turned the corner—or touched new lows. But even in the fast-moving stock market, recent history informs us. We study prior earnings to understand the potential for future ones. If we want to know whether a company will continue to grow, we must understand where its growth has come from so far. Stock prices change by the minute, but the tricks of the trade, the telling catch phrases, and the culture and practices underlying a company's shares are more constant. Just as in sports, the players and the prices change, but the essence of the game stays the same, continuing to offer insights into whether we buy, sell, or hold.

Consider the issues with Starbucks at this nadir. Throughout 2005, executives were pedaling hard to keep growth frothy, opening stores at a faster pace and ratcheting up the promise of future expansion. At the same time, the company was moving away from its core coffee business, adding breakfast and books to its stores and dabbling in music production and movies.

Now, investors must decide if the latest downturn is a function of a consumer pullback or if it's a sign that Starbucks has finally matured and reached the point where rapid growth is no longer likely. If it's the latter, it may be time to move on and find another faster-growing stock instead. All companies reach this point eventually—it's happened to Wal-Mart and Dell, Southwest Airlines and JetBlue, Chico's and Costco—and only a few, like Apple, truly find a new mission.

But what if consumer spending is the real culprit? If so, this downturn could be just another respite on the way to new highs. That means the lower price is an opportunity to hang on and maybe buy more. Long-time Starbucks investors have seen at least four other occasions when the stock has fallen as much as 50 percent before rebounding. If that's your hunch and you're right, you may benefit in ways the pros never will. Under pressure to perform each quarter and each year, most will dump a stock in a downturn and move one, potentially missing the turnaround.

If we're going to buy and sell individual stocks rather than simply investing in mutual funds, we have to accept that there aren't any simple answers. We have to do our research. We have to pay attention to our investments. And we have to understand how the game is played. Go for it—and good luck!

KAREN BLUMENTHAL
Dallas, Texas
June 2008

Introduction

FOR NEARLY TWENTY-FIVE YEARS, I've made my living as a financial journalist and yet the stock market continues to mystify me. One day seemingly good news can send a stock plunging; the next day bad news can send it climbing again. On any given day many stocks seem to move quite independently of any rational reasoning. (This revelation doesn't embarrass me as much as you might think. I've been married nearly the same amount of time and I don't really understand why my husband does certain things either.)

Of course such shortcomings don't keep any of us from trying to interpret the mysterious, from trying over and over to extract clues that will bring some order to the daily chaos. That's especially true with stock investing. We could plop all our savings into a basic stock-index fund and be done with it, or carefully pick the top-rated or best-known mutual funds as the safe-deposit box for our money. Instead many of us venture into this Oz-like place called Wall Street on our own, in our spare time, hoping we can somehow defy the odds and generate better returns than the broader market itself.

We do this knowing full well we would never challenge Tiger Woods to a golf game or the Williams sisters to a tennis match with a realistic expectation of winning; but somehow it seems okay to try to match wits with Wall Street professionals and all their technology, agility, and experience. After all most of them fail year after year to beat the market themselves. I've come to believe that our desire to invest on our own isn't driven so much by greed and hubris as by our need to control our own futures. So much rides on these purchases: Make a few really great choices and you can win a down payment on a new house, or maybe a college education for the kids. Make some rotten calls and you can watch your whole retirement vanish.

There is plenty of advice available about how we could go about this business on our own, from the classics of Benjamin Graham and Philip Fisher to the more modern gurus who shout at us from the magazine racks and the financial channels on cable TV. Many of them require a rigid commitment to a particular philosophy that reminds me of the many diets I've tried—they're interesting and exciting for a while but tough to stick with for the long run. Over time we lose our discipline and play hunches, like gambling on that new store where your teenage daughter shops or buying on tips from friends or family.

We plunge ahead, often acting on little more than instinct, even as so many of the rules of the stock-investing game have changed in the wake of the technology-stock boom of the late 1990s and the bust of the early 2000s. Companies have more restrictions on what they can say, and Wall Street has new rules to follow. Meanwhile powerful computer programs silently buy and sell millions of shares a day, sniffing out tiny patterns in stock prices in the hope that pennies per transaction will add up to substantial profits. Big securities firms are trading more heavily for their own accounts. And billions of dollars are flowing into hedge funds, unregulated investment funds for the very wealthy that are shaking up the market with aggressive trading strategies. All these factors create more formidable competition for little investors.

Instead of more advice and juicier tips, what we small investors needed, some colleagues suggested, was a different approach, an effort to demystify this mysterious Stockland. Maybe if we knew more about what to look for and what questions to ask—if we understood the importance of expectations, the impact of earnings, the influence of stock buybacks—we could make smarter decisions. That led to another idea: What if we tracked a well-known stock for a year, the same way a die-hard fan follows a football team? By looking at the stock through the eyes of those who owned it, admired it, touted it, traded it, or otherwise tried to make a living from it, certainly we could coax some of the market's secrets into the open. And if we uncovered guidelines to go by, rules of thumb that we could apply to our own specific philosophies, wouldn't that make us better investors?

It felt like a worthwhile mission. Then the question became, which stock?

Having covered a range of industries, I immediately started looking at retailers and restaurants, finding those businesses far more interesting and understandable than, say, a software maker or pharmaceutical company. But the first few stock charts were disappointingly dull. Then, remembering the small Starbucks store in the basement tunnel under my Dallas office building, I punched the stock symbol into the computer. The line that popped up on the screen stunned me. This was an investor's masterpiece, a consistently healthy, growing contributor to the American dream.

The long ride was impressive enough. Since going public in 1992, the stock had soared year after year, with only a couple of short breaks. Four stock splits had aided its rise, the last in 2001. Now at an age when many companies would be maturing and slowing down, it was still growing at a furious speed. And investor hopes were clearly sky-high: In late 2004 Starbucks had a market value in the neighborhood of $25 billion, more than four times its annual sales and about sixty times its earnings. Could it keep up the pace?

Beyond its stock-market prowess, Starbucks' story was a very human and very American success story, a company built on coffee, customer service, and intense loyalty. And like the stock market, Starbucks has become knitted into our culture. Just two decades ago, the lowly cup of coffee was barely a notch above tap water, something you expected to be widely available at airport terminals, auto repair shops, and night-time school meetings. Even if most of it was rot—weak, flavorless, and nearly see-through—it was cheap. Then Starbucks swept across the country and suddenly people from coast to coast were standing in line to plunk down up to $4 for a coffee-and-milk concoction served by a cheery barista in a green apron.

By 2005 some 35 million people a week visited Starbucks stores worldwide, many of them stopping by several times. Seduced by the taste of its dark-roasted coffee, a generation of discerning drinkers now shunned the freeze-dried and canned stuff in favor of carefully roasted beans, preferably freshly ground and recently brewed. An even younger crowd came to expect java steeped in milk, covered in foam, and sweetened or blended into a milk shake–like treat. While changing what we drink, Starbucks also changed where we go to meet friends or work on PTA projects and even how we talk. Just try asking for a medium coffee instead of a "grande."

The clincher for me though was its Nasdaq stock symbol: SBUX. By following that stock we could, to paraphrase the famous saying, follow the bucks. And that's exactly what we'll do for a year.

Starting in **January** we will meet buyers and sellers of Starbucks' shares as the company comes off a phenomenal year and get a sense of their expectations for the company and the stock and what clues might signal where the stock is headed.

In **February** we'll attend the annual shareholders meeting, the one time the company talks directly and publicly to all its shareholders, to begin to understand the various ways the company shapes investors' hopes and expectations.

Then in **March** we'll take a detour to understand the stock itself by tracing its history and its impact on the company, its founders and longtime holders.

From there we will move into **April** and the nitty-gritty of what makes a stock move and why, digging into where Starbucks' growth comes from and whether it is sustainable.

In **May** we will look at the significance of stock buybacks, which sometimes can be more for show than effect and can be an expensive gamble. But when buybacks are done for the right reasons, by companies that are otherwise sound, we'll see how they can make a difference to the stock in the long run.

We'll spend **June** looking at the multiple approaches of investors and how professionals assess stocks. Some focus only on the financial numbers, like the company's sales increases, earnings growth, and cash flow, while others study management, demographics, or global opportunities. But nearly all of them have a specific set of goals and stick with them.

In **July** we'll see how stock is traded and how that might impact your buying or selling.

We'll put Starbucks back under the microscope in **August** to see how its brand and reputation can create an economic moat that separates it from the pack and boosts its share price.

In **September** we'll see why the stock splits announced may be more meaningful than we thought, and in **October** how monthly sales reports feed the market's short-term neuroses while providing important clues to long-term investors.

In **November** we'll spend time with an analyst to watch how information moves from the company to investors and back, and where the professionals have advantages—and a few disadvantages.

In **December** we'll take a last, closer look at earnings and the effect of the earnings expectations game on the stock, and show how investors' additional research can help them make better choices.

Finally in **January** we'll see how a group of professionals and a group of amateurs assess their Starbucks holdings to answer that most vexing of questions: When should I sell?

When we're done, we'll have witnessed the quirks and some of the inner workings of Stockland, a fascinating place where a company's performance and investors' expectations continually criss and cross, creating investing opportunities. We'll see what drives stocks up and down, and how different people can make absolutely opposite bets and both still come out ahead. And we'll see how putting some extra effort into your portfolio and investing for the long term can, in fact, even out the odds for small investors. So let's go to the very beginning of 2005, where our first mystery is unfolding. After a terrific holiday season, Starbucks stock is falling. Why?

1

January

★ A NEW YEAR ★

There's a difference between a good company and a good stock

O n the first trading day of 2005, the stock of Starbucks Corporation took a breather. The price dropped more than $1, to $61.14, on about twice the usual volume of trading. For investors it was a chance to cash out some gains, especially since the turn of the calendar would keep the profits away from the tax man for another year.

The pause seemed like a well-deserved break following a glorious year for the company that taught America to love lattes. In 2004 more than 1,300 new stores were opened, keeping Starbucks near the top of the list of the nation's fastest growing retailers. The chain expanded in France, Spain, and even China, and its international business turned solidly profitable for the first time.

In the spring American consumers quaffed up a rich concoction first invented in London stores to celebrate Wimbledon, the Strawberries and Crème Frappuccino. A few months later the company's first-ever special drink for autumn, the Pumpkin Spice Latte, debuted to even more acclaim. In October an across-the-board 3 percent price increase on beverages, the company's first hike in four years, added to the top line. Then during November customers flocked back to enjoy the holiday lineup of Peppermint Mocha, Eggnog, and Gingerbread Lattes. Starbucks even seemed to have an unerring musical ear: The album of Ray Charles duets that it coproduced, *Genius Loves Company*, coincided with the Oscar-winning biographic movie and, unexpectedly, the singer's death. With the CD on prominent display on Starbucks counters, the chain sold hundreds of thousands of copies, helping the album go multiplatinum and become the singer's best-selling record of all time. *Genius Loves Company* would later win eight Grammy awards.

With everything clicking, Starbucks hit one financial home run after another. Sales went through the roof at stores open at least thirteen months, a key measure of retail success. While the company predicted that so-called same-store sales would grow 3 percent to 7 percent each month, give or take, the actual same-store sales growth began to jump in double digits: 12 percent in January, 13 percent in February, 12 percent in March, 11 percent in April, only retreating back to single digits in the slower months of August and September. By the end of the company's fiscal year on October 3, 2004, Starbucks' revenue had soared 30 percent, and earnings had rocketed up by 46 percent over the previous year. The year's profit, $389 million, or 95 cents a share, beat Starbucks' own early projections by 10 cents a share. It was, by all accounts, a remarkable performance.

The stock had climbed steadily all year, but in the last three months of 2004 it skyrocketed, propelled in part by a tepid stock market that suddenly turned hot after the November elections. Starbucks officials, recognizing the stock price might be overheating, tried to cool some of the fervor. In a press release announcing that overall November sales had jumped 26 percent and same-store sales had grown 13 percent, Howard Schultz, the company's chairman and chief global strategist, warned, "It is important to note, as we have said in the past, that comparable store sales growth of the extraordinary level achieved in November is not sustainable." Instead, he said, same-store sales of 3 percent to 7 percent were "the right level for longer-term expectations." The stock price climbed some more.

During the trading day on December 30, 2004, Starbucks briefly hit an all-time high above $64 a share, almost double where it started the year. After slipping a bit on December 31, it would end 2004 at $62.36, up a jaw-dropping 88 percent. By contrast the Standard & Poor's 500 Index rose a healthy, but far less robust, 9 percent. Both *The New York Times* and the *Financial Times* singled Starbucks out as a new economy stock market winner, putting it in the same crowd as technology gems Apple Computer, Google, Yahoo!, and eBay.

Those who hadn't owned the stock wished they had. John F. Jostrand, manager of William Blair & Company's Growth Fund, told his investors in his firm's annual report that the fund's stock picks had performed fairly well in the year. But the portfolio had lagged the S&P 500. One significant reason? The fund had declined to own Starbucks and eBay, giving it a "weak relative performance" compared with the broader index.

In other words, their success made the Blair fund look bad.

Though Sharon Zackfia, the research analyst at the Chicago brokerage firm, had recommended Starbucks as a "buy" all year, the fund managers didn't own it or eBay "due to their significantly high valuations."

Starbucks was in fact very pricey—and had been for virtually its entire public life. In the parlance of Wall Street, it was a hot growth stock. Unlike "value" stocks, which were attractive because they represented some kind of discount or bargain to their true value, growth stocks might carry a price way over and above any rational assessment. Value stocks were grounded in analysis, but growth stocks ultimately were a leap of faith, a belief that sales and profits would continue to grow and grow, and that investors would jump at the chance to pay princely sums for that expansion.

At the 2004 closing price, buyers of Starbucks stock clearly had grand expectations for their investment. They were paying more than $60 a share for a company that had recently earned less than $1 per share, a price-to-earnings ratio of roughly 65. By contrast, the typical stock was selling for about 20 times earnings per share. The price-to-earnings ratio was something like an SAT score for stocks, a number that let investors compare stock prices within industries and between them. That measure of relative price, as I would learn on this journey, could be a large part of the stock-purchase equation—or largely overlooked. Professional investors bought and sold for all kinds of reasons, and both the actual price and the price as it compared with others were just two of them. When new clients hire Voyageur Asset Management to manage their pension or retirement money, the fund managers buy the same portfolio that everyone else has, regardless of the price at the time—just like when you or

I buy into a mutual fund. So Voyageur was buying Starbucks for new clients even as the stock hit new highs.

In Akron, Ohio, Robert Stimpson, a portfolio manager for Oak Associates Funds, was busy assembling a brand-new mutual fund. After working for eight years as a financial analyst at Oak and other firms, he now had his own pool of money on which to build a reputation. For several months he had been sorting through technology names, financial services companies, and energy stocks for just the right mix for his Rock Oak Core Growth Fund, a diversified alternative to the well-established, much bigger White Oak Select Growth Fund, which focused on the volatile businesses of health care, technology, and financial services. Starbucks hit Stimpson's radar screen early and stayed there.

Tall, slim, and serious, Stimpson knew Starbucks was an expensive stock, but he was willing to pay a premium for consistent growth, partly because he was looking to own the stock for as long as three to five years. He liked Starbucks' potential to expand around the world and the appeal of its coffee to people young and old. He liked its aggressive store-opening plans, and he particularly liked its steady sales and profit growth, increases that were so year-in and year-out consistent, you could chart them with a ruler. Few companies that size were expanding so fast.

He saw the stock as a key part of his fledgling $10 million fund, but, he admitted, this high-priced diamond could languish in his portfolio, or worse, act as a drag on his whole fund just as he was pulling out of the gate. "I wish I had the opportunity to build the initial position at a lower price, but timing the market is very difficult on January 1," he said. Starbucks' price "scares me a little," he added, "which is why it's not a top five holding" in his portfolio. On January 3, the year's first trading day, he bought 900 shares of Starbucks stock at $61.07. Over the next few days, he added 1,200 more shares at prices between $60 and $60.32. It quickly became one of his ten largest holdings.

By contrast Don Hodges, working from a historic mansion converted into a comfortable office near downtown Dallas, looked at Starbucks' price in the new year and had a different reaction. The seventy-year-old money manager had made a good living investing for several hundred clients, but one of his favorite ventures, a small mutual fund he ran with his son, hadn't won the kind of investor attention he thought it deserved, despite some impressive returns.

Slowly that was beginning to change. The previous spring *Fortune* magazine had asked him for a stock pick. He recommended Starbucks, one of the better-known stocks in his eclectic mutual fund portfolio, which included companies of all sizes and industries. Hodges had watched the stock and felt like its strong sales and fast growth would send it upward. When Starbucks did climb, the Hodges Fund got a nice jolt—and a second nice mention from *Fortune*. By year end the fund was ranked first on several lists of top-performing funds in its category. Now those top-of-the-charts rankings were bringing in new investors.

To keep them Hodges needed more winners like Starbucks. But did he still need Starbucks?

Hodges, whose soft-spoken, slow-talking style was more undertaker than Wall Street whiz, began to wonder. From his vantage point, Starbucks was looking pretty overpriced. If that were true, the racehorse in his portfolio could quickly become the mule, underscoring that old Wall Street adage that there's a big difference between a good company and a good stock. On January 5 he dumped 10,000 of his fund's

40,000 shares at $61.02 a share. "I still think Starbucks is probably one of the outstanding companies in America. They seem to have done everything right," he said not long after his sale. In fact, two or three years from now, with thousands more stores open, the stock "more than likely is going to be higher than it is now," he said. But that might not be the case this year.

His hunch paid off. That afternoon after regular trading ended, Starbucks said that its revenue for the crucial month of December, the biggest sales month of the calendar year, had climbed 22 percent from the year before. More impressive, same-store sales had jumped 8 percent from the previous year. Customers clearly still craved Starbucks' coffee, its gift cards, its mugs, and all the goodies that went with them.

It was great news. But it wasn't what Wall Street expected to hear. Investors had come to expect more caffeine-laced results to justify that overheated stock price. The analysts who tracked the stock had predicted same-store sales would be 9 to 11 percent higher than a year ago. The actual number wasn't just a cooldown; it was a letdown.

The next day in heavy trading on the Nasdaq Stock Exchange, the company's shares slid 3 percent, falling nearly $2, to $59.74. The next day the share price dropped again. The next trading day, January 10, Don Hodges sold another 5,000 shares at $58.75—and Robert Stimpson picked up 1,300 for his new fund at a similar price, $58.67. But sellers outnumbered buyers and the stock lost another 3 percent in value, tumbling like a toy clunking down a staircase. In fact every day for a week the stock fell, until it had dropped 10 percent of its value, or about $2.5 billion of shareholders' wealth.

Less than two weeks into January, the stock that every portfolio wanted to boast about in late December was a stock that many could do without. Fundamentally nothing had changed. The company continued to open its predicted number of stores, customers stood in line morning after morning, and billboards and in-store posters touted a new product, a rich drinking chocolate called Chantico, an elixir intended to bolster afternoon and evening sales.

On January 26 the company reported record first quarter profits for the quarter ended January 2 and raised its estimates for its fiscal 2005 net income, telling investors it now expected to earn $1.15 to $1.17 a share, up two to three cents a share from its previous projection. That should have been a pick-me-up, but Wall Street again was disappointed. Stock analysts at some of the big brokerage houses already were projecting year-end earnings in the new range. And they heard a cautionary tone in the company's comments on an earnings conference call with big investors: Between the lines, Starbucks' executives were saying the breathless double-digit same-store sales growth of 2004 was over. At least for the time being the sales growth in existing stores would be in the range of 3 percent to 7 percent, solid—impressive even—but not the superstar levels of a few months before. The next day the sinking whoosh coming from the stock was the sound of air escaping from investors' inflated expectations—and the deflating of the price-to-earnings ratio. The shares dropped $2 more, to close at $53.03. They would rebound only slightly in the last couple of trading days in the month.

Beyond the company's comments there had been just one key clue that the stock might be headed for an adjustment—had investors been watching closely. Academics had long noticed that buying and selling by insiders—that is, executives and directors—can be a signal about where the stock price might be headed. Howard Schultz, the energetic company leader who knew Starbucks better than anyone, exercised some stock options every year, but he tended to sell mostly when the price was up. In October both he and Orin Smith, then the chief executive officer, exercised stock options and sold the shares when the price was in the low $50s. Smith, who had announced his planned retirement in March, reaped a $59 million profit, while Schultz made a little more than $10 million.

But in the last ten days of the year, as the stock price moved from $59 into the $60s, Schultz stepped up his selling. He exercised options and then sold close to 500,000 Starbucks shares, giving him a late December profit of more than $26 million. When the required disclosures were made with the Securities and Exchange Commission in the week between Christmas and New Year's, hardly anyone noticed.

Months later in an interview, Schultz acknowledged that there had been "an artificial rise" in the stock price at the end of 2004. But had the stock ever been overvalued? "No," he said emphatically. "The stock is undervalued. I've said that since we've been public."

In another interview he shrugged off the timing of his sales. "I don't remember that," he said, when asked about the transactions. "How much did I sell?"

When reminded he added that he and his wife meet with advisers who make estate-planning recommendations, often resulting in year-end sales. His last previous sale before October 2004, however, had been in summer 2003. And in previous years he had sold stock in February, March, and June, as well as December.

"I gotta tell you," he added, "if we caught the high, we were fortunate."

Fortunate, indeed. But it takes far more than luck to build a multibillion-dollar business—and a personal fortune—by putting high-priced cups of coffee into millions of hands a week. It takes audacious ambitions, a crystal-clear focus, a willing public—and a popular publicly traded stock.

2

February

★ THE ANNUAL MEETING ★

"You get the shareholders you deserve." — Warren Buffett

T he year's rough start left some investors and analysts skittish, and the news in early February didn't help. After the close of regular stock trading on February 2, Starbucks reported that January sales at stores open at least a year grew 7 percent—exactly the growth it had predicted. But analysts and big investors were still looking for friskier results for comparable store sales, sometimes called "comps," revved up by Christmas gift cards. Once again they were disappointed.

The next day Mark Kalinowski, an analyst with Smith Barney, changed his recommendation on the stock to "hold" from buy, telling clients that new traffic to the stores was slowing and operating profits were flat despite the price increase. In a research note, he sheepishly acknowledged that he probably should have recognized that the run-up in the price at the end of the year came from a tactic known as "windowdressing": Some mutual funds managers wanted their investors to think they were clever enough to own the best stocks of the year, so they scrambled to buy Starbucks shares as the year came to a close, knowing the stock would show up in published lists of their year-end holdings. As soon as the calendar turned, however, they would dump the shares in favor of more promising prospects.

"In hindsight, we should have downgraded the stock entering calendar 2005, ahead of the 'portfolio windowdressing' effect that hampered the stock in January," Kalinowski wrote, noting that it wasn't too late for investors to back off.

Already in a nervous state before the one-two punch of a disappointing sales increase and an analyst downgrade, the stock plummeted on February 3, a day when the broader stock market was mostly flat. More than 16 million Starbucks shares were traded, about 4 percent of all the company's stock. The price plunged $4.43, to close at $49.57, a one-day loss of 8 percent that would turn out to be the company's single worst day of the year.

In barely four weeks, more than $5 billion in stockholder value had evaporated. Though Starbucks' same-store sales were growing at nearly twice the average of fast-food restaurants, suddenly some investors and stock analysts were beginning to wring their hands. Was the slowdown in sales growth from 2004's wicked pace a sign that fewer new customers were coming in the door? Were there simply too many stores chasing customer dollars? Was the autumn price increase the main engine now keeping sales climbing at existing stores? After growing so fast for so long, was Starbucks finally facing a growth stock's most fearsome foe, saturation?

In the dance of expectations between a company and Wall Street, a mutual rhythm can be hard to maintain. Companies make predictions and promises and then try to at least match them over quarters and years. But the folks on Wall Street are buying and selling every working hour of the day. They want to know not just what has recently happened, but what will happen next, vacillating regularly between hope and fear over the outcome. Right now fear appeared to be winning.

But Starbucks would have its say soon. The company's annual shareholders meeting, the one time during the year when all shareholders have a chance to hear the company's viewpoint, was coming up. Here was the company's opportunity to deliver its best sales pitch for its shares, uninterrupted and unfettered by any faraway analysis. And like almost everything else at America's most popular coffee purveyor, the meeting was to be a slick, well-organized, and highly polished affair, something akin to a Las Vegas show served up with a venti-size cup of love.

To hear Starbucks' point of view and see what actual shareholders thought, I traveled to Seattle for the February 9 meeting and arrived at the city's opera hall well before the 10 A.M. curtain. On the chilly plaza outside, Starbucks employees in their signature green aprons cheerfully welcomed arrivals. Inside servers handed out free lattes and samples of the new Chantico. Guests helped themselves to an array of scones, breakfast rolls, and muffins piled high on long tables. In an overflow hall, shareholders posed for photos with a cutout of the charismatic Howard Schultz.

A team of Starbucks staffers had planned this $300,000 gala for months, deciding what entertainment should be featured, which of the company's accomplishments should be highlighted, and settling on a special theme—this year the coffee tree, with roots in the company's coffee heritage, the trunk reflecting the core relationship with employees and customers and the branches representing innovation. Then about 175 pounds of coffee, 600 gallons of milk, juices, and more than 10,000 pastries had to be ordered.

Three days before the event, eighteen-wheelers rolled into Seattle Center to deliver audio equipment and huge screens so that all the action on the stage could be broadcast, rock-concert style. Trucks also brought in four palettes of coffee beans, tea, CDs, and other goodies for five thousand take-home thank-you bags.

All this was for a tradition as old as the existence of corporations themselves. Ever since the first company charters were issued by national governments, company stockholders have gathered regularly to check on their investments and quiz managers about the company's business. In the seventeenth century, British courts found that a shareholder's right to elect directors and vote on company matters was so precious that by law, the responsibility could not be transferred to someone else. The shareholder was obligated to show up, to give advice and to vote.

The same principles took hold in America, and as early as 1797 shareholders of a Baltimore insurance company protested the president's $2,500 a year salary as exorbitant, especially because the company's prospects were "dark and gloomy." In their regular duty to elect directors, stockholders in the 1800s sometimes ousted the whole board and replaced it with newcomers. But as companies grew in the late 1800s and early 1900s, so did the number of owners, from dozens to hundreds to many thousands. When the numbers got so large that attendance at meetings was unrealistic, states gave shareholders permission to turn over their voting rights to others. By the 1920s professional managers, not owners, were often in charge, and the little investor fell further and further away from how the company was run.

The once feisty annual meeting became, for the most part, a lifeless proceeding. There were exceptions: Environmental and political activists, knowing that corporate chiefs would have to pay attention, came to see the public gatherings as a prime place to stage a protest or take the microphone during the question-and-answer sessions at the end of the meeting. When a takeover loomed or company officials engaged in particularly scurrilous behavior, dedicated shareholders might show up to complain. But for the most part, the annual shareholders meetings of the late twentieth and early twenty-first centuries were short and deadly dull, with stiff executives delivering PowerPoint reviews of the company's results and then quickly calling for votes on company directors and the auditing firm.

By contrast Starbucks' gathering was a celebration not just of coffee and a popular store, but of an investment with a spectacular record. After the company went public in 1992, its most loyal local investors had come together annually at its roasting plant in Seattle, mostly to hear Schultz share his vision and ambitions for bringing good coffee to the United States and then the world. As the company grew, though, new and special features were added to the annual meeting—a little theater, personal testimonials, and a Schultz favorite, the "popular culture" video featuring snippets of Starbucks jokes and stories from the likes of Jay Leno, Oprah Winfrey, Regis Philbin, and David Letterman.

The meeting reached a crescendo in 2004 when Starbucks filled the city's 2,900-seat opera hall. Shareholders were treated to videos, acrobats, and unicycles, and a personal story from one of the company's longtime roasters.

Kathy Berd, a Seattle potter, shareholder, and investment-club member, thought that was fun enough. But then the company introduced a new CD of favorite songs chosen by the singer Emmylou Harris as part of its plans to sell more music in its stores. The executive making the announcement told the crowd, "the only thing better than this would be if Emmylou were here," Ms. Berd remembered.

Then to the crowd's surprise, Emmylou Harris came out to perform, singing "Red Dirt Girl" and John Lennon's "Imagine."

"I'm thinking, *no way!*" Ms. Berd said. "It was pretty cool."

Given last year's highlights, the company planned on more than 5,200 attendees for 2005. But Starbucks, worried that it couldn't accommodate everyone who wanted to come, required stockholders to reserve their seats through Ticketmaster, limiting tickets to two per shareholder. Unfortunately the mailings carrying the information arrived over several days, and by the time some investors got the instructions, all the tickets were gone, leaving a number of those who were left out as hot as steamed lattes.

Inside the hall I mingled with an array of shareholders—retired Boeing employees, farmers, young couples, old couples, and stay-at-home moms. They came mostly from Seattle, but also from all over Washington State, California, and Oregon and points farther away.

One happy ticketholder was Theresa Collier, a self-taught investor who owned Starbucks shares herself and in her two sons' education accounts. Ms. Collier, who sold children's books in schools and people's homes and worked as a seasonal tax preparer, relied on an investment philosophy that could have come from a children's fantasy novel, based as it was on "moats" and "stars." Using Morningstar.com's ratings, she looked for companies with a "wide moat," or a strong competitive advantage. And she considered buying when Morningstar gave those "wide moat" stocks its highest five-star rating, meaning it believed they were significantly undervalued. Using that theory she had done well with shares of Citigroup and Johnson & Johnson, two dividend-paying stocks that brought in a little extra income to supplement her part-time work.

But Starbucks' stock didn't pay a dividend. And even at its current downtrodden price, the stock was still a Godiva-like investment in an M&M world. So how did Morningstar rate it?

It got one star, she admitted. "They think it's a great company—it's just overvalued." But she stuck with it, in part because she liked its management and its rapid growth.

Soaking up the passion of these stockholders, I started to chat with a store manager in the overflow auditorium. Suddenly I was busted. A Starbucks media relations team member, wearing a headset and microphone, spotted me interviewing, an apparent no-no. I was in midsentence when she broke in and cut me off. "I understand you're a reporter," she said, looking more like the Secret Service than my Starbucks friend.

Yes, true, I told her, but I'm in the middle of a conversation. "May I finish, please?"

"No," she told me, "You have to stop." The store manager, turning pale, quickly backed away. I tried to hand him a business card as the Starbucks Secret Service kicked into action. She shouted into her microphone, "I need media relations! Media relations, are you there?" People nearby moved away. There was no truce to negotiate.

The friendly chitchat ruined, I walked out of the hall, worried that security might usher me away for interviewing without permission. Every facet of the event was carefully orchestrated. Reporters who checked in properly were assigned an escort and whisked to a media room deep in the bowels of the opera hall. Later they were seated in boxes in the upper levels, luxurious for sure, but also miles away from shareholders, directors, or executives who might have insights to offer.

I took up a new post in the freezing parking garage—but this was no romantic Deep Throat rendezvous. The arriving shareholders were cold and in a hurry to get to the free coffee. Most were long-term investors who simply shrugged off the recent price decline as something that stocks do. A couple from Spokane had owned their shares ten years. A mother-daughter pair had been in since the initial offering in 1992, and a gentleman whose business card read "Clairvoyant and Spiritual Counselor" had purchased shares after the second stock split because he had a good feeling about it.

Soon, though, it was clear that a significant group was missing: the real company owners. Individual shareholders held about 30 percent of the stock, a high percentage for such a well-known name. But 70 percent were owned by institutions like Capital Research and Management Company, which runs the giant American Funds; money managers like TCW of Los Angeles, which takes care of more than $100 billion of other people's money, and Voyageur Asset Management. These were the buyers and sellers who could make the stock price hop with a sale or purchase of several million shares. But no one from those firms made the pilgrimage. Neither did Robert Stimpson, the shepherd of a new fund.

The pros, it turned out, had had their own meeting at

Starbucks headquarters back in October, two days of intense, fact-heavy presentations full of details about store sales, growth patterns, international plans, and marketing approaches. As the largest owners, they could command one-on one meetings alone with top management, who traveled several times a year to visit big investors in their own offices. When the big guys had questions, they could directly phone a top official, instead of stopping with the junior employees who answered the investor-relations office telephones. And while they got a few freebies, mostly they walked away with armloads of stats for their computer models and insights available only by Webcast to the hardy souls who had the patience (and computer hookups) to listen.

The analyst conference is really about "a lot of information," explained Peter Tremblay, the Starbucks director of public affairs who coordinated the annual meeting shindig at the Seattle Center. "The shareholders' meeting has a lot more passion and emotion."

Or, as Howard Schultz put it, "The meeting has really become a brand-building tool."

In other words Starbucks' gathering of the little guys was a revival for the faithful, the loyal, long-term shareholders who didn't need a spreadsheet to believe. They believed in Starbucks and its ability to brew profits that would, in turn, brew a stock destined to grow and grow and grow and grow. They believed in the power of the stock market to send their kids to college, provide for their retirement, or maybe even to make them rich. Never mind that they were amateurs, and that investing in individual stocks day in and day out could sometimes be as risky as betting on the ponies at the track. Despite the meltdown of Enron, frauds at WorldCom and HealthSouth, and the crash of both the Dow Jones Industrial

Average and the Nasdaq Stock Market in 2000, nearly half of all U.S. households owned a stake in public companies in 2004, either directly or through mutual funds, up from just 40 percent in 1995. For them—and for most Americans— the stock market was now as much a part of their daily life as fast food, religion, and coffee.

As the shareholders settled into their seats at 10 A.M. and the music from the Pike Place Market Singers ended, it was clear that the ticket scheme hadn't worked quite as planned. Empty seats stuck out like the missing teeth in a little kid's mouth. But those who were there came to hear the gospel, and Starbucks wasn't about to disappoint them.

Actors opened the meeting with a reenactment of the morning rush at a Starbucks store, and after introducing company directors, Schultz reminded the crowd how far Starbucks had come from when he joined the company in 1982. Back then, he said, "There were four retail stores in Seattle and the big dream at the time, candidly, was one day maybe we would open up in Portland, Oregon—and that was a stretch."

By the time the company went public in 1992, there were 125 stores. "And here we are today," Schultz said, launching into his salesman's patter, "and looking back, it's a stunning accomplishment, the growth, the development of the company with 9,000 stores in 35 countries, the equity of the brand being at an all-time high in terms of its respect, not only in the United States, but around the world."

In the two hours that followed, Starbucks executives delivered the feel-good message the shareholders had hoped for. Schultz highlighted the contributions of Courtney, a disabled worker in a Seattle store who can't hear or speak "but she has the heart of a lion" and thanked Courtney's parents for bringing their daughter "to the Starbucks family." Herbie Hancock, who was producing a CD to be sold in Starbucks stores in the fall, made a surprise appearance (for free) to play a piano solo, "My Funny Valentine."

In the "popular culture" video, Regis Philbin got laughs when he poked fun at the company's "bewildering" menu, noting, "You don't see the word coffee anywhere." *Jeopardy!* offered a whole category on the coffee company. And Jerry Seinfeld riffed on a late-night talk show, saying, "People seem to feel when they have a cup of coffee that they've opened a small business or something. They pull out laptops and Palm Pilots," he said, "and try to look like they've got quite a bit going on, you know, with their half-caf moka-choka ya-ya."

Then, with the company's longtime president and chief executive Orin Smith retiring in March, there were special good-byes to say. Smith reminisced about the company's phenomenal growth to a $5.3 billion company from a $100 million enterprise in 1992. Sure, he said, the company's growth rate had slowed from 60 percent a year in the early days to a mere 20 percent or so now. But, he added, "it had to do that, or you literally would have to make room in your homes for another Starbucks."

Perhaps aiming his message at current skeptics, he told the assembled that all along, doubters questioned how much the company could expand. "When we went on that road show in 1992," he remembered, "most of the people we talked to didn't think we could have 500 stores. If we had told them that we would have 9,000 stores in 12 years, they would have locked us up." In opening stores, he added, Starbucks had done more than dot the landscape with green-and-white signs. "We've changed the way customers live their lives," he said, "how they start their day, where they meet, and even how often, how they reward themselves and oftentimes how they feel."

He finished the review with a familiar refrain, the kind of bottomless optimism that long-term shareholders love to hear. "We are still in the early chapters of the Starbucks story," he told the crowd. "For those of you who have come here every year for the last twelve years, you've heard that every time. So, you must be thinking, either these guys need a remedial reading course or this is a very long book. And I'm glad to say it is a very long book."

Finally he turned to Schultz. "Howard, it's come to this," he said, clearing his throat to push back the welling emotions. "I just want to thank you and let you know how much you've mattered to me, how much all those times meant, the joy and the laughter, the tears. Thank you so much."

After highlighting Smith's contributions and support, Schultz had the audience pulling out hankies again. "I didn't rehearse this part," Schultz told the crowd, his voice breaking. "I don't know how best to say this, other than to say I love Orin Smith."

Shareholders dabbed their eyes. "The only thing missing," the *Seattle Times* wrote later, "was Oprah."

The stock got its share of adulation too. The audience gasped when executives, using charts on the huge video screen, reminded shareholders that Starbucks' shares had soared nearly 5,000 percent between the company's public offering and the end of 2004, far, far more than the Standard & Poor's 500 Index or the Dow Jones Industrial Average or the overall Nasdaq stock index. A $10,000 investment on that June day would, after four stock splits, be worth $480,000 now—a performance of Microsoftian proportions.

That the stock—that soaring symbol of the company's

astonishing success, the one thing that had brought all these people together—was in a rare slump was almost unspoken amid the celebration at the annual meeting. To the smaller long-term investors here, the more than 20 percent drop was just one of those market corrections, a pause to let others catch up before Starbucks rejoined the race. In fact some investors had come to the meeting hoping to hear that the company would announce its fifth stock split now that the price had climbed over the $50 mark, around where it had split in the past.

Schultz didn't offer up that prize. But he did briefly acknowledge "the dip in the stock" in recent days. "I was told not to say that," he told the audience, as if to apologize for his indiscretion in commenting on the current stock price to the stock's owners. "But it's really bugged me that the stock would go down on 7 percent comps." He paused for a punch line. "I know the lawyers are freaking out right now." The audience laughed, and he moved on.

By the time executives got to the real business of the day, electing directors and the auditor and approving a new employee stock-option plan, the meeting had stretched beyond two hours and the opera hall resembled an arena in the last three minutes of a lopsided basketball game. The last piece of business, shareholders' one chance to voice concerns or ask questions, brought only two people to the microphones. One woman asked for more women in the topmost ranks of management. And then a deaf shareholder, signing his question, finally brooked the unpleasant issue. "I had noticed in the last week or so," a translator said, "that the stock has declined and I'm wondering if you can comment about that."

"I'd love to," Schultz answered, almost before the translator had finished.

It was an overachiever's curse, he explained. "Despite the fact that we consistently try and provide guidance of 3 to 7 percent, when we overachieve so often, many people don't listen," he said. Then when the company simply meets its predictions, "people believe that we perhaps have disappointed." Despite the stock-price drop, he said, "we're quite certain that long-term value for our shareholders will be significantly increased if, in fact, we maintain our commitment to the things that we talked about today."

With no other questions, the meeting adjourned. Shareholders filed out to grab a last free drink and to pick up a goodie bag (or two) stuffed with Tazo tea, coffee beans, a CD, and a Borders gift card, in honor of the new agreement for the company's Seattle's Best Coffee brand to run the bookstores' cafés.

For the investors who might have been a tad worried about the stock, the message was right on point. The company would continue to soar; the stock was merely in a lull before its next rise.

The reporters who covered the meeting didn't exactly see it that way. Some saw the company's chairman and chief global strategist trying to talk the stock back up. Within a few hours the Associated Press reported that Schultz "lashed out" at investors for driving the price down. The Dow Jones News Service said he complained about Wall Street. The next day the *Seattle Post-Intelligencer* began its story by noting that the audience laughed when Schultz "lambasted the inflated analyst expectations that depressed the company's stock value."

Schultz, interviewed later, said his comments had been blown out of proportion: "As an outsider looking in, I'd say if not 100 percent of the time, then 90 percent of the time, the media always sees the glass as half-empty." Analysts, he added, had the same affliction. His job wasn't to worry about what Wall Street was fretting about. Rather, he said, "at the end of the day, the only thing that matters is whether or not wo execute." He didn't need to talk up the stock. If the company grew as it should—and promised it would—"the stock is going to take care of itself," he said. "It sounds so trite— but it's true."

3

March

★ THE STOCK ★

Printing paper money

ith Starbucks' stock well established now, Schultz could downplay his role in the current price. But the stock itself and the enormous wealth it had created wouldn't exist had Schultz not been the stock's most determined and enthusiastic salesman in the early years of his company's life.

Following the annual meeting, I took a detour to learn more about the history of the stock. The shares had, for the most part, settled into a narrow zone, trading between $49 and the low $50s. After the company reported that in February 2005 same store-sales increased a stronger-than-expected 9 percent, the stock briefly climbed to $55 in early March, but then slid back down. The price still seemed rich, and the month's big promotion for caramel, with Caramel Macchiatos and three kinds of Caramel Frappuccinos featured on store blackboards and posters, couldn't generate much excitement. This seemed like a good time to take a look back.

In their most basic form, stock sales finance a company, allowing entrepreneurs to expand much faster than they could from their own resources and giving a fledgling enterprise far more flexibility than debt would allow. If we knew more about the genesis of Starbucks' stock, I reasoned, including how it grew, how it built such a passionate and loyal following, and how it won broad public support, then we would see not just how the stock market works, but why it works as well.

As it turned out the shares that won over the hearts and brains of so many loyal investors were first delivered in 1985 on the dining table of a Seattle osteopath. Ronald Margolis liked to dabble in small start-up companies on the side. He made a good living in a gynecological practice. But as a fairly active investor, he had made a lot of money playing the options market and trading municipal bonds he thought were "misvalued."

Margolis didn't know Howard Schultz, but their wives knew each other. And when Schultz's wife, Sheri, told Margolis' wife, Carol, that her husband was looking for investors in a new business, Carol suggested that the two men talk. At the time Schultz was itching to go out on his own and looking for seed money, the first real investment in his dream. A salesman by trade he had spent the last three years as the marketing director at a small Seattle institution called Starbucks Coffee Company.

Starbucks sold fresh roasted coffee beans, but Schultz saw far more possibilities there. He wanted to open his own coffee bars serving Italian-style espresso and other drinks brewed from Starbucks' beans. He wasn't after one experi-

mental store. He saw a whole chain of coffee sellers, starting
with four to eight right off the bat.

Schultz brought a carefully crafted business plan to their
meeting, but Margolis waved it off. The doctor said he just
wanted to hear the thirty-two-year-old's vision for this new
company. "Everybody has a business plan to show and everybody has projections to show you," Margolis said. "You can
look at all those things but you have to understand that
they're just projections. They're not real."

Instead, he said, he looked for something far more intangible, the potential of the person sitting across from him.
"The real questions are," he said, "are you dealing with an
honest person and do they have enough energy and ambition
to continue? And the next thing—will their ego allow them to
hire the right people?" The young man sitting at his table
brimmed with enthusiasm about Starbucks' coffee. He was
absolutely insistent people would line up to buy his fancy
drinks, even if they had never even heard of espresso before.
And he was dead certain that he was on to a truly big idea.
But even given that, why would Margolis hand over his own
money for this?

"He was risking everything to start this company," Margolis said. "It looked like he had the energy and the ambition to
do it—and I took a chance."

Margolis asked Schultz how much he needed, and on the
spot wrote a check for $100,000. With that he became the
first stockholder in a radical new venture, owning more than
100,000 shares in a coffee dream, priced at a mere 92 cents
a share.

With Margolis' money in hand, Schultz was able to sign
up a few others, including Arnie Prentice, a mild-mannered,

soft-spoken insurance and financial services executive who also had become something of a local "angel" investor. In addition to providing cash, the earliest investors signed on for the long haul, becoming part of a network of advisers that would, in just a few years, encircle Schultz and his growing company like a large, loving, and protective extended family. They provided not just money, but support, advice, and connections, helping to bring in more and more funding until the company was big enough to attract the most coveted investor of all, the public.

Margolis, after investing himself, approached fifty or more of his doctor friends, trying to pry $25,000 investments from them. None would bite. The big businesses in Seattle at the time were manufacturers like Boeing and the giant department store, Nordstrom. The big-box, deep discount Costco Wholesale sold its first shares to the public in late 1985 and that dynamic software company called Microsoft was about to do the same. Big concepts and big ideas were hot, and it was hard to see the prospects in a chain of coffee shops so small that each would fit in a two-room apartment. Who could possibly see that the shop might one day spring up in seemingly every major shopping area in urban and suburban America, in thousands of variations? Margolis could convince only a few personal friends to back the idea.

For those who took the time to look beyond the basic questions, it may have been possible to see that Schultz was on to something big—but probably not. A scrappy and competitive New Yorker who can take over a room when he's wound up, Schultz had grown up in government-subsidized housing in Brooklyn and found his way out through a football scholarship to Northern Michigan University. When the football gig didn't work out, he stayed in Michigan, earning a degree in communications, and then becoming a salesman, first for Xerox and then for a seller of plastic tubs and housewares called Hammarplast. In the early 1980s Schultz took his first trip to Seattle to see why a small Seattle customer was buying so many of Hammarplast's simple plastic cones used to make drip coffee. There he became enamored with the coffee business. He and Sheri gave up good jobs to move west in 1982 so that he could join Starbucks, then just a handful of coffee-bean stores and a mail-order business.

Starbucks had been founded in 1971 by three coffee-loving friends, Jerry Baldwin, Gordon Bowker, and Zev Siegl, who were far more interested in literature, history, and gourmet food than in business. Inspired by Peet's Coffee & Tea out of Berkeley, California, they had hoped to convince Seattle and the Pacific Northwest to replace the sawdustlike brew that came out of grocery-store cans with a flavorful, high-quality coffee made from carefully selected fresh-roasted beans. After cooking up the idea, they worked on the name. The original choice, said Baldwin, was terrible, something that "sounded more like a law firm than a coffee company." In yet another conversation about what to call the venture, someone suggested Starbo, a onetime Washington mining town. Then Bowker blurted out, "Starbucks." It had the right ring, it was easy to spell and impossible to mispronounce. Later at the library Baldwin found a nice literary connection: Starbuck was the first mate in Herman Melville's *Moby-Dick*. (Starbuck was also a main character in the play and 1956 movie *The Rainmaker*.)

Siegl sold out in 1980, and by the time Schultz showed up, Starbucks was a solid small business with a strong regional reputation and a devoted customer base. Schultz caught Bowker's and Baldwin's contagious passion for rich, dark-roasted coffee. But always the impatient New Yorker, he almost immediately wanted more. He believed the company could expand faster and be far more successful if it sold coffee not just by the pound, but by the cup.

Schultz's autobiography, *Pour Your Heart Into It,* and the official company history date the concept behind the modern Starbucks to a business trip that Schultz took to Milan, Italy, in 1983, where he first witnessed the power of the Italian espresso bar as a neighborhood gathering place. With Italian opera in the background, the stores were full of energy, camaraderie between customers, and the daily joy of exquisite—and strong—coffee. *"This is so powerful,"* Schultz wrote, his own emphasis added. *"This is the link. . . .* What we had to do was unlock the romance and mystery of coffee, firsthand, in coffee bars." He was so moved with his epiphany, he said, that he found himself physically shaking.

But the trip was only one part of his big idea. Schultz also had his eye on an equally powerful, but less emotional, aspect of selling coffee in a cup: Eye-popping profitability.

After all, the markup on a pound of coffee, after transportation costs, roasting, and selling, would hardly be more than double the cost. And people could buy only so many coffee beans each week. A cup of coffee, while a smaller transaction, had much more potential for both profit and repeat business. He saw that firsthand on a business trip to San Francisco when he happened by a housewares store. There about a hundred square feet of space had been carved out and fitted with a pass-through window. Inside were eight or so coffeepots on burners, with perhaps a half dozen different varieties and a couple of decaffeinated versions. From 6 A.M. to 10 A.M. a steady line formed outside the window as a worker poured one Styrofoam cup after another—bang!

bang! bang! bang!—selling each for the hefty 1980s price of $1 a cup.

Schultz was mesmerized watching dollar after dollar pass through the take-out window. He called a friend, Scott Greenburg, a young lawyer who was building his legal business by helping clients raise capital, to tell him about this discovery. Greenburg recalled that Schultz was curious about every aspect of the little operation: "How much does it cost to make a cup of coffee? What is this guy's overhead? How long does it take to pour the cup?" The answers were pretty clear: There wasn't much fancy footwork or gee-whiz technology to the idea, but there was plenty of money to be made.

Schultz's bosses at Starbucks were willing to let him experiment with a coffee bar in a corner of a new store, but they resisted changing their business from a successful bean seller to something more like a restaurant. Their resolve grew stronger when Starbucks jumped at the chance in 1984 to buy Peet's, the original purveyor of high-quality dark-roasted coffee. Once Starbucks and Peet's were one company, Baldwin and Bowker weren't interested in changing its focus— but they were willing to help Howard Schultz pursue his vision. Though it was heavy with debt from the Peet's purchase, Starbucks itself invested $150,000 to help Schultz design and launch his own coffee bars, which would use Starbucks coffee to make fancy Italian coffee drinks like espressos, cappuccinos, and caffè lattes, an espresso-and-steamed-milk combination.

Schultz and his lawyer pal Greenburg wrote the original business plan for the coffee bars at Schultz's kitchen table. Giving the business the difficult to spell and nearly impossible to pronounce name of Il Giornale (il jor-nahl-ee) Coffee Company, a play on the daily Italian newspaper, Schultz had to come up with a way not just to sell coffee, but to bring customers back again and again. It was in this plan that he wed the ideas that would later attract so many investors: the romance and history of Italian espresso, the traditions of the European coffeehouse, and the wonderful profit margins of selling dozens and dozens of cups of coffee or caffè lattes for a dollar or two a piece.

Almost instinctively Schultz was on to a trend gathering steam in the mid-1980s. Consumers had pulled back during the steep inflation and high energy prices of the late 1970s and early 1980s, buying tiny gas-sipping cars and scrimping on goodies. To cut costs, manufacturers had cut back too, shrinking box sizes and even candy bars. But as inflation began to ease, the enormous Baby Boom generation moved into young adulthood and was ready to play. Couples with two jobs had delayed starting a family and now had more discretionary money to spend. They snapped up Coach bags, bought designer clothing, and ate rich—and expensive— Häagen-Dazs ice cream. Toyota, sensing a missed opportunity, began to design its new Lexus luxury car line, recognizing that Americans were willing to pay handsomely for a well-made, high-end brand. While Schultz's notion of fine coffee and a warm and inviting atmosphere would make a distinctive stopping place, it was steeper-than-usual prices that truly made the plan a workable business and investment. "Not everybody can go to Tiffany's, but everybody can afford a buck to buy a great cup of coffee," Greenburg said. "Even way back then, it was obvious."

When the first Il Giornale opened in a Seattle office tower in April 1986, Schultz was still scrambling to raise an additional $1 million plus to open his next several stores. But his dreams were as big as ever. That May he distributed a corporate manifesto to the fledgling company's few employees. Titled "When It Comes to 'Establishing the Il Giornale Difference . . . '" Schultz's goals were nothing short of ambitious—and visionary:

"Il Giornale will strive to be the best coffee bar on earth. We will offer superior coffee and related products that help our customers start and continue their work day. We are genuinely interested in educating our customers and will not compromise our ethics or integrity in the name of profit. Our marketing will emphasize quality and service, not price.

"We will set aggressive goals and drive ourselves to achieve them. We recognize this is a unique time; when our coffee bars will change the way people will perceive the beverage. . . .

"As a corporation, we wish to be an economic, intellectual and social asset in communities where we operate. But beyond that, we expect our coffee bars to enhance the environment in which people work. . . .

"We care deeply about what we do."

In the single-spaced, page-and-a-half template for a month-old operation, Schultz described not just his dream of a far bigger company, but also an unusual retailer, one that would be incredibly demanding of its employees, yet would treat workers decently; one that would not just sell a product, but that would change customers' attitudes as well. It should have been just an outrageous example of a salesman's hubris—except that it more or less became true.

Dawn Pinaud bought in. She had helped Schultz with his coffee bar experiment at Starbucks and jumped to Il Giornale to be the manager of the very first store. The Starbucks coffee bar sold only one size of espresso drinks. But Il Giornale wanted to convey a different image, something far more exotic than a simple cup of joe. Multiple cup sizes and the now-familiar domed lids were ordered. Schultz, Pinaud, and a couple of other members of the new company debated how to jazz up the basic small, medium, and large. Since the stores were designed around the concept of Italian coffee bars, they wanted distinctive names. "Short" became the moniker for the 8-ounce small and "grande" for the 16-ounce large. But the medium, 12-ounce size? Someone suggested "alto." Instead the group settled on "tall."

In time, "short" fell off the menu (though most stores still sell it on request) and a nearly Big Gulp–size, the 20-ounce "venti" was added, leaving the stores with the bizarre "tall" for small and "grande" for medium. Other Italian-sounding names followed: doppio, macchiato, misto. What some people might find hokey became for others like secret passwords, a language shared by those elite, special customers who knew and understood what the coffee was about.

The initial store, a mere 800 square feet, caught on quickly, serving nearly 1,100 customers a day within the first year. While the Starbucks bean stores kept retail hours, Il Giornale opened its doors at 6:30 A.M. to catch the morning rush. Copying traditional Italian coffee bars, it even sold panini sandwiches. A second store opened six months later.

While the new employees were getting to know their customers and preaching the virtues of espresso, Schultz was running into dead ends in his quest for money. Without a well-known name or a proven concept, he had been turned down by more than 200 possible investors. At least, though, he had help from his first investors and a new hire named Christine Day.

Day, then the young mother of a newborn, had worked for a financial services firm specializing in private placements, which was now relocating. A former client of hers, Arnie Prentice, told her about a fellow who was raising money for a new venture who needed someone to run his office. Day interviewed with Schultz on a Friday. "He was really intense," she remembered. "The last person had quit because she couldn't work for him."

That weekend Schultz hounded her to see if she would take the job. She wasn't sure she should work for anyone that tightly wound. But her husband saw the Starbucks roasted coffee they had sent home with her and gave his advice. "He said, 'You get a pound of this a week?' I said, 'Yeah.' And he said, 'Take the job!'"

She began automating the payroll, taking over the ordering, and helping with administrative duties. But because she had called clients in her old job and asked for $125,000 checks, Schultz began to ask her to follow up with his potential investors. "Howard would give me a list every day of the people he wanted called to see if they would send their checks in," she said. "Pretty soon he figured out he could give me the list of people who he had barely spoken to and I would call."

The money came in slowly until a contemporary of Schultz's, Steve Sarkowsky, brought his father, Herman, to the store. The elder Sarkowsky was a prominent businessman who had made his initial money in homebuilding, and at the time he was an owner of both the Portland Trailblazers basketball team and the Seattle Seahawks football team. Investing in start-ups had become something of a side business, though he kept his priorities straight: He missed out on becoming an early investor in Costco because he didn't want to give up a great doubles tennis match to investigate the concept.

Schultz's zeal impressed the elder statesman. So did the prices Il Giornale was charging. "I figured, geez, $1.50 for a cup of coffee is almost as bad as paying $2 for a hot dog at the ballpark," he said. He invited Schultz to make a pitch to two friends with whom he sometimes invested. All the previous rejections had dimmed Schultz's ambitions only a smidge. The original business plan called for a hundred stores in five years, but Schultz scaled it back to maybe seventy-five. Still he saw a chain that went well beyond Seattle and the Northwest. Sarkowsky and his friends were impressed enough to invest $750,000, completing the first full round of financing, about $1.3 million at $1.65 a share. The initial stockholders had placed their bets.

With that cash Schultz bravely went to Vancouver, BC, for a third store. Then within a year the unexpected happened: His old partners at Starbucks decided to slim down, selling off all their other brands and wholesale businesses to concentrate on Peet's. All of Starbucks' assets—seven stores, one under construction, a roasting plant, and the established name—were for sale. Schultz could quickly more than double the size of his little venture and, more importantly, make a much more marketable brand his very own.

There was just one hitch: One of the large outside Il Giornale investors also saw the value of Starbucks, and threatened to cut a deal on his own to put the two companies together, making it *his* company, not Schultz's. In a tense meeting, the investor told Schultz that he had put up the original money and essentially owned the company; the move would be his call. Schultz was so distraught by the meeting that he hardly made it to the lobby before the tears came. The young entrepreneur, now all of thirty-four years old, had been blindsided, and now his big dream was on the line.

Luckily his other investors rallied behind him. With Starbucks as the prize, raising the necessary money, $3.6 million, was much easier and the price was higher, $2.40 a share. Most of the earlier investors put in more money to make it happen—with one exception. Starbucks itself, which had put up the very first dollars for Schultz and his Il Giornale, gave up its stake as part of the sale.

In the process Schultz learned a painful but valuable lesson. Other people's money was crucial to building a business, but so was something less tangible: loyalty. If his investors hadn't bought into his passion and his goals, if they hadn't invested in *him* as well as a retail idea, he could easily have been pushed out. From then on he would look for a personal commitment not just from managers and rank-and-file employees, but also from the larger investors and even the jaded Wall Street types who would soon come courting his business. If they saw the same potential and believed in the same dream he did, they would stick around for the long haul and preach the Starbucks story to a wider audience than he could ever reach alone. In time that kind of support might be just as valuable as the financing they provided by purchasing shares.

After the 1987 purchase the Il Giornale stores changed their name to Starbucks, and the voluptuous brown Starbucks siren turned Il Giornale green; over time, she also trimmed down and lost her ample breasts, belly button, and tail-like legs. Once again Schultz's ambitions grew. Now he promised investors that he could have 125 stores in five years. By then the company might be big enough to sell shares to the public to fund its growth.

While still digesting the purchase, Schultz made his most audacious move: He opened a store in Chicago. Determined to show that his coffee idea would work anywhere, he figured a cold, big city in the Midwest was the perfect place to prove it. Unfortunately the citizens of Chicago didn't immediately get the message. The first store faced the street, not the lobby of an office tower. Three more stores opened in the next six months. People didn't rush to go there.

With so much expansion in so short a time, the bigger company developed a voracious need for new cash. It needed money to lease and design new stores, build big computer systems that would support its growth to 200 stores or more, and hire people to keep the operation moving. Within a year after buying Starbucks, Schultz was asking investors for even more money, this time $3.9 million at $3.30 a share. Two years later in need of ever bigger investments to fund its ferocious growth plans, Starbucks went looking for the next stage in start-up financing, venture capital, seeking far bigger dollars in exchange for a sizable stake in the fledgling company.

Craig Foley worked at the time for Citibank's Chancellor Capital and had invested in technology and health care companies, as well as retailers like Costco. He had heard about Starbucks from an associate who visited Seattle regularly. But on a trip to Chicago, Foley stopped in one of the city's new Starbucks stores. He wasn't impressed. The store was empty and it wasn't particularly clean. The experience left him cold. "I said, 'interesting concept, but where are the customers?'" he remembered.

Once again the Seattle connections made the difference. Schultz had recruited Jeff Brotman, the founder and chairman of Costco, as both an investor and a paid adviser. Brotman knew Foley and called him to ask a personal favor: Would the investor take another look? Foley agreed, meeting with Schultz in New York and visiting stores in Seattle, Portland, and Vancouver. Ultimately his firm put in about $4.5

million. Altogether Starbucks raised $13.5 million in early 1990 from venture funds and other investors, at $3.75 a share.

With bigger money coming in and the expansion continuing, the company began to gussy itself up to seek the public's money. Howard Behar, a seasoned executive, joined the company in 1989 and helped turn around the struggling Chicago market. Orin Smith, an executive with proven financial skills, was recruited the next year. Some of the local Seattle angels who had gambled early on the company were gently asked to step down from the board in favor of the out-of-town venture capital investors and directors with bigger résumés. In 1990 the company turned profitable for the first time.

Schultz also was able to reap some rewards from his labor. He cashed in stock options for about $1.5 million. In late 1990 the company loaned him the money to buy 80,000 shares at 99 cents apiece, charging him just 3 percent interest at a time when the bank rate charged to corporate customers was around 10 percent. A year later the company loaned a group of seven executives $3.7 million, including $2.1 million to Schultz, so they could buy stock at $9 a share as part of the last private placement, which raised about $20 million.

To expand beyond its 126 stores, the company was ready to go after bigger money: selling stock to the public. But before it started that process, it created a stock-option plan for employees, dubbed Bean Stock, a play on both the coffee bean and Jack's fast-growing beanstalk. Under the plan, employees who are at the company as of April 1 of a given year receive options early the following year to buy shares equal to about 14 percent of their pay. A part-timer making $10,000 a year who was employed as of April 1, 2004, would have received options in early 2005 to buy $1,400 of stock, or about twenty-six shares with an exercise price of $54.64. The options vested, or became exercisable, over four years. That employee could sell a quarter of those shares after October 1, 2005, and would pocket a profit if the stock price had climbed. With the introduction of the plan, Starbucks began calling its employees "partners," emphasizing they were all in the game together.

Just as Schultz thought it crucial that his employees be committed investors in the company, he was insistent that the investment bankers who would sell Starbucks to the masses bought into his vision of sowing Starbucks around the country. Dan Levitan was working in Los Angeles for Wertheim Schroder, a middle-tier investment firm. A new colleague had heard of Starbucks and wanted to check it out. Coffee consumption in the United States had been in decline since the 1950s, and Levitan was skeptical, but he agreed to go. Once in Seattle in mid-1991, he was surprised to see lines forming at a store and to hear the cabdriver rave about the coffee. Schultz's unbridled enthusiasm impressed him.

Later when Schultz visited Los Angeles on a business trip, the two had dinner. "He believed in his company and wanted to see if I believed in it," Levitan said. At the end of 1991, when Starbucks raised its last private money, Levitan told Schultz that he thought the price was too cheap. Schultz challenged him. If so, then Levitan should buy some. Levitan invested.

Still the testing wasn't over. Schultz would call to say, "We're opening a store on Tuesday in San Francisco. Goldman Sachs is sending a guy." Levitan stewed. His firm sent flowers instead of a representative. An intense man with close-cropped hair and bundles of nervous energy, Levitan came to believe that Starbucks and Schultz had great potential, and he began to work "24 by 7 trying to think how I was going to get the Starbucks business."

It wasn't that initial public offerings were especially lucrative. Fees for IPOs were about 7 percent of the value of the shares sold, split among all the firms in the offering. Starbucks would be raising maybe $20 million or $25 million, a modest amount even in the early 1990s. At that point, though, Starbucks was bigger and more established than many companies that wanted to go public, and it was clearly a hot prospect. Once an investment banker was in the door, the relationship could pay off many times over, especially if the company grew like Schultz boasted it would. Plus the pickings were pretty slim that year.

To choose the lucky bankers to take the company public, a beauty contest was held in spring 1992. Seven firms were invited to make presentations over two days after first answering pages and pages of detailed questions. In addition bankers had to take a tour of the roasting plant with an assistant of Schultz's, who surreptitiously reported back on their excitement about and interest in the business. Ultimately Alex. Brown & Sons and Levitan's firm were chosen to be the underwriters.

The next step was to prepare an offering document or prospectus explaining the business that would support the 1.5 million shares to be sold to the public. Current shareholders also planned to sell 600,000 shares in the offering. After the sale the company would have about 13 million shares outstanding, with more than 80 percent still owned by the original shareholders. To make their pitches, the investment bankers, Schultz, and Smith went on a two-week "road show," starting in New York and Boston. From there they went through the Midwest, Denver, and down the West Coast, sometimes hitting two cities a day to talk with groups of investors at breakfast and lunch, and to meet with big potential investors in one-on-one meetings. At those meetings the investment bankers would ask for orders to buy shares, looking for investors who would ask for at least 10 percent of the deal. Of course the investors wouldn't actually get 10 percent of the offering, but the bankers wanted to whip up enough desire for the stock to be sure it would launch successfully.

The idea, said Peter Breck, a venture capitalist who was then a managing director of Alex. Brown, "was to create plenty of appetite for the stock so they will have unrequited demand." Then after the initial shares were placed, enough investors would still want the stock that the shares would climb or hold their own in the first few days of trading.

The road show also went to Europe because Schultz knew even then that he wanted to build a global company. At a presentation in Zurich, Breck recalled, Schultz showed a photo of a barista drawing espresso into a Starbucks cup. One potential investor was appalled. "You mean you serve the coffee in the paper cup?" he asked. "It will never work." And with that he got up and left the meeting.

In preparation for the initial offering, the four-letter stock symbol was chosen from a list of available options. Lone Star Steakhouse & Saloon had gone public in March 1992, snapping up the most logical symbol, STAR. From what was left, SBUX jumped out as the best choice, capturing both the company name and the future value of the shares.

As with all his investors, Schultz was partial to those professionals whom he felt really understood his vision and would ask the bankers if they could make sure those folks got shares. He also wanted customers to have a shot at the stock. Alex. Brown set up an 800 number and hired extra staff to field calls from potential small stockholders. "It was a complete nightmare for us," Breck said. "Everybody who ever had a latte before wanted to buy the stock."

When the road show was over and orders were in hand, the underwriters tested what price the public would pay. In a difficult market for new stocks, they concluded there was enough demand to raise the price beyond the initial estimate of $14 to $16 a share. Ultimately the offering price was approved by a special committee including Schultz and other Starbucks directors.

On June 26, 1992, Starbucks became a publicly held company, selling stock to the public at $17 a share, a price that was more than 40 times its current earnings and $1 a share above the estimated price—an impressive feat at the time. On the first day of trading, the stock soared to $21.50, giving Starbucks a market value of more than $270 million.

Behar and Smith went to dinner that night, both to celebrate their success and Smith's fiftieth birthday. Behar had sold a house before he joined the company, making $140,000. Half had gone into buying a small new house and the other half had been invested in Starbucks' stock. Given that he had lost money on his investments before, he had no idea how this one would turn out. But that night they ordered champagne and celebrated that they were now, officially, millionaires. "That was giddy," Behar said.

The company would return to the public debt and stock markets several times to raise money to fund its growth, and its stock mostly climbed. In the early days Starbucks sometimes traded at 60 and 70 and 80 times its earnings per share. Occasionally investors would worry about its expansion or its business model and the shares would slide, losing up to half their value. But then the festering issue would be resolved and the stock would take off once again. Only twice had Starbucks stock finished down in a calendar year; it also had declared stock splits in 1993, 1995, 1999, and 2001. Over time, though, most of the earlier investors sold at least some of their stock, in part because their financial advisers urged them to diversify. But few of them sold all of it.

Dan Levitan still owned shares—and now ran a venture capital firm with Schultz. Craig Foley, Herman Sarkowsky, and others all made good money in many other investments as well. But they all talked about Starbucks as "we" and not "they," and said they would have a hard time selling the Starbucks stock they still owned. "I do have an emotional attachment to it," said Foley.

For early holders who held on, Starbucks' stock was one of those rarest of investments, the kind that started as a slow drip and turned into a flood. Christine Day received options for helping to complete the first financing, which later helped her make a large down payment on a house on a lake. Jennifer Ames-Karreman, another early employee, used Bean Stock and options she received as a manager to earn an executive MBA, to work part-time while her children were young, and to share some of the bounty as gifts to her family.

Schultz, from almost nothing, amassed a fortune in the neighborhood of $1 billion. His combined stock options and stock holdings totaled more than 16 million Starbucks shares, valued at more than $800 million in early 2005. In recent years, in addition to annual salary and bonuses of about $3.5 million, he had received annual options to buy at least 500,000 shares. Wealth from Starbucks stock allowed him to become an early investor in eBay and to become the lead owner of the Seattle SuperSonics professional basketball team from 2001 to 2006. But he was vague about what it meant to him personally, saying only, "I think it's given many of us the ability to do things that we've only dreamed about," including, in his case, creating a family foundation to help the less fortunate.

To discourage employees from focusing on the price, Schultz said he made it clear that he didn't want Starbucks to post its stock price in the office and he didn't want it highlighted or discussed. Unspoken was a different reality: The stock is a crucial part of the company's past, present, and future. It was the fuel that funded its early growth and gave it the flexibility to expand at an almost unheard of pace. Now that the company generated enough cash on its own, the stock took on a different meaning. It was a valuable currency for compensating upper-level executives, an incentive that excited and rewarded rank-and-file employees and the turbocharged flourish that gave Starbucks an extra glow, that sealed its status as a hot, hip, twenty-first-century corporation.

As such, Schultz was understandably protective. When the media glare was harsh or some analyst would raise skepticism about the company's prospects, he felt the criticism personally. "I think that in order to succeed at this level, you have to take this personally," he said. "This isn't a job, it's the work of your life and the responsibility you have to more than 100,000 people and their families. I take it personally because it's a reflection of everyone who works at this company."

Though Schultz wouldn't say this either, the stock was also his ultimate "I told you so." In the earliest days, while he was still raising money and his wife was pregnant, the company had trouble paying vendors and making payroll. Schultz himself went a year without a salary. His in-laws came to visit and his wife's father asked him to take a walk with him. "While on that walk," Schultz said, "I guess you would say maybe we had a come-to-Jesus meeting about my responsibilities, which I took very seriously. Basically he was concerned about the course that we were on, and asked me when I was going to get a job and give up this hobby."

Schultz asked one of his investors, Jack Rodgers, to reassure his father-in-law. By then Rodgers was in his mid-fifties and already had retired from two careers, twenty years in management at IBM and more than fifteen as a franchisee of McDonald's, Benihana, Red Robin, and Athlete's Foot stores. Investing in a bank here and a radio station there, Rodgers also had joined a small-business investment company with eleven others. When Schultz showed up looking for money, Rodgers agreed to investigate the coffee concept. The two hit it off, and Rodgers recommended that his group invest $250,000. But his partners turned him down. They wanted hot technology investments, the kind that might increase fivefold in five years, not hot coffee.

Instead Rodgers became a major individual investor and a consultant to Il Giornale and then Starbucks, to be paid in what he and Schultz referred to as "worthless" stock options. Calm, patient, and affable, Rodgers became a "wise man" for the impulsive, high-intensity Schultz, or as Schultz put it, "the gray-haired assistant coach on the bench who's seen it all before."

Rodgers took Schultz's father-in-law to his country club for a round of golf and lunch. "He was the nicest guy," Rodgers remembered. "But he was sincerely concerned." By then Rodgers had seen Schultz in action—and he was personally involved. He reassured the father-in-law and told him "he had every reason to be very proud of his son-in-law."

Even so Rodgers couldn't have predicted that hitching his third career to the youthful Schultz would "turn out to be the most important financial decision of my life." In the beginning days, he helped run side operations like the mail-order business and restaurant sales. He helped get Starbucks coffee into Nordstrom's cafés and worked to get Starbucks into its first airports, where it could introduce customers to the coffee that would eventually come to their neighborhoods.

During the earliest years, he purchased roughly 100,000 shares, mostly at $2.40 and $3.60 a share, though he also bought a few at $9 before the public offering. He also received options to buy about 100,000 shares in lieu of pay. He sold some to diversify his holdings and gave a fair bit to his four children and their children and a family partnership. Still even with the stock in a bit of a slump in early 2005, the oldest shares were worth hundreds of times what he paid for them.

"I have benefited more from my Starbucks stock than my other two careers—and other investments—and my Starbucks stock is substantially more meaningful," he said. He and his wife tried to keep their Starbucks holdings to no more than 70 percent or 75 percent of their portfolio, but for many years that was a struggle. "It's tough to reach our self-imposed diversity strategy of selling Starbucks stock," he said.

Ron Margolis, the first investor, didn't have quite the career of Jack Rodgers, but the stock was just as lucrative. He invested in the company several times and put about $10,000 in Starbucks stock in a trust for his young daughter. Though that stock eventually was sold, the trust grew to more than $4 million.

He ran into some legal troubles in the early 1990s unrelated to Starbucks, but by 1992, when Starbucks was sold to the public, his initial investment was worth nearly $2 million. He recalled vacationing in Santa Fe and seeing the new price in the newspaper. It hit him that a dollar change in the stock would be more than he could earn in a year of practicing medicine. Some of his shares funded a small charitable foundation, some were sold, and a good number went to Carol in a late-1990s divorce. But he still owned more than half a million shares in early 2005, valued at roughly $25 million. That amazed him.

"I didn't have a particular thought of what it was going to become, but I never ever had a thought that a new culture would be started," he said. "I thought it would be a relatively successful group of coffee shops."

Never much of a coffee drinker, he said he mostly buys the sweet, icy Frappuccinos when he goes to a store. But he doesn't go that often. "I think the coffee is terribly overpriced," he said.

4

April

★ THE GROWTH ★

A store-opening machine

People who bought shares of Starbucks may have thought they were investing in fine coffee or cheerful servers or even the marketing genius of Howard Schultz. But they were also buying the skills and savvy of people like Doug Satzman.

Satzman, a big, outgoing fellow in his early thirties, was a Starbucks director of new store development, leading a San Francisco–based team that scouted locations and picked the best ones for new Starbucks stores. If Satzman's group did its job right, it would open about seventy stores in his northern California and Reno/Tahoe, Nevada, region in 2005, while other teams around the country would open seventy-five to one hundred stores each. Altogether 1,500 new locations were expected to dot Mother Earth during the Starbucks fiscal year ended October 2, 2005, giving the chain more than 10,000 total outlets.

And thanks in large part to its new stores, Starbucks' sales and profits would grow at double-digit rates—sooner or later pushing the stock price up as well.

That's because in Stockland, almost nothing is more valuable than productive growth. We buy stocks because we believe they will be worth more in the future than they are today. How much they go up depends heavily on two factors—the dividend, or the cash paid back to shareholders, and earnings growth. Since Starbucks didn't pay a dividend—it used most of its cash flow to build new stores and update old ones— investors looked to its remarkable earnings growth to keep the stock price soaring. So our next logical stop to understanding why Starbucks' stock kept climbing was to understand how Starbucks grew.

Where a company's earnings come from isn't always obvious. Some chains that franchise, for instance, may make more money from loans to franchisees or from marking up the food or other products they sell to them than from healthy sales and profits at the franchised outlets. An automaker may earn more from car loans than from selling cars, or occasionally more profit will come from a company's small subsidiary than its main business.

Starbucks itself was nearly ubiquitous: It peddled bottled Frappuccino through a joint venture with PepsiCo, moved bags of whole beans through grocery stores and marketed a to-die-for coffee ice cream (try the Java Chip) through a deal with Dreyers. You could get Starbucks coffee from your office coffee service, at restaurants, or even on a flight with United Airlines. But those were mere hobbies compared with the main business. The vast, vast majority of Starbucks' sales and profits came from selling latte after macchiato after Frappuc-

cino at its stores. And the vast, vast majority of Starbucks'
growth came from successfully opening new outlets. It was,
in short, a store-opening machine.

While it might seem like Starbucks could put up a coffee
shop in the middle of a cornfield and customers would come,
it was actually much more challenging to consistently build
the kinds of stores that generated ever-growing sales over a
number of years. Starbucks accomplished it on several levels:
It built a coast-to-coast empire in the United States and expanded internationally. It built its own stores and licensed its
concept to others, which helped it expand faster than it could
alone. And in projecting that it could continue to increase
sales at least 20 percent and profits 20 to 25 percent a year
over the next five years, Starbucks executives mastered the
expectations crescendo. Every couple of years, their vision of
how big the company could become expanded, sending a
clear message to investors that today's growth was just a taste
of bigger possibilities down the road. In turn those projections and that optimism fired up its stock price well beyond
its obvious value and kept its price-to-earnings ratio at a
plump and fluffy level.

To see how all the pieces fall into place, Satzman took
me on a tour of his territory, starting on the corner of Mission and Fourth streets in San Francisco, where he tried
to explain one of the most baffling aspects of the Starbucks
phenomenon.

To our right was the Metreon, an entertainment mall
near the city's convention center with sixteen movie theaters,
arcade games, restaurants, and a small but spiffy Starbucks
store. Satzman's team had just approved a kiosk store inside an elegant thirty-nine-story Marriott hotel just across

Mission Street. And to our left, across Fourth Street, was—you guessed it—a spacious Starbucks store. Three Starbucks on four corners.

Then Satzman pointed to the fourth corner, where the Mission campus of City College of San Francisco ran for half a block or more. "We actively contemplated putting another unit in there," to be run by students, he said, with complete sincerity. The demand was sufficient, he added, but they weren't able to work out the logistics of a student-run store.

Three Starbucks on four corners wasn't always enough, after all.

"If you're over here," Satzman said, referring to the Metreon, "you are not likely to cross the street. If you're in the hotel, you might be going to the right to Market Street, where the shopping is"—in the opposite direction. The folks in the movie theater or the hotel might never bother to go outside to find the full-fledged Starbucks store. "Where a lot of our growth is is driving that incremental cup that someone may not have planned to buy," Satzman explained.

Starbucks first saw this phenomenon in Vancouver in the early 1990s, when lines grew long in a small store on a busy corner. A second spot became available kitty-corner to the first store and Starbucks took it. To everyone's surprise, both stores did well as people came to the corners from different directions and moved on. The logic was so simple that it almost sounded like a corporate version of that old chicken joke:

"Why did Starbucks cross the street?"

"To get to the customers on the other side."

Satzman got his start in real estate with Ritz Camera, then Blockbuster Video wooed him away with plans to open 500 stores a year for the next three years. The big expansion lasted about a year, until sales started to slip, a harsh reminder that merely opening a store doesn't mean the strategy is working. Blockbusters' big plans were scaled back.

Satzman joined Starbucks more than five years ago, working first in the Washington, DC, area and then transferring to San Francisco. Now as part of Starbucks' U.S. field staff of about 200 real-estate people, he found the retail coffee business drastically different from the video-store experience. "In reality, demand for specialty coffee is growing faster than we and our competitors can add stores combined," he said. The push to add stores, he added, "is really driven by demand."

We walked through the Metreon store, a mere 300 square feet elegantly squeezed into a space that would otherwise be a lobby. There was no need for a ceiling. The store was primarily a counter with a space-age sign and enough room for three or four employees. (Though this seemed small, Starbucks even had an extra-small version, designed to fit in about 250 square feet.) Building out the space required relatively little capital, so the store made sense even with low-to-medium sales.

The hotel store, since it was licensed, didn't require any company capital at all. Across the street the bigger store, at 1,600 square feet, was just about the typical size for a new store. On average such a store would cost about $390,000 to open in 2005 and would turn in first-year sales of about $900,000. That's a sales-to-investment ratio of 2.3 to 1, a more-than-healthy return on the funds required. And since Starbucks stores tend to take two to three years to fully mature, the sales should grow a bit faster at the new stores than at old stores for a couple of years.

The sales-to-investment ratio drove every decision to open a store, but Starbucks had other reasons for larding up a dense urban neighborhood or downtown with more than one outlet. Despite many efforts to build sales later in the day, most Starbucks stores rang up at least half their sales before noon. A store could handle only so many customers at a time, even with two or three cash registers going, and in the morning lines often grew. No matter how badly people wanted a latte, if the line looked too long, they'd keep walking—maybe to a competitor. Opening another store nearby was the retail equivalent of basketball's boxing out, stationing yourself under the basket to get the rebound so the other team doesn't. The new store might take some sales away from the original location, but it could lead to far more sales overall. Jim Donald, Starbucks' CEO, said one Texas store manager complained that his store's sales of $1 million a year had flattened because of a new store across the street. But the new store, a drive-through, was on track to bring in $3 million its first year. So in the same vicinity Starbucks was now pulling in $4 million a year from two spots rather than $1 million or $3 million from a single store.

Once Starbucks knew it could open three or four stores within five or eight blocks of each other, the more delicate question became, How many is too many? Initially the popular thinking went, there was room for about one coffee shop per 25,000 people. But as both Starbucks and competitors proliferated, the presumed number fell toward one shop per 10,000 to 15,000 people. Some towns have far more than that. The geographic Web site ePodunk.com noted that Falls Church, Virginia, near Washington, DC, population 10,377, and Katy, Texas, near Houston, population 11,775, each had eight Starbucks in town, making them perhaps the most caffeinated suburbs in America. Looking at total coffee shops in metropolitan areas, market researcher NPD Group found that Anchorage, Alaska, might have that title, with almost three coffee shops for every 10,000 residents. Not surprisingly the Seattle area, with more than 260 Starbucks stores and many competitors, came in second—and the San Francisco area came in third.

Research showed that customers would travel only a few minutes to buy coffee—or maybe six to eight minutes, tops. So for Satzman and his team, minutiae mattered. Was the location on the side of the street where people head to work? Was it on the end or the middle of a shopping center? Even a slight bend in the road "can really have a demonstrable impact on your business in the short run," said Launi Skinner, Starbucks' senior vice president of store development. "If we were to place a store right on the off side of that bend, it just takes people that much longer to see that we're there," Skinner said. "If it's a street that's a major thoroughfare, it could take them months before they realize we're there."

In assessing a site, she said, Starbucks estimated the nearby population, what percentage of the population drinks coffee, how many cups of coffee competitors were selling, and "how many more cups of coffee do we think we could sell in that particular market?" Technology made the job easier. Cities, for instance, provided traffic counts on most major thoroughfares. Building landlords knew how many people worked in an office tower and how many passed through and could estimate income levels. Beyond the obvious information, like the transactions at each store, Starbucks kept a detailed database of information about all its stores, such as ranking on five grades how easily someone could get into and out of a store, each with a different impact on sales. Starbucks had software that drew on that data to estimate a store's first-year sales.

Satzman drove me to our next location in San Francisco, explaining that Starbucks liked to enter a market with a splash, picking a high-profile intersection that everyone knows, a strategy it called Main & Main. Once in place, it expanded to multiple locations. In San Francisco Starbucks moved in as soon as a noncompete agreement with Peet's, its former owners, expired in 1992. Its first spot was at Union Street and Laguna, a popular, high-profile shopping area, and from there it grew to 68 coffeehouses in a city of about 800,000 and about 375 in the broader Bay Area.

We pulled up to a seven-year-old store, once a controversial one. The store at Ninth and Howard was situated like a 7-Eleven, just behind ten gasoline pumps. The gas station's mini-mart was next door, as was a Burger King. It was a high-traffic corner near a hospital, with lots of cars streaming by, but Starbucks officials weren't sure they wanted to be that close to a gas station and fast food. "For a long time, this was a no-fly store," Satzman said.

To appease concerns about mingling with the other retail riffraff, the store had only a front door, rather than having interior doors that connected it to its neighbors. The store now was also one of just a handful that were open around-the-clock, an experiment to see what kind of nighttime demand there might be. Turned out, there was plenty. Satzman said that in the middle of the night, the customers might include a taxi driver, a police officer, an ambulance driver, and hospital staff.

On the way to look at an urban store in Oakland, Satzman explained that he and his team of four real-estate people, four construction managers, and three designers tracked a number of potential properties at once. Once at the store, he parked in a large lot across the street and pulled out an area map. Current stores were marked with green dots. Target stores with Starbucks outlets got a red dot. To assess the potential customer base, yellow dots recorded parking garages and the number of spots they had; larger buildings were marked with their leasable space and their occupancy rates. Other numbers detailed traffic counts from the Bay Area Rapid Transit system.

Satzman's team drilled in on finding where the growth would be over the next five years—where the new communities and shopping would spring up, where businesses would move, where the traffic will go. He pulled out an aerial map of Stockton, California, a growing community about eighty miles east of San Francisco. In an area with a couple of stores within two to three miles, a new housing-and-lake development was under way. Starbucks was considering grabbing up a site that might not have a great first year, but would be there as the community fills in and grows.

Once real estate got its eye on a site, it worked with the operations folks, who will have to run it—and all of them would be compensated, in part, on how their new stores performed. Then the two groups compiled a huge packet of information, including site design, an environmental review, and the lease, which allows some kind of exit within three to five years if the location doesn't work, as well as options to extend the lease if the store succeeds. Next came information on parking, traffic, and demographic details on the population within two to three miles. The other Starbucks nearby were reviewed, as were competitors; then sales for the next ten years were forecast based on the historical trends in the region. Before a decision was made, however, the operations and real-estate managers piled into a car and toured the site and area one more time. Because stores take a year to eighteen months to select and open, Satzman had largely lined up his 2006 openings and was working on 2007.

The big, quaint Oakland store we headed to, trimmed in yellow and decorated with a sign shaped like a coffee cup, was in a transitional neighborhood a few blocks from downtown. The store, opened a year ago, was part of a joint venture with former Los Angeles Lakers star Magic Johnson to open stores in lower-income, more diverse communities. In addition to trying to encourage economic development, the stores also gave a nod to Starbucks' expanding customer base. In the mid-1990s, the typical Starbucks customer was an affluent white college graduate. But newer customers, according to a 2004 company survey, were somewhat more likely to be minority and had an average income of $55,000 a year, down from more than $80,000 for long-timers.

Still the Oakland neighborhood was rather no-frills, and Satzman had been concerned that the store would fall short of initial goals. It didn't. On a weekday afternoon, most of the seats were filled with people reading or visiting in quiet conversation. Our group of Satzman, a Starbucks marketing manager from San Francisco, and a Seattle media relations manager seemed almost boisterous by comparison.

Fortified by a grande cappuccino, Satzman headed out again, pointing out a new push to build stores on main highways, even if that meant putting a store in tiny towns like Buttonwillow, California, or New Braunfels, Texas. Company officials have said they see the potential for more than 500 high-volume, off-highway stores on the nation's interstates, advertised with billboards a few miles ahead and huge "lollipop" signs visible from a distance. The company has already addressed one hitch: When people left the highway for coffee, a line often formed first at the bathrooms. Starbucks doubled the bathrooms in newer highway locations, Satzman said, and may consider adding even more.

In Pittsburg, about forty-five miles east of San Francisco, Satzman pulled up to a new store, a former Wienerschnitzel hot dog restaurant with a coveted drive-through. For years Starbucks executives balked at opening drive-throughs, fearing that something so fast-foodlike would sully its brand. But beginning in fiscal 2004 about half of all new company-owned stores included a drive-through window, which required more employees, but also rang up much higher sales than traditional stores.

To make this one work, Satzman said, Starbucks had to convince the landlord to tear off the huge yellow triangular roof and build a new flat one, with a little angle in front. It also asked the landlord to spruce up the center, which was sagging from age. Inside the store looked much like any other Starbucks, with the brightly colored signature pendant lights, the wooden counter design and the rounded "hand-off" bar, now a laminated surface that will last longer than the old wood ones. An early real-estate executive, Arthur Rubinfeld, helped set the standard for the Starbucks look, encouraging designers to focus on what customers see when they walk in, particularly the items between waist and chest high. In other words, stained woods went out front, plastics in the back. To save money and work, ceilings and ductwork were painted dark colors rather than finished with drab acoustical tile. Floors might be nothing more than concrete. Sofas and soft chairs were welcoming, and round tables were preferred over square or rectangular ones because they were more casual, and a single person sitting at one looked less alone.

Roughly 80 percent of the store design was standard issue, but the rest was up to the real-estate and operations team—and their budgets. The group could spend more on one store than another as long as the whole portfolio met its targets. One store in the Belltown neighborhood of Seattle added curtains. Others had murals. At this old hot dog stand, the old restaurant's booths, a Starbucks rarity, were still intact on one side of the store. On the other side was a bookcase, giving the area a more kid-friendly appeal. "Each store is like a snowflake," Satzman said.

That was somewhat less true of the kiosks in grocery stores and hotels, which were crammed into regular store space. Starbucks executives often boasted that Starbucks didn't franchise like nearly all the fast-food giants, but that told only part of the story. In truth Starbucks did something very similar: It had a large network of licensees, a kissin' cousin to franchising. Rather than sell a franchise territory to an individual who could open stores in that geographic area, Starbucks licensed the right to open stores in certain locations, such as airports, hotels, and groceries, to other companies for a fee and a percentage of sales. It also sold its coffee, mugs, and other inventory to its licensees—at a profit. HMS Host, for instance, operated Starbucks stores at airports where it held the concession rights, and those little outlets generated almost as much revenue as a typical company-owned storefront.

In the later 1990s Orin Smith, the company's longtime number two to Schultz, said he began to see far more opportunity in licensing, especially to supermarket operators. He feared, he said, that sooner or later someone would open stores in the nation's 25,000 groceries. "I didn't want to see somebody else's brand in several thousand supermarkets because overnight I'd have a national competitor," he said. By late 2004 Safeway, Albertson's, and Kroger owned hundreds of licensed Starbucks kiosks inside their grocery stores, and Target ran Starbucks outlets in its discount stores. Hotels sold so much branded Starbucks coffee that they wanted their own Starbucks espresso bars too.

Smaller in size than a regular store, these mini coffee bars in stores and hotels brought in perhaps $250,000 to $300,000 each in annual revenue to the operators, maybe a quarter of the sales of a company-owned store. But they helped Starbucks quickly add to its store count and nab captive customers. Keeping the service standards up was challenging, as the employees worked for the licensee, not Starbucks. But since Starbucks didn't have to pay rent or staff the stores, more of the licensing revenue dropped straight to the bottom line—one way profits would grow faster than sales.

Overseas Starbucks often entered new countries with licensees or in joint ventures where it had a small ownership. That gave the company access to local expertise and had the added benefit of keeping most of the start-up costs (and potential early losses) off the company's books. Later when operations in the country were more established, Starbucks often increased its stake or bought the venture for a modest sum. In recent years, as the overall store count exploded, U.S. and foreign licensees opened more stores (937 in fiscal 2005) than the company opened on its own (735 in 2005).

Starbucks needed international expansion to sustain its status as a growth stock, but it came in fits and starts. Starbucks had entered Tokyo in 1996 with a splash and had slowly been building stores in Asia, but its international presence was still small in 1998. That year Starbucks bought a London-based company called, conveniently, Seattle Coffee Co. If the company looked familiar, that was by design. Scott and Ally Svenson, Seattle natives living and working in London, discovered they missed their hometown coffee. Ally quit her job and opened a coffee shop in Covent Garden in 1995. Her husband joined the business a year later, just as the first of their four sons was born. Within three years, they had sixty-five stores in the United Kingdom, Southeast Asia, and the Middle East. The couple and their investors were planning for an initial public offering when Starbucks came knocking with an offer of more than $80 million in stock.

The purchase gave Starbucks an instant presence in London and a toehold in Europe. It began to expand more rapidly, opening hundreds of stores, with Japan and the United Kingdom remaining the largest markets. The growth was rockier than in the United States however. In the United Kingdom competition, lax service, and unusually high rents at stores opened after the Seattle Coffee purchase hurt results. In Japan same-store sales actually began to fall in mid-2001 as the Starbucks fad cooled and the number of competitors exploded. In an effort to reduce costs, food quality declined and some locations turned out to be duds.

In both countries new management, a renewed focus on service, and closing some stores staunched the losses, and Starbucks' international business recorded its first sizable profit in fiscal 2004. Still for all its talk about international expansion, Starbucks recorded 84 percent of its revenue and more than 90 percent of its operating income from U.S. operations.

That dependence was clear in April, when disappointing March sales numbers were reported. Smith had just retired after five years as CEO and fifteen years as a top executive, and Jim Donald, a former supermarket executive, took the top operating spot. The company said that in March, same-store sales rose just 6 percent, in part because of a later start to

Starbucks' annual brewing sale, when it cut the prices of its big-ticket coffeepots and espresso makers. It was the third underachieving month so far this year, and the smallest monthly same-store sales increase in more than two years. Take into account the fall's 3 percent price increase, and the true growth was more like 3 percent, which would have been the softest sales month since the company emerged from a nasty slump in early 2002. The market shrugged off the long-planned management transition, but not the sales. The next day the stock dropped $1.63, or 3 percent, to $50.50, and the following day, it dropped more than 3 percent again.

In mid-April, Bear Stearns analyst Ashley Reed Woodruff raised her rating on the stock to "outperform," but that didn't halt the decline. On April 20 the stock bottomed out during the day at $44.58, a 29 percent drop from year-end as investors fretted about the company's future earnings and growth.

But the next week Starbucks came through for them. On April 27 the company reported cheerier results for the second quarter ending April 3, saying that net income climbed 27 percent to $101 million, or 24 cents a share, right on target with the company's earlier estimate that it would earn 23 to 24 cents a share in the quarter. Revenue for the second quarter rose 22 percent to $1.5 billion. Even better, officials raised their year-end target once again, increasing it by two cents, after increasing the fiscal-year earnings estimate by two cents a share in January. Now, officials said, Starbucks expected to earn $1.17 to $1.19 a share for the full year.

And its same-store sales, the ones that had been giving investors such heartburn? In the coming months they would be "at or slightly above" the high end of its 3 percent to 7 percent target range, meaning monthly sales numbers should warm up once again.

Investors were reassured and the stock began to rebound. The next day the stock price jumped $2.15 to $48.56 on double the usual volume. Goldman Sachs raised its recommendation to outperform, the fourth positive vote from stock-brokerage analysts in recent weeks. Within a few days the stock crossed $50 again, plus some, and held there.

In recommending that clients add Starbucks stock to their portfolios, the analysts cited the company's planned store openings, its consistent earnings growth, and the beaten-down stock price. To do that, they had to make a convincing argument that a stock trading at about 40 times its fiscal 2005 earnings, and more than 30 times next year's projected earnings, was a good purchase. Classical financial gurus, like Benjamin Graham and his most famous disciple, Warren Buffett, might have a hard time buying that. They encouraged investors to look for stocks of growing companies whose stock prices understated the potential of their earnings or dividends to grow, or that were low enough that investors would have a "margin of safety" in case the company didn't do as well as everyone expected. If the investor made a good call, the earnings went up and the stock price rose even more as the price-to-earnings multiple grew, the equivalent of Stockland heaven.

The value-stock gurus warned against buying stocks like you were buying from Tiffany's, paying a premium for the name, the blue box, and the reputation. "Consciously paying more for a stock than its calculated value—in the hope that it can soon be sold for a still-higher price—should be labeled speculation," Buffett wrote.

The professionals who recommended or bought Starbucks tried to justify its high price by firing up the spreadsheets. Some tried to project out the company's future cash flows and estimate their value today, concluding that the stock still had a little more room to expand. David Palmer, a stock analyst with UBS Investment Research, recommended buying Starbucks in part because of how it stacked up next to other wowie-zowie consumer companies. He looked to a measure called the "PEG Ratio," the price-to-earnings to growth calculation, or how the P/E ratio relates to the company's actual growth rate. When Starbucks traded at about 40 times its fiscal 2005 earnings and was projected to grow about 25 percent, he calculated its PEG at 1.6. That was below the PEG ratios the stock market awarded to well-known consumer stocks like Coca-Cola, Kraft, PepsiCo, and General Mills. A value investor might question whether those PEG ratios were inflated or note that the PEG might go up if earnings growth merely slowed a little bit. But Palmer saw them as benchmarks for what growth investors were willing to pay, arguing that Starbucks should trade at a ratio similar to those peers.

Still others simply tried to do the math. Assuming Starbucks could maintain the same P/E ratio—a brave assumption—its stock should grow 25 percent a year if its earnings grew 25 percent a year.

Unfortunately the stock market was never so predictable. And there was a significant catch: No company grew at a fast pace forever. At some point it simply ran out of profitable places to go or got so big that adding on billions and billions of dollars of sales a year became nearly impossible. For retailers the turning point in the stock market usually came sometime after they opened about half the stores they could possibly open, whatever that was. Once investors came to believe the company had matured and growth was permanently braking, the market could be ruthless. Not only would the stock price tumble, but the P/E ratio would sink from its lofty perch, even if the company continued to increase earnings at an above-average rate. The combined effect of a compressing P/E ratio and a slowing growth rate was a stock that could skitter sideways or slide, sometimes for years on end.

It was this Stockland slippery slope that growth company executives dreaded most. It wasn't just that executives' wealth was tied up in the stock price; employees received stock options, too, and a long run to nowhere could blister morale and send promising talent fleeing for more lucrative opportunities. To avoid that, Starbucks executives' challenge was to manage Wall Street's hopes so that investors didn't expect too much and then punish them for shortcomings, or expect too little and not cherish the stock enough. So while opening stores at a rapid pace, Starbucks executives also needed to convince investors that the company's potential was still far from unmet.

It did that by gradually moving its goal posts farther out every few years. In the early 1990s, when it had just a few hundred stores, it predicted 2,000 stores by the year 2000. Smith said the executives were being cautious in their estimates. Even so he added, "A lot of people didn't pay any attention to it because it sounded pretty outrageous."

When Starbucks came close to that number, executives told investors that they believed it could ultimately open 20,000 stores worldwide.

In mid-2002, when it had just over 5,600 stores, the company upped that estimate of its potential to 25,000 stores with a not-so-subtle nod to its steep stock price and its built-in promise of more, more, more. "We believe the key to building shareholder value is continued rapid growth coupled with solid financial results," Schultz said in a press release. "Increasing our long-term global store target to 25,000 locations reflects the enormous worldwide acceptance and demand for the Starbucks Experience and emphasizes the significant growth that lies ahead for the company."

Then at its analyst meeting in October 2004, Starbucks raised the target *again*, to a long-term goal of 30,000 stores. Once more, it said, it had come to realize its opportunities were far greater than it ever believed.

When would it reach that level? Officials wouldn't say.

For many analysts, money managers, and other investors, believing the numbers—and supporting a price-to-earnings ratio in the stratosphere—wasn't all that hard. McDonald's had more than 30,000 outlets worldwide, and people were still devouring Big Macs at new locations. Similarly Subway had more than 18,000 U.S. stores. Clearly people drank coffee far more often than they ate hamburgers or sandwiches (except, maybe, for Subway's pitchman, Jared).

And for those who might shake their heads and question where the growth would really come from, Schultz and other Starbucks executives increasingly had an answer: China.

Christine Day, Schultz's onetime Il Giornale office manager, climbed the corporate ladder to president, Asia/Pacific in 2003 and accepted a challenge: Build a $4 billion business in Asia. Arriving in China, she was stunned at the urban growth and the business opportunities. The Starbucks stores there had low labor and operating costs, making them highly profitable even at lower volumes. The customers tended to hang around and to eat more, enjoying trout pâté sandwiches, egg salad and shrimp sandwiches, and the classic Starbucks blueberry muffin. Meanwhile new rules allowed Starbucks to open stores without partners and distribute its own goods.

Day and her team set about taking digital pictures of the twenty biggest cities, their large buildings, the designer brands in stores and on people, and the proliferation of cars. The perception was that "people still ride bikes," she said. Moreover she saw a genuine threat. If Starbucks didn't move quickly, it could face a situation like Australia, where local and international competitors had secured the top market share.

"If we didn't get in and build the brand presence and build the loyalty now, some things like what happened to us in Australia would happen, where the competitors would start to outgrow us really rapidly and the good real estate would be gone," Day said. Coffee loyalty was on the line in, of all things, a nation of tea drinkers.

Over several months she brought back details of the potential to Schultz, the executive team, and the board, and China began to move up the list of important markets. While the internal vision was about getting a leg up on competition in a fast-changing market, the message for investors was somewhat more starry-eyed.

Starting with a slow, low drumbeat at the October 2004 analyst meeting, Starbucks officials highlighted China "as its next big international opportunity." The beat grew stronger and louder in Starbucks' second-quarter earnings, when it noted the opening of its first company-owned store in China.

On the earnings conference call with analysts, Schultz led off his comments with an almost breathless elaboration on the possibilities ahead. The size of China's population and its economic growth "have inspired all of us at Starbucks to put an accelerated focus on our expansion in this unusual, unique market," he said. "We believe Starbucks is quickly becoming a part of the daily lives of many consumers who desire one of the highest quality coffees in an inspiring and comforting environment."

The acceptance of the brand, he went on, "has exceeded even my high expectations and highlights the tremendous opportunity that is even greater than we originally thought." He didn't offer any details on how many stores Starbucks might open there in the next year or two. (Nor did he note that only 120 stores were then operating in mainland China, fewer than what Starbucks operated in, say, Dallas–Fort Worth.) But he told investors that "we view China as one of our biggest growth opportunities and believe it could ultimately become one of our largest international markets."

In May the pitch to investors continued. Martin Coles, president of Starbucks Coffee International, told journalists in Hong Kong that long term, China could become Starbucks' second-largest market, after the United States. When? He didn't say, nor did he offer how long it would be before China actually had a financial impact on the top or bottom lines.

Later Schultz practically bubbled with energy talking about the expansion ahead for Starbucks. We met at the bustling Starbucks in Seattle's University Village, one of the busiest outlets in the world. (The number one store, in case you were wondering, is at London's Standsted Airport.) Straight across the parking lot was a smaller store, next to a Crate & Barrel. The Barnes & Noble bookstore there served Starbucks as well.

Despite the thousands of stores in operation, Schultz saw nothing but growth ahead. "We are embryonic. We are so early on," he liked to say. Over a casual Sunday lunch in a café, the executive was animated as he tore through a list of the possibilities. Prototype stores in nearby Renton were experimenting with a new way of selling whole-bean coffee. Two experimental music-and-coffeehouse outlets were about to open, mixing CDs and café. A test in Minneapolis might finally mean Starbucks had developed a way to sell freshly brewed coffee through a vending machine. A new bottled Frappuccino would be out by year end. The company had yet to conquer such enormous markets as Brazil, Russia, and India. But what most captured his imagination was China.

"We didn't realize over the last couple of years how big and what an opportunity China would be for the company," he said. "That's one of the reasons why I think we're still so early on in the growth and development of the company on a worldwide stage."

The P/E pump was primed: More fast growth was on the way.

5

May

★ BUYBACKS ★

Buying higher profits

ometime after Starbucks' stock began its dive early in the year, it caught the attention of an especially interested buyer, one with a fair bit of cash on hand, plenty of borrowing power, and an exceptional insight into the company's business. Like a lot of potential buyers, this one was enchanted with the combination of the company's potential and its beat-up stock price.

The exact date the big investor began snapping up the stock wasn't clear—it didn't have to say. But by early April, before the stock hit its low for the year, the investor had spent an impressive $335 million to acquire 6.5 million Starbucks shares, enough to rank it among the company's fifteen largest shareholders.

In May the silent and unexpected buyer revealed itself—as Starbucks. And it indicated it would buy even more shares.

Typically in Corporate America the

operations people run the main show, building the business and the brand, which generate the profits and cash flow, which, in turn, feed the stock price. But the financial folks have a few potentially stock-enhancing tricks of their own. Buying back the company's stock is one.

Quietly, between late winter and late summer 2005, Starbucks bought enough shares that, if it were an outside investor, it would have become its own largest shareholder. That a company's management can secretly go into the stock market and buy its own shares, knowing all that it knows about its own business and its prospects, ranks among the quirkier aspects of Stockland. If the buyer was an executive with the company, he or she would have to disclose the purchases within a couple of business days. Very large individual investors and institutional buyers also had to disclose their purchases in various filings. But a company buying its own shares got to play by different rules. When the company's board authorized it to purchase a certain number of shares, the company publicized the decision. But when—or if—the shares were actually purchased was revealed only way after the fact, usually deep in the footnotes of quarterly and annual financial filings.

Stranger still, Wall Street usually applauded the stock purchases. Researchers found that when companies announced plans to buy their own stock, or when their boards gave them authorization to buy more of it, the stock price initially rose only modestly, by about 2 percent. But for many companies, the price climbed by a fair bit more than the market over the next four years.

On the surface, the reasons were pretty simple—and maybe too simplistic. When companies sold stock or issued stock options, they might dilute the holdings of other shareholders. But if there were fewer shares outstanding, the thinking went, then the goodies the company generated in the future, especially the earnings and the cash flow, would be shared by fewer people, meaning a little bit more for all the shareholders who hung on. Harley-Davidson, for instance, purchased so many of its shares by mid-2005 that its earnings per share for the second quarter rose to 84 cents from 83 the year before, even though its net income declined 4 percent. Thanks to its buyback, the motorcycle maker said that it expected its earnings per share to jump 10 to 13 percent for the year, instead of previous estimates of 5 to 8 percent. In theory the higher earnings per share would also fire up the stock price.

The other concept was a somewhat more dastardly assumption: If the company wanted to spend its own money on its shares, it might well know something good about its future that the rest of us don't know. In fact in a survey of 384 financial executives, 85 percent said they believed share repurchases sent a message to investors about management's confidence in the company.

For that Warren Buffett might get some of the credit. In the mid-1970s he convinced the management of the *Washington Post* that its stock was trading for far less than the actual value of its assets. Using excess cash to buy the shares cheaply would benefit shareholders and the company, like cutting a pizza into fewer pieces so there would be more on each slice. Over time the *Washington Post* purchased about 40 percent of its outstanding stock. Its net profit grew impressively, but with fewer shares in the marketplace, its earnings per share grew even more. So did the return on shareholders' equity, a much-watched measure of how well a company is using investors' dollars. Other Buffett investments, including

Coca-Cola and Wells Fargo, also bought their shares at low prices, with good results.

Twenty-five years later, though, Buffett's view had changed. In the early days, he said, the wisdom of the original purchases "was virtually screaming at managements" because stock prices were relatively so low. But "that day is past," he said in a 2000 letter to Berkshire Hathaway shareholders. "Now, repurchases are all the rage, but are all too often made for an unstated and, in our view, ignoble reason: to pump up or support the stock price."

Indeed knowing that investors thought fondly of buybacks, companies sometimes simply announced plans to buy their stock for the same reason baseball players took steroids—to juice their results. One academic study noted, "One reason that firms may announce a buyback program may be to mislead investors and, perhaps, in an indirect way, manipulate stock prices."

The purchases could also be ill-timed—and disastrously expensive. In the boom of the late 1990s, carmakers and airlines, among others, spent huge cash sums to jolt their shares. General Motors forked over more than $9 billion from 1997 through 2000 to purchase more than 20 percent of its outstanding shares. US Airways spent more than $800 million on buybacks in 1999, even as it posted quarterly losses, while Delta Air Lines paid $2.4 billion from the late 1990s through 2000 to buy its shares, offsetting stock options. When those industries hit the skids a few years later, their stock prices were far lower and that cash was long gone. But it wasn't forgotten. In 2005 Delta, operating under bankruptcy-law protection, asked a judge to void union contracts and impose wage cuts to help keep it operating. Judge Prudence Carter Beatty responded with a tongue-lashing, accusing the company of throwing away precious cash a few years before "in order to make (the) stock market price look good."

That wasn't a new accusation. As far back as the 1920s, some companies manipulated their stock prices by buying and selling their own shares. But the fascination with stock buybacks was a relatively recent phenomenon. In the early part of the twentieth century, dividends were divine, the way to reward stockholders for a company's good performance. Shareholder advocates would demand bigger dividends from recalcitrant managers, arguing that the profits, after all, were the *shareholders'* money and they deserved to get their hands on some of them. In fact because stocks were considered riskier than bonds, for many years the dividend yield on stocks, the actual cash return on a stock purchase, exceeded the interest rate paid on government bonds. That trend didn't reverse until 1958, when dividend yields fell below bond yields and kept shrinking. With more cash on hand, companies plowed more of their profits into expanding their business. To the shock of longtime market watchers, stock prices surged.

In 1982, after years of debate, the SEC set four standards for purchasing one's own shares, saying that if companies followed those rules, they wouldn't be accused of market manipulation. The guidelines were easy enough: A company could use only one broker or dealer a day to make its purchases, it couldn't buy during the frantic opening or closing of trading, it couldn't pay a price higher than the last independent trade, and it couldn't buy more than 25 percent of its average daily volume.

For old-line companies a regular dividend remained a symbol of solid corporate citizenship, proof that management was adept enough at generating profits that shareholders could take some money to the bank every single year. But in the 1980s new, fast-growing companies like Microsoft and Dell burst into being and ballooned so quickly that paying out a piece of the profits was unthinkable. Every dime was turned back into building the technology giants.

Eventually many businesses reach the point where they no longer need to invest all the cash back in the operations and their excess cash grows. Even as the big technology companies moved into the league of the world's largest enterprises and their cash accounts bulged, they held off for years on giving shareholders a regular allowance. (Microsoft finally paid an annual dividend in 2003 and switched to a quarterly payout the next year.) For one, there were tax consequences. Companies paid taxes on their profits, and then, when they paid dividends from those profits, individuals had to pay taxes as if the distributions were regular income. That changed in 2003, when the tax rate on corporate dividends was dropped to a maximum of 15 percent. By contrast, with a buyback only those who sold their shares for a gain had to pay taxes.

In addition, to the modern entrepreneur, dividends had become so fuddy-duddy, so unsexy. For a sizzling growth company, a regular quarterly payment to shareholders would be like letting the hair go gray and the belly sag. How could the stock market award a company like that the kind of premium price that marked it as hot and desirable? Holding off on a dividend could keep the image youthful, recognizing that maybe you were in the middle years, but you still had the moves to attract attention.

At the same time companies needed to make better use of the bloated cash reserves from their business profits than merely collecting the low interest rates of the late 1990s and early 2000s. Buying their own stock gave them a way to return some cash to shareholders without committing to a regular payout—even if many of the shareholders didn't know the buybacks were going on. In 1998, for the first time, U.S. companies paid more for their own shares than they paid out in dividends. In 2005 companies in the Standard & Poor's 500 spent a record $349 billion buying their own stock, up from a record $197 billion in 2004. The amount spent on stock buybacks even began to exceed what companies put into capital improvements, a stunning admission that managers apparently couldn't find better business investments for their cash.

Exactly what Starbucks was up to with its buybacks wasn't clear on the surface. While some companies liked to make a big announcement about their plans to purchase their own stock, Starbucks tiptoed through the process. The first clue came in the second quarter earnings report on April 27, and then it was seen only by those who like to cozy up with the table called "Consolidated Statements of Cash Flows." About halfway down the table, which shows where a company's cash comes from and where it goes, was a line, "Repurchase of common stock," that revealed Starbucks had spent $335 million on buybacks in the fiscal second quarter, compared with $40.7 million in the same quarter a year ago.

Ironically, as Starbucks was buying, many money managers still considered Starbucks' stock to be priced somewhere in the stratosphere. In early May *Barron's* reported that a poll of 175 money managers had ranked Starbucks as one of the market's most overvalued stocks, right up there with Google, eBay, and Yahoo!. A few days later, Starbucks announced a jump in April same-store sales of 9 percent, apparently benefiting from this year's sale on brewing equipment, which had taken place in March of the previous year. The stock rallied, climbing 3 percent to close at $52.24.

On May 5, after the close of regular stock trading, Starbucks said in a press release that its board had given approval for management to buy up to 10 million Starbucks common shares, even though 5.7 million shares could still be purchased under a previous board authorization. There was no mention that the company was still snapping up its own shares.

That admission came on May 10 when the company filed its quarterly 10-Q financial report with the SEC. There, in footnote eight on page nine, it said it had purchased 6.5 million shares at an average price of $51.12 for the quarter ended April 3. The company then noted that it had 12.1 million shares authorized for purchase as of April 3 and that the board had authorized 10 million more shares on May 5. It finished the footnote by saying it had 15.7 million shares remaining for purchase as of May 5. The reader who was comfortable with word problems worthy of a junior-high math exam could total the authorizations, 22.1 million, subtract the 15.7 million shares that still could be purchased, and deduce that Starbucks had purchased 6.4 million more of its shares since early April.

Starbucks' public statements were just as cryptic. In the May press release, Michael Casey, the chief financial officer, said the approval to buy more company stock "reflects the continued commitment by both the Board of Directors and Starbucks leadership team to pursuing opportunities that return value to our shareholders."

Did that mean Starbucks was trying to bring up the stock price?

"No," Casey said in an interview in his office, where the Boston native has lined the walls with photos of great moments from Boston Red Sox baseball and Boston Celtics basketball. "If that happens, that's fine. We always want the stock to go up. But that's not the purpose of buying the shares." Nor, he said, had Starbucks set out to buy a certain dollar amount of its own stock or to try to offset shares that it issued as stock options to executives and employees, as other companies often did.

He had other reasons. With the business strong and growing, Starbucks was rolling in cash. For the last few years it had generated more than enough hard dollars to cover the hundreds of millions of dollars needed to open new stores and remodel old ones, with some left over. The funds hanging around the balance sheet like a bored teenager had increased too. At the end of fiscal 2004 Starbucks had more than $600 million in cash and short-term securities. A major buyback put that cash to work and also gave Starbucks an excuse to add a little debt to its balance sheet, evening out its capital structure. The company did just that in August, agreeing to a $500 million credit line from a group led by Bank of America, its first significant borrowing in a decade.

Of course Starbucks could have used its cash pile for its first dividend, but Casey and the rest of management weren't ready for that kind of long-term commitment. Should Starbucks encounter a great acquisition or expansion opportunity, it wanted the freedom to leap on it. "Stock buybacks are much more flexible," Casey said, as onetime Celtics stars Kevin McHale, Larry Bird, and Robert Parish looked on from a photo over his shoulder. "Once you institute a dividend, there's an expectation that you're going to continue to pay it and that you're probably going to raise it in the future. . . . At some point in time, we may decide that a dividend is appropriate, but today we want to maintain the flexibility."

The other significant factor, he said, was "an opportunity to buy back shares at what we think is below the fair value of the company." He measured that value the old-fashioned, long-term way, calculating the company's projected cash flows for the next fifteen years, and then estimating what they were worth today. Forget the price-to-earnings ratio or other measures that showed Starbucks' stock was trading in nose-bleed territory. Based on Starbucks' finance department's assessment of its future results—and it should know better than anyone—the shares were undervalued. What the real value was, Casey wouldn't say. But over the next couple of months, as the stock bounced from about $46 in April to $56 in early June and then back down again, the company was buying its shares in the low $50s and below.

The sensitivity to price played out in the way Starbucks actually executed its purchases. Using a different brokerage firm each quarter as allowed under the rules, Casey would give the brokers a matrix. For example, he might ask them to buy back 100,000 shares a day at up to $50 a share. But if the price fell below $49, they could buy 200,000 shares, and if it fell below $48, 300,000 shares. Brokers were asked to shoot for the volume-weighted average price each day—but if they managed to pay less, Starbucks paid an incentive. Companies usually want their stock to go up over time, but when they were buying, they didn't mind taking advantage of price declines.

Clearly Starbucks saw benefits from the buybacks. But were they also good for Starbucks investors?

That answer was murkier. Certainly the company did have the cash available and it didn't take on much debt. To stock market professionals, buying shares was a far more palatable way for a healthy company to spend cash than making a bad acquisition or investing in something off-base, like, say, Internet companies. Reducing shares outstanding also helped Starbucks bolster its third quarter earnings per share by about a penny, enough to make a difference in the reported number. But the improvement in earnings per share was partly offset by some other real and potential costs: The small amount of interest Starbucks paid on its new debt and the lost interest that Starbucks might have received from that cash had it not been used for buybacks.

To those who study such things, the biggest issue was whether the stock itself was a good buy. To answer this, we could return to Buffett, who said, "There is only one combination of facts that makes it advisable for a company to repurchase its shares: First, the company has available funds—cash plus sensible borrowing capacity—beyond the near-term needs of its business and second, finds its stock selling in the market below its intrinsic value, conservatively-calculated."

The latter, of course, was the catch. Without Casey's insight and the natural optimism of an insider, it would be tough for an individual investor to figure the future cash flows, the required capital spending, and the appropriate discount rate. Ken Charles Feinberg, co-portfolio manager at Davis Selected Advisors, offered another route. Investors could look at the earnings yield, the upside-down version of the price-to-earnings ratio. That number was the earnings, which were just north of $1 a share for the previous four quarters, divided by the stock price of say, $50, giving Starbucks an earnings yield of 2 percent. That was much less than the company would get investing in government bonds. But if Starbucks' earnings climbed by 25 percent a year, as it had projected, the earnings would about double in three years. Then the earnings yield on those $50 shares would double, too, to 4 percent, something closer to what Starbucks might receive for its invested cash.

If Starbucks could keep the expansion intact, the earnings could double *again* in three years. That would give those $50 shares a more impressive yield of 8 percent—and now we're talking some value. That's the power of growth. Depending on your optimism and perspective, the buybacks might well be worthwhile by that measure, though the company didn't appear to be buying the shares below their intrinsic value, conservatively or liberally calculated.

Like many things in Stockland, there was no way to know whether a buyback was a good deal until you had some hindsight. If Starbucks' prospects and earnings remained strong, its growth continued, and its earnings and stock price climbed, the money likely would have been well-spent. But if growth slowed or the company needed cash, investors might look back with regret.

For now the jury was out. The stock continued to trade between the low and mid-$50s, and when the opportunity presented itself, Starbucks was buying.

6

June

★ THE INVESTORS ★

Winning by not losing

June started on a positive note, when on the first day of the month, Starbucks said its same-store sales climbed 7 percent in May—exactly what analysts were expecting. The stock had been slowly ratcheting up into the mid-$50s, and after the sales were announced, it held there, higher than it had been for most of the year.

A few small developments fed the company's insatiable need for growth. Hilton Hotels said it signed a licensing agreement to add more Starbucks outlets inside Hilton, Doubletree, and Embassy Suites hotels. And Starbucks said it was increasing its stake in its partnership in southern China to 51 percent from just 5 percent. The price was a pittance—less than $15 million—but the move underscored the message that the company would be expanding there.

Now that I understood Starbucks'

growth and knew what it looked at when it bought its own stock, the next logical question was, who were the other players in this stock? And what do they consider when they buy? That piece of the journey took me from coast to coast, starting in at the big Los Angeles money manager, TCW.

There over lunch in the firm's comfortable private dining room, stock analyst Nick Bartolo pulled out his Starbucks spreadsheet. To assess the stock for his firm's portfolio managers, he had built an extensive financial model, taking into account how many stores Starbucks might open, how fast sales might grow, and what its profit margins might be. He had estimated how much it would spend to open those stores, the depreciation it would have to record and the taxes it would pay. Because his projections went out to 2016 and he printed the whole model on one page, the sheet looked like someone had covered it with tiny rows of pepper.

But it was nothing to sneeze at. Riding on the analysis was a $700 million investment in Starbucks' stock.

While a waiter took orders from the day's menu, Bartolo, a late-twenty-something accountant who was just a year or so out of an MBA program, explained that he quantified the stock's value by estimating its future cash flows—much like Starbucks assessed the stock itself. While taking into account the company's projected sales growth, taxes, and profit margins, Bartolo's model looked at how the company was faring now, as well as what would happen if the growth rate slowed or other projections weren't as rosy.

Bartolo also looked for comparisons to estimate how big Starbucks could really become. In key markets Dunkin' Donuts had 15 stores for every 100,000 people; Starbucks had about 6.5. Another way to look at the question: The

United States had between 35,000 and 40,000 post offices. Could there be just as many Starbucks stores?

"Investing is a range of possibilities," he said. His job—indeed, every investor's job—was to handicap the various outcomes. From private company dining rooms to home dining tables, investors constantly weighed the possibilities of where Starbucks might be going—and often came to opposite conclusions. After all, even when a plethora of sellers pushed down a stock price, someone was buying, concluding, for whatever reason, that the stock was worth owning.

In the three to four million Starbucks shares that changed hands every day, all the daily duels of the marketplace took place at once. One investor might act on a hunch or a shred of news, while another might put the detailed analysis of several highly paid analysts and managers to work. Short-timers looked for tiny swings that might produce quick profits, either up or down, while long-term holders focused on trends that would sustain a stock over many months or years. Technical traders studied endless squiggly lines of stock-price movements to see if they could spot an excess of buyers or sellers who would send a stock in a single direction. Momentum investors knew that stocks on the rise tended to keep climbing—at least until something happened and they started to fall. (And then they really, really fell.) Analysts at Motley Fool recommended Starbucks—and those at Morningstar discouraged it.

In the quirky world of Stockland, many of them could be right all at once, depending on when you bought the stock and how long you planned to own it. In investing, as in religion, there were multiple approaches and answers, and people tended to be faithful to their own ways. Since no one was right all the time, most money managers simply hoped for more good years than bad ones and enough really good stocks to overwhelm the more common mediocre ones and the genuine stinkers. Shawn Price managed the $1.2 billion Touchstone Large Cap Growth Fund, which owned Starbucks from the summer of 2004 into 2005, but sold out in January and April. He made a profit of about $5 a share, which helped, but it didn't make Starbucks a standout. "We make about 85 percent of our profits on about 35 percent of our stock picks," he said.

In the industry the various kinds of investment managers were rated not on how much money they actually made for customers, but on how they fared relative to the broader market, often the S&P 500 Index, or compared with similar funds. That meant if the broader market or that particular sector was down 20 percent for the year and the fund was down merely 15 percent, the manager was a winner—even though many investors might feel otherwise.

About 53 percent of Starbucks' shares outstanding were owned by portfolios specializing in growth stocks, not surprising given the company's aggressive store growth. (In addition ten of the nation's fifteen largest large-cap growth mutual funds owned Starbucks stock in the late summer and early fall of 2005.) Another 19 percent of the shares were owned by S&P 500 funds and others that simply mimicked the well-known stock market indexes.

Even for those institutions with enormous sums invested in the coffee shops, the reasons for holding Starbucks shares were as different as the drinks on the menu. What was notable, though, was that most managers had a basic method and philosophy and stuck with it, buying when a stock fit their key criteria and selling when it didn't. Based on quarterly filings with the SEC, the biggest holder was a mutual fund giant just down the road from TCW, the American Funds. The funds were sold through brokers and investment advisers with an upfront commission and were part of Capital Research & Management Company, a quiet firm still partly owned by its founding family, the Lovelaces. The American Funds owned about 22 million Starbucks shares, more than $1 billion worth, with about half held by the Growth Fund of America, the nation's largest mutual fund. Even though it was a large stake, Starbucks was so far down the list (and maybe so far down in value for the year) in the giant portfolio of more than $100 billion that it wasn't even named in the Growth Fund's annual report dated August 31, 2005. Like most big-company growth funds, this one was heavy with technology stocks, like Microsoft, Google, and Texas Instruments, as well as well-known retailers like Target, Lowe's, and Best Buy, and energy companies.

The fund had outperformed the standard market indexes for several years, which it attributed in part to its unusual structure. To reduce the reliance on the whims of a single manager, each fund had a team of managers, each with a portfolio to run. The fund's analysts also had the power to buy and sell shares. Because the fund's management was broken into pieces, "every stock in the portfolio is a high conviction name for one of us," said Rob Lovelace, a senior vice president and third-generation fund manager. The structure "encourages them to run a tighter portfolio. We don't need to buy a number three or number four bank."

The size of the Starbucks holding in the Growth Fund indicated that it might be a top ten choice of at least one portfolio manager and maybe a top three for another. But because managers had autonomy in what they owned, it was conceivable that one could be buying a stock and another could be selling the same stock for the same fund.

Sands Capital, based in Arlington, Virginia, another of Starbucks' top five holders with about $900 million in stock, put a premium on sustainable above-average growth in profits. The company, which managed just $16 billion in assets, also looked for leadership in the company's industry and little debt.

At TCW all growth-stock investments were expected to produce strong and sustainable cash flows and to have financial report cards that topped their industries. But those financial results were seen as the effect, not the cause, of other less-measurable traits. TCW looked for companies with products that dominated their industries, or with a cost advantage that skinned the competition. It wanted businesses that were relatively hard to copy, and management groups with a winning record.

Bartolo, who followed about twenty other stocks closely and another thirty more generally, was attracted to Starbucks' unit economics, the way it made money in each store. Many of the company's biggest costs were fixed—its rent, its utilities, its equipment—which meant that as the store's sales grew, the profits could grow faster. "Each incremental same-store sales dollar is very valuable," he said, since an increasing percentage of it should flow straight to the bottom line.

While analysts for brokerage firms—what Wall Street called the "sell side" of the business—printed up and distributed reports for customers detailing their thinking, "buy side" analysts—whose firms make purchases for their portfolios— generally kept their work close to the vest. Once known as Trust Company of the West and now a unit of the French financial giant Société Generale, TCW managed more than

$100 billion on behalf of wealthy individuals, mutual fund holders, and government and corporate pension funds. Since TCW didn't want the rest of the world to know what it was up to, Bartolo's "buy" recommendation on Starbucks was for internal eyes only.

But his recommendation didn't mean portfolio managers would follow it. TCW was Starbucks' second-largest shareholder at the end of 2004, owning nearly 19 million shares valued at more than $1 billion. Then a new manager came into one of its institutional funds (one separate from the main growth funds), prompting some customers to pull out, which in turn forced some stock sales. The manager took this as an opportunity to remake the portfolio, selling a few million Starbucks shares in exchange for his own favorites in the second quarter of 2005.

On the flip side, Stephen A. Burlingame, one of two TCW portfolio managers overseeing about $27 billion in growth-stock investments, had also sold some Starbucks holdings in late 2004 when the price soared. But now with the stock down about 20 percent from the high in fall 2005, he was holding tight to it. His portfolio held just twenty-six stocks and typically owned them for three to five years, making the firm an unusually long-term investor. As such Burlingame cared as much about the atmosphere Starbucks had created, which encouraged repeat business, as he did about the number of stores it was opening.

Starbucks "is more of a ritual and less of a product. No one has ever created that sort of environment before," he said. "It's a toll bridge that you have to cross to start your day."

Given that, he looked at it as a subscription business. If people paid about $4.25 every time they visited, and they visited frequently, how much would they be worth to the company over the long run? If Starbucks could sell more CDs or sandwiches, could it maximize the revenue per visit? "We actually think that the lifetime value of customers at Starbucks is a lot higher than what the market thinks," he said.

He met with Starbucks' executives when they came through his office and attended a couple of investor conferences where they spoke, giving him confidence that the company's special environment would translate overseas generally and in China specifically. "Our expectation is that International over the next five years will be a meaningfully bigger share of the pie," he said.

His biggest concern? That customer service would slip, especially at licensed stores like those in airports, discouraging customers from going back to their regular stores. "The day I get a McDonald's customer-service experience, it's over," he said.

IN SHARP CONTRAST to these Los Angeles–based TCW professionals, Theresa Collier—whom we first met at the annual stockholders' meeting—was an amateur, a Seattle mom who started investing almost as a hobby but nowadays sees the work more as a regular job. A nurse by training, she quit the business after twenty years to spend more time with her teenage sons and work part-time selling Usborne books in area schools and homes and as a tax preparer during tax season. Many days she spends an hour or so at the computer working on her portfolio.

Her first investment—in the company that owns Usborne, Educational Development—was a huge hit. She invested heavily in it between $2.50 and $3.50 a share, and rode it up to a peak of $13. It was risky business for someone who drove a 1994 Saturn with 80,000 miles on it and who had paid off her home. But her success with that investment created a nest egg for further investment, and she set a goal: to make $50,000 in 2005 to supplement her income and that of her husband, who worked for the city-owned utility company.

Talking over coffee at a Seattle Starbucks, Collier, a slight and unassuming woman who could easily disappear in a crowd, explained that in the early part of the year, her investing bordered on day trading. She figured, admittedly simplistically, that if she made a $250 profit on 200 trades, she would make her goal—not including the cost of commissions. "It's definitely gambling," she said, "but with the odds in my favor." She traded the Chicago Mercantile Exchange, an unusually volatile stock, twenty times, making a $20,576 profit. Time Warner tended to move between $16.50 and $18, and since the price was low, she could buy a fair bit each time. She even traded Starbucks three times, for a $4,000 profit. She kept her commissions down by using online trading firms, paying less than $10 a transaction.

After a few months and some time with investing books like Philip Fisher's *Common Stocks and Uncommon Profits,* she decided her trading was too dangerous and went in the other direction, focusing on long-term investments. To learn more about smart investing she prowled the Web, trying sites such as Motley Fool, which she found too promotional, and Morningstar, which began rating stocks in 2000 after years of rating mutual funds. On Morningstar, for about $130 a year, she became a fan of the firm's popular Vanguard Diehards message board for mutual-fund investing advice. And she found recommendations of stocks that were undervalued and that had those all-important economic moats. Her twenty or more stockholdings included such recommended Morningstar stocks as Citigroup and Anheuser-Busch.

But Morningstar wasn't hot on Starbucks. The price was just too high, and the stock carried a mere one-star rating into February, when it moved up to two stars and then, briefly, three. Carl Sibilski, the Morningstar analyst who followed the company, looked at the cash flows and its ability to grow. In the first half of the year, he valued the stock at $43 a share and then raised it to $46—roughly the stock's brief fifty-two-week low. But he recommended buying only if the stock was in the $33 to $36 range, which, of course, it never was. "We like Starbucks as a company, but as an investor, we're worried that too much focus is currently on the good news and not enough attention is being paid to the fact that even highly successful business operations can and do have missteps along the way," he wrote in June.

The number of Morningstar "5-star" stocks varied, depending on the opportunities and what the broader market was doing. Pat Dorsey, the firm's director of equity research, said that investors who bought only the top-rated stocks would have realized about a 10 percent annual return. But the value-oriented approach wasn't as good at identifying true "1-star" stocks. After all, those who avoided Starbucks in 2003 and 2004 missed out on a big run. "That's an area we're looking to improve on," Dorsey said.

Because Morningstar wrote solely for investors and wasn't selling investment banking services to the company or stock trading to clients, it could be far more bearish than most analysts. It also encouraged investors to think long term—like years. "We think people should own stocks, not rent them," Dorsey said.

Theresa Collier was coming to the same conclusion, recognizing the risk she was taking in trading the same stock over short periods. She also had a few stumbles along the way, losing money on some investments. For instance, at one point trading online she accidentally bought 1,000 shares of a company called Iron Mountain when she meant to sell them. She sold her whole stake at a loss. But she was still sitting on real and paper profits on a portfolio that exceeded $500,000.

She was also still a big believer in two expensive high growth stocks—Starbucks and Whole Foods—despite Morningstar's ratings and her changing philosophy on investing. Though she owned just 100 shares of Starbucks, she saw a higher price ahead. "I am fascinated with China," she said. A colleague at H&R Block whose wife is Chinese told her that an emerging class of young people would be ideal customers there because they wanted to embrace new things and reject the old. "They don't want anything to do with the older generation," he told her.

In Dallas, Don Hodges was on a roll. The little mutual fund he started in 1992 with his son won a Lipper award for the best three-year performance in its "multi-cap" category, and now money was finally coming in.

At the end of 2003 just $40 million was invested in the fund, less than what the bigger mutual funds might plow into a single stock. With so little invested Hodges couldn't pay the big brokerage firms to market his fund to their investors, so individuals had to find and call the Dallas firm directly to invest. In contrast some of the biggest U.S. mutual fund companies, like American Funds and Putnam Investments, paid fees to brokerages for selling their funds to individuals, a practice known as "revenue sharing." In exchange the brokerages might offer only those funds to their customers—whether they were strong performers or laggards—or they might give only those funds access to their stockbrokers, making the brokers more likely to push those funds. The practice was legal though it was supposed to be disclosed to customers. In a crackdown in 2004 the SEC fined Edward D. Jones & Co. $75 million for failing to tell its customers that it primarily marketed seven preferred mutual fund groups because the groups paid for the access.

By the end of 2004 the assets in Hodges' fund had grown more than 50 percent, to $64.4 million. But Hodges still had more ideas than he did money to invest. Early in 2005 he was still fond of Burlington Northern, the rail company, and then tiptoed back into Krispy Kreme, which had been hammered after an accounting scandal. After selling 15,000 of the fund's 40,000 Starbucks shares in January, he kept an eye on it, and by February, with the stock down roughly 15 percent, he began to reconsider. It still felt expensive, but his gut said the market had punished it enough. He bought 15,000 shares at prices between $51.08 and $51.31. "I'm comfortable buying it here, even though I know it's high risk," he said.

As an investor Hodges' approach was a combination of study, analysis, and the intangible intuition that comes from years of experience. A native of Canadian, Texas, near Amarillo, he had started as a broker for Merrill Lynch, Pierce, Fenner & Smith in Oklahoma City in the early 1960s, and eventually became president of a regional brokerage out of Dallas. Unhappy with the endless meetings of top management, he hung out his shingle for First Dallas Securities in 1989. In addition to his mutual fund, he managed some $450 million of clients' money.

First Dallas had three stock analysts on staff, but they focused on smaller, mostly regional companies like hotel operator La Quinta and Palm Harbor Homes, a Dallas seller of manufactured homes, some of which made it into the mutual fund. Hodges got most of his Starbucks information by reading Wall Street analyst reports and just watching the company himself. "One of the things I've said for a long time is, the market can teach you to be a good investor if you're just a good observer," he said. He was impressed with Starbucks' growth, with how customers sit down and stay, and with the plastic gift cards that hold cash for the company. "How many of those cards are lost, or put in a pair of trousers and hung in the closet?" he wondered.

Though Hodges had been in the business for decades, he admitted to still becoming emotionally involved in the investing process. He fretted that individuals lost faith in stocks after scandals at Enron, Tyco, and Krispy Kreme. "I think you can get as drunk on money as you can on booze," he said of executives who have gone astray. He seethed when talking about executive pay and the enormous severance packages given to executives who were sent packing. "Why should a chief executive get any more than the guy in the mailroom, who's worked there all his life, when he leaves?" he asked, after ranting about the tens and hundreds of millions paid to some recently departed executives.

From Hodges' viewpoint, investing for others was hard enough when the market turned against you, without fraud and bad behavior coming into play. He remembered 1974, when the market was in such a downward spiral that he would buy a stock and "before a client even paid for it, you'd be down 20 percent." The misery was repeated in 2001 and 2002, when every industry seemed to be sinking. During

those months clients had sharp words for him. Hodges recalled one customer who bought in at the peak in early 2000
and sold at the bottom. "I kept saying, 'Stay in the boat.' He
called and said, 'You have ruined me, you have ruined me.'"
Hodges wrote him a letter trying to explain and apologize.
In 2003, the market soared 34 percent. But even three years
later Hodges could taste the client's pain. "I still have com-
passion for this guy," he said.

Hodges' emotional investment in his work sometimes in-
fluenced his investments. When Sirius Satellite Radio signed
Howard Stern, Hodges dumped the stock. "I just want to feel
like what we make money from, we can be proud of," he said.
A Morningstar mutual fund analyst, however, in noting that
the fund was volatile and had high expenses, also warned that
Hodges might miss growth opportunities by making decisions based on social issues when it wasn't a socially responsible fund. Still, Morningstar gave the fund four stars.

To Hodges, however, there were plenty of good companies to choose from and a few wouldn't make or break his
fund's performance. In addition to avoiding shock-jocks, he
wouldn't invest in alcohol or tobacco. In April he read in an
analyst's report that Starbucks had joined with Jim Beam to
market a Starbucks coffee liqueur. As a teen he had drunk to
excess, but quit after a bad car accident. Despite his admira-
tion for Starbucks, he didn't want any part of the new business, however small. He sold the fund's Starbucks shares,
some at a loss, at prices between $48.65 and $50.74.

"It kind of made me sad because I like the stock," he said.
"It's a good company and they've been good to us." He didn't
mind that some of his close friends drink—or that Starbucks
chose to sell the liqueur. "But I'm not going to be an owner of

it," he said. "I don't want to make a profit off what they're doing."

In May the assets of the Hodges Fund crossed $100 million for the first time and kept growing. They would reach $264 million at the end of 2005, a year in which the fund climbed 17.26 percent—without any help from Starbucks.

In AKRON, OHIO, rookie mutual fund manager Robert Stimpson and his Rock Oak Core Growth Fund were off to a bit of a slow start. He had bought 3,600 Starbucks shares at an average price around $60 in January, added 2,000 shares in March at a price around $52, and then made slight adjustments, selling 200 shares in May and buying them back in June.

His confidence about the company hadn't wavered. "The growth opportunities are still intact and remain very robust," he said.

For a mutual fund, performance was the lure to bringing in investors, but a newcomer had no record and few tricks for attracting them. Stimpson's company, the Oak Associates Funds, based in Akron, Ohio, had much bigger and more established funds, including the White Oak Select Growth Fund, with $1.1 billion in assets invested in about twenty-five stocks, all of them in technology, health care, and financial services. During the boom White Oak had blown the lights out, but in recent years it had been volatile and often disappointing. Clients began asking for a more well-rounded fund, and Stimpson hoped to provide one.

His Rock Oak fund was started with company and existing shareholders' money, and Stimpson spent about four months searching for stocks that met his four main criteria:

A strong product line with the power to influence prices and deliver consistent growth, the potential for global reach, innovative approaches, and a business that caught the demographic wave by, for instance, catering to baby boomers or young people. He chose Starbucks without building his own financial model or talking with company executives. Instead he relied on public information and Wall Street brokerage reports. He concluded that he especially liked its international opportunities, including its potential to have 15,000 stores outside the United States, and its efforts to add Frappuccinos and other drinks that appealed to teenagers. Store growth was another factor, as was the consistent growth record, even though he had to pay a premium for it. He figured he could pay a steeper price because he intended to own the stock for up to five years.

But Starbucks' first quarter woes, combined with price drops in eBay and UPS, helped send the new fund down 4.1 percent in the first quarter. With the decline, the assets in the fund fell below $10 million as well. The second quarter was going better, but not nearly well enough to make up for the slow start. Stimpson expected new inflows of cash to take time. New funds, he said, often don't bring in new money until they have at least a one-year record, but more commonly three years of experience.

Rating firms like Morningstar didn't help much. It didn't review the Rock Oak Fund because it was too new, but it trashed the White Oak Select fund for its heavy bets on unpredictable sectors, giving it one star. Analyst Christopher Davis noted that Stimpson had no prior record running a fund, and he fretted that the staff could become strained as Oak opened Stimpson's new growth fund and a new small-cap fund. "All in all, this isn't an attractive package," Davis wrote.

———

HEDGE FUNDS have been the hottest funds in recent years because a few of them have turned in jaw-dropping returns. The often secretive funds seek to make money regardless of what the rest of the market is doing, but the lightly regulated funds aren't for the fainthearted. Many use debt as part of their investment strategy, sell stocks short, buy complex derivative securities, or trade using complicated and proprietary mathematical formulas. And the cost of participating can be enormous: In 2005 the typical fund charged a 2 percent fee, or $2,000 on a $100,000 investment, *and* took 20 percent of any investment gains right off the top.

Even so an estimated 8,000 hedge funds were managing more than $1 trillion in 2005, up from $400 billion in 2000. In the overall ownership of Starbucks stock, hedge funds appeared to be, at best, bit players. Ownership data collected by Thomson Financial showed that hedge funds typically had small holdings in the stock at the end of each quarter—usually far less than 1 million of the 400 million shares outstanding. But the snapshot at the end of the quarter didn't always give the whole picture.

Consider Renaissance Technologies, a firm with offices in Manhattan and on Long Island that was regarded as one of the world's most successful hedge funds. Founded by a noted mathematician, James Simons, Renaissance traded millions of shares a day using highly sophisticated mathematical models that were so secretive even its own holders didn't understand its strategy. All they knew was that the company's seventy PhDs built models based on massive amounts of data that looked for statistical relationships between stocks and tried to make money from them with quick trades. On Wall

Street such firms were called "quants" for their quantitative work, or "stat arb" hedge funds because they used intense statistical approaches to ferret out slight price differences between securities, a process known as arbitrage.

Renaissance's Medallion fund had earned an average annual return of about 34 percent between its 1988 creation and 2004—even though it charged up-front fees of 5 percent *and* took 44 percent of all investment gains. Even if you had the money to invest, you couldn't get into this fund now. It closed to new investments in 1993. (In 2005, though, Renaissance began raising money for an even bigger hedge fund, designed for institutions and requiring a *minimum* investment of $20 million.)

In this rapid-fire trading of highly liquid stocks, the computers sometimes selected Starbucks. Whether they moved the price, attracted other kinds of trading that moved the price, or simply added to volume was impossible to say. Filings compiled by FactSet Research Systems showed that the firm owned as little as 200,000 shares at the end of 2004 and as much as 1.1 million shares at the end of September 2005. But neither the computers nor the insiders really cared. Nor did they care if the company reported significant news or if the Federal Reserve raised interest rates again. Instead they looked for action, volatility, and connections.

"We don't know anything about the stocks we invest in," said a spokesman. "We're not an investor—we're a trader. Warren Buffett is an investor."

So that was it? It was just what the computers wanted to do? "It's certainly not because I woke up this morning smelling the coffee," he said. "To us, it's a ticker symbol and a bunch of data points."

———

IN A NEW YORK office near Rockefeller Center, not terribly far from Renaissance, one of the hardy short sellers in Starbucks stock had set up shop in leased space in someone else's office. Walking from the official office, with its color-coordinated carpet and cubicles, into this investor's den could hardly be farther, both in geography and appearance, from TCW's private dining room. On simple wooden desktops stacks and stacks of reports and files filled in most of the spaces between the computers. The decor was far closer to college dorm room than New York hedge fund.

The investor, a bearded and pudgy middle-aged man, refused to allow his name to be used. Like many short sellers, he bordered on paranoid. Speaking with intensity, passion, and a few expletives, he worried that companies that identified him as betting against their stocks might go after him, noting that short sellers—who borrow stock and sell it, hoping to buy it back at a cheaper price—were sometimes threatened or followed. And he was certain that he wouldn't be able to ask questions on conference calls if company executives knew he was hoping their stocks would fall.

By nature short sellers are an odd lot. Given their investing bent, they tend to see the world as permanently out of whack and in need of adjustment. In a stock market full of Winnie-the-Pooh optimists, they are the Eeyores. At the horse track, this investor said, "most people try to pick the horses that come in first. We look for the ones that come in last. We're looking for three-legged horses."

But even for such naysayers, Starbucks was a hard stock to love. Despite its rich price and its endless potential for stumbling, the stock had gone up many more months than it had gone down. It had been such a heartbreaker for short sellers over the years that many wouldn't bet against it again.

The New York money manager, who ran a hedge fund that invested in about thirty stocks, long and short, and some short-only money, had been in and out of Starbucks a few times. A few years ago he made good money off Starbucks' ill-fated investments in the Internet. But this time he had made a modest bet, attracted by the more subtle questions about its growth. By his assessment the United States was overdue for a consumer recession. He was skeptical that people in China would pay Starbucks' prices for coffee.

Highlighting the tension between buyers and sellers, he looked at many of the same factors as TCW—and saw a completely different story. He thought the company's move to sell more food, CDs, and the like was moving away from its core business, a sign that the basic product might be losing steam. And he looked at the store economics and saw trouble. "If there's any slow up in their comp store sales number, God help you, because all their costs are fixed," he said. Because the first cups sold were expensive and the "nth cup" was almost free, a big drop-off in sales would quickly hurt profits.

"The question is, where's market saturation?" he asked. That was especially relevant because the market had placed such an enormous value on the stock. At the end of June 2005, Starbucks had a net worth that was about 60 percent of McDonald's market value, even though the hamburger chain had three times the sales and five times the profits. The fund manager clicked through a few more screens. The coffee chain, with a market value of about $21 billion, was worth a little more than either Ford or General Motors, huge companies that had fallen onto hard times.

In assessing stocks he and his partner went to analyst meetings, listened to company conference calls, and tore apart financial filings, which he described as "written by lawyers to keep people from going to jail." He also estimated his risk in each investment, using a "make three, lose one" formula. That is he was willing to bet on purchases that could make him $3 for every dollar he might lose, such as a stock that might rise up to $36—or fall as much as $12. He applied the same metric to his short sales, taking the risk that he might lose 25 percent or 30 percent of the value if the stock went up. In other words he wasn't just looking for his short positions to slip. He wanted them to crater, dropping by half or more.

He avoided companies that he thought were fraudulent, very small companies, and ones built on science or technology that had to actually work. For the year his fund was up a little. Pure short funds, however, are an investor's hedge against a nasty bear market, and aren't expected to actually make money in good years for the stock market. A West Coast short seller explained that the goal is to lose less than the S&P 500 goes up. "People do not invest with short funds for absolute returns," the investor said. "They want you to be cost-effective insurance."

Both short sellers had a cynical view of traditional portfolio managers. "People who make great fortunes are the ones who run counter to the herd," said the West Coast short seller. "The people who really invest well look where everybody else is and go where everybody isn't."

The New York investor believed many portfolio managers and other money managers owned Starbucks despite its high value because in the grand scheme of stock choices, Starbucks was a truly safe choice. Few bosses or customers would chew you out for owning it, especially since many other growth managers were likely to have it in their portfolios. And if your firm was competing for a 401(k) account, you'd want at least some of the same standard stocks your competitors had, or you'd risk looking like a freak in the bake-offs that companies and governments held to select their money managers. "Everybody wants to keep their jobs," he snarled. "Nobody gives a piss about the customers. Why should they?"

As I started to leave I asked if his commute had been affected by a musical performance on the *Today* show that morning that apparently had brought a crush of fans, crowding the Big Apple's streets at rush hour. He fumed. "Those are the worst things in the world!" He then ranted that the free performances were like an invitation to terrorists—reminding me that to market skeptics, disaster was always just a step away.

"There are two places you could blow yourself up on national TV—Times Square and here," he went on, gesturing toward Rockefeller Center. "Osama bin Laden could come with stuff strapped to him, and they'd let him go there."

Such was the life of a short—nasty and brutish.

7

July

★ THE TRADER ★

The moving business

E ven amid the steady stream of stories about multimillion dollar paydays and corporate excesses, the story that broke in *The Wall Street Journal* in July 2005 was a doozy.

A bachelor party for a top trader at Fidelity Investments in 2003, the newspaper reported, had started with a private jet trip from Boston to New York City and then on to South Beach in Miami, apparently paid for by a West Coast stock-trading firm. Another stock-trading firm paid for some of the hotel rooms. Over a fun-filled weekend, the guests dined at an expensive Miami restaurant and then enjoyed time on a yacht, paid for by yet another trading firm eager to win Fidelity's trading business. Guests on the yacht included bikini-clad women—and a dwarf hired to liven up the event. Among the activities that weekend: dwarf tossing, something that apparently involved a Velcro suit and Velcro "wall."

"Some people are just into lavish dwarf entertainment," Danny Black, part owner of Shortdwarf.com, told the newspaper.

The party attracted the attention of federal securities regulators, and not just for its entertainment choice. Regulators worried that Fidelity, the giant mutual fund that manages more than $1.1 trillion of Americans' savings and retirement accounts, might have directed some of its massive stock-trading business to the trading firms because of the favors it received and not because they offered the best value. In addition to highlighting an unknown demand for dwarf services, the investigation was notable for shining light on an arcane and often opaque corner of the market: the enormous business in the actual trading of stocks like Starbucks.

To a little investor the process of buying stock was sort of like turning on the TV and getting a picture—it just happened. Whether you sent in an order to buy Starbucks electronically or called a broker to sell your shares at the market price, you simply got a receipt back showing that the transaction had gone through. Did you get the best price possible? Hard to say. Was your order filled in seconds, minutes, or hours? Again hard to say. About all you knew for sure was that the stock was bought or sold and you paid a commission to the brokerage firm. And that commission cost could swing wildly, from a fixed rate of $7.95 to $12.95 per trade if you were a regular customer of an online discount broker to hundreds of dollars if you used a broker at a full-service firm for a big purchase.

All those charges added up to huge fees, $18.4 billion a year in total commissions paid to buy and sell stocks listed on an exchange, according to the Securities Industry Association, a trade group. Of that amount, institutions like mutual funds and banks paid about $11 billion in commissions, according to Greenwich Associates, a financial services industry consultant. Fidelity, for instance, was a huge trader; the company that stock traders called "Fido" accounted for up to 5 percent of the trading on the New York Stock Exchange or Nasdaq on any given day. Though it had a reputation for negotiating bare-bones commission rates, its totals still added up. Just five of its large funds—Contrafund, Magellan, the Low-Priced Stock Fund, Diversified International and Growth & Income—combined paid more than $160 million in annual stock-trading commissions, according to its filings.

Typically institutions and mutual funds paid brokerage firms up to 4 cents or 5 cents a share for trades, costs that came straight out of our mutual fund or pension-fund investments. Those payments covered not just the cost of traders and actual trading, but also the cost of stock analysts and their research on companies like Starbucks, a subject we will come back to in Chapter 11.

To understand this often-invisible territory of Stockland, in late July I visited the Jersey City, New Jersey, trading desk at Knight Equity Markets L.P., one of the nation's largest market makers in Nasdaq Stock Market–listed stocks. Starbucks would report its third-quarter earnings the afternoon of July 27, and I wanted to see how the market would respond, both before and after this important news, from an insider's seat on a trading floor.

The stock was still lukewarm by Starbucks' standards. As in May, June same-store sales increased 7 percent. But late in June the stock had stepped below $53 and continued to hobble between $50 and $53 for several weeks. Largely because both Starbucks' and McDonald's stocks were slumping compared with their year-end 2004 prices, stocks of big restaurant companies as a group were down about 5 percent for the year as of mid-July, while the S&P 500 was up 2.5 percent.

Sharon Zackfia, an analyst with William Blair & Co. in Chicago, saw the drooping price as an opportunity. She recommended Starbucks stock for her firm's "Current Better Values List," a bimonthly list of analyst picks that were expected to perform well over the next twenty-four months. The price was down, she noted, but more importantly, the price-to-earnings ratio had dropped to about thirty-six times the estimated earnings for the next fiscal year, below the average P/E range over the last five years. Analysts including Zackfia were starting to wring their hands over what would happen to Starbucks' same-store sales after the anniversary of the price increase passed in October. Zackfia predicted the stock wouldn't recover until after the October sales numbers were known, when investors would finally pay attention to its growth again. But to her that made Starbucks a good buy in coming weeks. In the short term, though, a positive earnings report could give the shares a jump start—and a weak one might send them tumbling once again.

Keeping a close eye on SBUX at Knight was Chris Rossetti, a trader and former middle linebacker for the Hofstra Pride who had studied finance with the dream of trading stocks on Wall Street. He interned at the American Stock Exchange before joining Knight in 1996. Only a few months before, he had switched from trading technology stocks to specializing in a smorgasbord of stocks, including restaurants, oil-services companies, and trucking and transportation firms.

Rossetti sat to one side of the massive trading floor in a two-sided row of institutional traders. Behind him were salespeople who talked to and took orders directly from clients. To his left another set of traders handled the retail trades that came in from individuals who bought and sold through Ameritrade, TD Waterhouse, E-trade, and the like. To monitor his long list of companies, he watched four giant computer screens filled with current prices, charts, and the latest bids, or the current offers to buy, and asks, the offers to sell.

This morning P. F. Chang's China Bistro, the Chinese restaurant chain, had warned that its quarter was "off to a very bad start," and its full-year earnings would be lower than expected. Investors were dumping their shares, sending the stock down until it reached a price that buyers were willing to pay. At one point in the day, the stock was down more than $9, or about 15 percent from its $63.12 close the day before, but now it was just down $6.50. "Some people don't care where it is, they just want to get it off their books," Rossetti said, as he clicked on prices on his computer screens. "Most likely, the stock is too low right now, but some people are still holding it down." Chang's bad news was pulling down other stocks, too, and Rossetti's screen displayed most of the restaurant group in red.

Stocks that were liquid, or that had plenty of buyers and sellers, didn't need much of Rossetti's attention. Most of their trading was done through the electronic networks that had exploded in recent years, allowing stocks to be traded almost untouched by the many people in this room. About 90 percent of the orders from individuals now were filled this way. And for a well-known stock like Starbucks, most buy and sell orders were routed directly into one of several electronic communications networks, or ECNs, where they were filled almost instantaneously or sat in line until the right price was available. Rossetti focused on the tougher stocks—the volatile ones, the big trades and the companies with relatively few shares.

Orders came flying in, some from one of three phone handsets in front of him, some via instant messages on one of his screens, and occasionally, one hollered from behind. A customer wanted to test the market by selling 25,000 shares of a $4 stock. If a buyer showed up quickly, Rossetti explained, the customer had let him know that more orders to sell would come in. But he wanted to start small so that he didn't show his hand; the client didn't want to artificially push the price down. Rossetti also worked trades of NutriSystem, the marketer of weight-loss products, a volatile stock that had been the subject of some rumors. One customer was buying 20,000 or so NutriSystem shares at a time; another was selling the stock.

A different client wanted to sell 25,000 shares of a thinly traded power transmission company. "It will be a miracle if they get that much done," Rossetti said as he looked for a chance to move some of the stock in pieces. Because volume in the stock was usually light, this amount of traffic might be noticed. "If anybody is watching, they'll be saying, 'There's a seller out there,'" he said. Yet another client wanted to sell yet another stock, but at the volume-weighted average price for the day, which meant parceling it out in small bits, trying to hit the average price that showed up on his screens.

Though they were also called traders, the folks with that job description at money managers or mutual funds had far different jobs, doling out their buying and selling to those who might be discreet or quick or cheaper than competitors. Those traders would call or transmit their orders to Knight's sales staff, who relayed the details to Rossetti or other Knight traders to execute. "All the traffic happens through the trader. We're the quarterbacks," he said. If the activity dragged, he would send a note out to Wall Street's electronic news systems, saying that Knight was interested in buying or selling a particular stock.

As one of his colleagues said, "We're in the moving business, not the storage business."

As a market maker Rossetti had the option of accepting another's electronic bid or offer or making the trade using Knight's own capital, then buying or selling to cover Knight's position later. In the olden days of a decade or so ago, market makers in Nasdaq stocks bought stock at the bid price and then sold it at the ask price, making a profit in the spread between the two, which was often measured in eighths of a dollar, or 12.5 cents a share or more. But securities regulations have changed drastically since then. Spreads between bid and asked prices have narrowed to as little as a penny in big-name stocks, and Nasdaq market makers now frequently traded straight-up with someone else and charged a commission.

On his far left-hand screen, Rossetti kept a tally of how he was doing that day, trying, of course, to keep the bottom line green. But he also knew he could take a loss "to do a good job for our customers." Afterward he would try to earn the money back or at least cut his losses—but he didn't have to.

"Loss ratios are an important part of our business," explained Robby Roberto, a Knight managing director who oversaw the sales and trading side of the business. Just as investors lose money on some stocks, trading firms had to take some losses on behalf of their big clients. "That's where the three-cent commission comes in," he said. "You are working for your customer."

Despite P. F. Chang's problems, Starbucks wasn't doing

much at all in the hours before its big announcement, for the most part going sideways. "It's fairly quiet," Rossetti said, taking a quick look before moving back to the work on his screen. "There won't be too much leaking out."

Today, though, he wouldn't wait to find out how the news came out. After matching institutional investors in trades in NutriSystem, Rossetti left early to take his two-year-old daughter Sophia to the circus.

Joe D'Amato, a quiet fellow with an easy smile, slid into a desk next to Rossetti's to pick up the trading. He still had 10,000 shares of another little stock to sell and he needed a buyer before the end of the regular trading day. After two 1,000 share blocks of the stock moved quickly at $17.20 a share, he guessed that a buyer was out there snapping up inventory. Immediately he offered—and unloaded—the remaining 8,000 shares at $17.20 each.

In the minutes before regular trading officially closed at 4 P.M. Eastern time, an order came in to buy 12,800 shares of Starbucks at the closing price. Every day, starting ten minutes before the close, the Nasdaq ran a little auction to set the ending price of the day, rather than using the price of the last trade that happened to cross as the clock ticked to the top of the hour. Traders submitted bids and offers, and a final number emerged.

Now it was about seven minutes until the close, and this client missed the window. But it was an important enough customer that Knight wanted to make sure it would get the closing price, whatever that turned out to be. D'Amato watched the prices flash. Starbucks' price was bouncing a bit between $50.35 and $50.42, and he had other trades to get done. Quickly he moved to buy 12,800 shares at $50.38—and ended up with 3,000 more shares than he needed.

The stock closed at $50.35, down 4 cents for the day. The move had cost Rossetti's account 3 cents a share, or $384—and D'Amato still held 3,000 shares in the account.

With earnings due out in minutes, he didn't want to be holding any of the shares at all. But he was able to move only 2,000 of his extra shares, this time at the closing price. His loss grew to $444.

Rossetti called to check in. "I lost $100,000," D'Amato teased him. (Actually the account was solidly up for the day.)

At about seven minutes after the hour, Starbucks' earnings headlines started to move, flying by on the newswires on the computer screen and running across the bottom of the four giant flat-screen televisions on the walls turned to CNBC and Bloomberg TV. Third-quarter earnings, the headlines read, were 31 cents a share, a penny ahead of estimates. The company was sticking with its estimates for the fourth quarter.

With the regular trading day over a small football flew by on the other side of D'Amato's desk. On the return flight it crashed into the desk in front of him, but he didn't look up. In after-hours trading, where prices tended to be more volatile because far fewer shares were traded, Starbucks' stock price almost immediately shot up to $52.

A colleague called. "Are you long on Starbucks," he asked. "Yes, up a G," D'Amato replied. But not for long. With a click or two, he sold the last 1,000 shares in the account at $52.10, making $1.72 a share—a $1,720 profit that more than covered the earlier loss. Then the stock began to retreat again, back under $52.

D'Amato smiled. "I got lucky," he said.

He finished his work and then pointed out the Starbucks stock chart. Traders keep an eye on moving averages because they almost paint a picture of the current market psychology in a stock, of whether the trend is up or down. The 100-day moving average, one gauge of where the stock had been, was just over $52. With the news, the stock had moved almost right to that average, he pointed out. Tomorrow, he added, if the stock held above $52, it would next run into a ceiling of sorts at about $53.45, the 200-day moving average on his screen. He didn't offer a specific reason, only that he believed the patterns of the market are consistent that way.

I headed back to the hotel to listen to the Starbucks conference call with analysts, but he was done for the day. The fine details of the earnings won't matter much tomorrow. Mostly Rossetti and his colleagues will need to know the broad landscape to get a handle on which direction the market may be moving.

The listeners to the call, of course, got all the gory details. In the hour-long chat, company officials covered all the numbers, noted the tenth anniversary of the popular icy Frappuccino drink and the release of an album by a new group, Antigone Rising. Earnings rose 29 percent, to $126 million, or 31 cents a share, for the quarter, from $98 million, or 24 cents a share, the year before. Revenue rose 21 percent, to $1.6 billion, helped by the opening of hundreds of new company-owned stores and strong same-store sales.

The company predicted it would end fiscal 2005 with net income of $1.19 to $1.20 a share, up from $1.17 to $1.19 a share before. It planned to open 1,800 stores in fiscal 2006, up from 1,500 in 2005. It also estimated that revenue in fiscal 2006 would increase by 20 percent and earnings would grow 20 to 25 percent, to $1.44 to $1.47 a share, before the cost of expensing stock options, a new accounting requirement. That meant the stock was trading at about 42 times current earn-ings and about 35 times the next year's projected profits.

Analysts asked whether Starbucks would continue with more assistant store managers, to give it a deeper bench as it grows, and inquired about possible price increases, sales of lunchtime sandwiches, and coffee sales through grocery stores. In their reports the next morning to their own sales-people and customers, they noted that the company had beat their expectations and most of them highlighted strong oper-ating margins in the U.S. business, helped by increased traf-fic and somewhat lower dairy costs. Those reports would help brokerage firm salespeople pitch big investors, which almost certainly would generate trading in the stock.

Trading was at the heart of Wall Street, the absolute core of what Wall Street firms did for a living. But as much or more than in any other industry, technology was roiling this busi-ness. In the 1980s, currency, bond, and stock traders were the "masters of the universe," the swaggering Wall Street types who cut million-dollar deals in seconds on the phone, made trades that brought in fat profits and took home outsize pay-checks. Since then, however, commission rates for stock trad-ing had fallen from more than 10 cents a share to an average of 4 cents a share, a 60 percent drop, and they are still falling. At Knight, which specialized in trading and didn't offer in-vestment banking or traditional research services, the average commission on stock trades was 3 to 3.5 cents a share.

Trading volume had ballooned, to be sure. But growing electronic networks, which hardly existed until the late 1990s, were grabbing much of that market share at a much lower price—as low as 1 to 2 cents a share. "You put your order in with a price, people see it and they respond to it," said

Christopher R. Concannon, executive vice president, transaction services, for the Nasdaq Stock Market. "It's a little bit like eBay, but much faster."

Trading on the New York Stock Exchange was still quite old-fashioned. Every stock was assigned to a "specialist" who kept track of the market in those shares. Even orders submitted electronically had to cross through that specialist's system. But at Nasdaq, Concannon estimated, roughly 60 percent of the volume was executed by these networks—that is, a computer directed the trade to a particular system and—boom!—the stock was matched with a buyer or seller.

This shift, combined with the other changes in how Nasdaq stocks were traded, turned the business upside down. At Knight revenue plunged 46 percent between 2000 and 2004, to $625.8 million. In 2000 more than $1 billion in revenue had come from handling both sides of Nasdaq transactions and booking the spread; in 2004 that business provided just $251 million in revenue. The money it brought in from charging commissions and fees had grown tenfold to $276 million, but it wasn't nearly enough to make up the difference. Like many Wall Street firms, Knight was trying to build other businesses, like managing investments for others, offering services like program trading and some technical stockmarket research. But steady profits were still on the horizon.

Industry wide, the pay for traders and salespeople was still good—in the $200,000 to $300,000 a year range for a successful equity trader with just a few years experience. A top salesperson could earn $800,000 to $1 million a year—but that was still less than in the golden days, when the potential pay was much higher.

More change was coming. In April 2005 the New York Stock Exchange agreed to merge with one of the largest electronic networks, Archipelago, and Nasdaq agreed to buy another, Instinet, putting the two marketplaces in the center of the revolution. For investors the sweeping transformation meant that trading commissions should continue to come down, good news for mutual fund investors and pensioners because trading expenses should decline.

The revolution in trading also benefited small buy-and-hold investors. Retail commissions were lower than ever before, trades were executed much faster, and investors could actually buy and sell at the prices they saw on their computers, rather than working from outdated information as they had in the past. Knight's business might be struggling, but "there's never been a better time to be a retail investor," said Thomas M. Joyce, Knight's chairman and CEO.

The shift, however, was more of a mixed bag for little investors who hoped to profit from stocks that they owned for a few hours, days, or weeks. Increasingly they were competing against huge investment funds that were quicker and could trade far more cheaply than any individual. More and more, less visible players were trading in enormous volumes, many using complex mathematical formulas to try to profit from the tiniest moves in the market. I got the message when one of the folks at Knight pulled up a list of big traders in Starbucks stock in June and a company named Lime popped up near the top. Lime? Clearly this wasn't Goldman Sachs.

It turned out that Lime Brokerage was an affiliate of hedge fund Tower Research Capital and was started in 2001 to offer faster trading services to the burgeoning hedge funds business. Headquartered in an old building with a funky rooftop garden in New York's Tribeca neighborhood, Lime's kitchen and break area was almost larger than its workspace. But on a typical day it traded 150 million shares on behalf of fewer than 100 customers, explained Michael Richter, executive vice president and chief financial officer.

The soft-spoken Richter, an accountant by training, was in his late fifties, old enough to remember working with real people. Early in his career, when he worked for American Express, he oversaw 300 clerks whose job was to type up letters of credit, each with their specific terms and conditions. The advent of the word processor in the early 1980s helped streamline that part of the business, so that each document didn't have to be hand typed.

Twenty years later, Tower and Lime realized that traditional brokerage systems were set up to handle many customers placing one or a few orders a day. But quantitative hedge funds, those that relied on fast, fancy mathematical models, needed the opposite, the capacity for one customer to trade hundreds or thousands of times a day. (The firms were sometimes called "black-box" traders because their methods were completely opaque. Since they were limited partnerships, they didn't have to disclose details to the public.)

Lime created a system that allowed hedge funds to use the brokerage to connect directly to electronic markets that match buyers and sellers in the blink of an eye. "Think of different garden hoses," Richter said, like a quarter-inch garden hose and fire truck hose. "If you try to connect your fire truck hose to a garden hose, it wouldn't work.

"In one respect, what we've designed are very big, fast pipes."

On a typical day, more than 12 million orders passed through those pipes. Using elaborate formulas, the funds offered to buy or sell shares to catch moves or needs in the market. But if the transaction wasn't completed in a second or two, the order would be cancelled and another one made.

"Some are trading in and out all day, looking to make a penny or two and get out," he said. Others would be long some stocks and short others—say, long Coke and short Pepsi—in hope of catching some hard-to-see spread.

With such high-volume dealing, trading costs mattered. Buying or selling through an electronic market cost 35 cents per 100 shares traded. On top of that, Lime charged 25 cents per 100 shares for providing the pipes, bringing the total cost to 60 cents per 100 shares, far less than the three to five full pennies-a-share commissions, or $3 to $5 per 100 shares traded, that institutions paid traditional market makers.

Even with such tiny fractions, Wall Street, of course, had found a way to make a profit. In the electronic-trading world, traders could provide "liquidity" by using their own money to act as buyers and sellers, just as old-fashioned market makers like Knight did by buying or selling shares for their own accounts. If the hedge funds provided liquidity, they didn't pay the electronic markets, but instead received a rebate of 20 cents per 100 shares.

Richter explained: Suppose a stock's current price was $30 bid and $30.02 asked, meaning that the most a buyer would pay at the moment was $30 and the least a seller would sell for was $30.02. "For whatever reason," he said, "your model says the price is going to go up." So the hedge fund stepped in and bid to buy shares at $30.01, putting the fund ahead of all the investors at $30. If someone took that bid, the fund would be credited with providing liquidity in the market, for offering a penny more than everyone else. For that the fund's total cost would be 5 cents per 100 shares traded— Lime's charge for the pipeline of 25 cents minus the 20 cents rebate.

Then if the fund turned around and sold the shares at

$30.02, it would make a $1 profit on 100 shares, and pay a total of 10 cents in costs for the two transactions, after paying Lime and receiving its rebate from the electronic marketplace. "You made nine-tenths of a cent (a share) on a trade," Richter said. "Life is good."

Use the computer to trade tens of millions of shares that way, and you could actually make real money.

My head still spinning, Richter offered a tour of the office, with several spots splashed with lime-green decor. Most of the employees were on a different floor, including a group of fewer than ten who handled all the orders, dealt with exceptions and exchanges and other tasks. Behind the main pod of employees, Richter clicked through several locks and opened a door to the computer room. A number of computer servers sat on rows of racks, as innocent as stuffed animals on a child's shelf.

"The servers are ours and our customers," he said. "Some of the customers like to put their machines here." Lime supplies real-time market data, and putting the computers side-by-side speeds up how fast they can communicate—and trade. When information changed, clients simply tweaked their programs.

As the door closed the machines no longer looked so innocent. In my mind's eye, I could see their calculating innards clicking away, buying, selling, buying, selling, completely invisible except for the volume they roll up on unknown stocks' daily tally. No human hand, no analysis of sales or profits, no economic forecasting, and clearly no emotion to get in the way. Their sheer independence gave me chills.

Creepy as it seemed, there will likely be far more of that in the future. It was hard to figure how much of the current trading was solely computer or mathematically generated, but some estimates put it at about 10 percent. Even if that grew, and even if the percentage of trades that institutions routed directly to electronic networks continued to grow, the stock market would still need market makers like Knight and Rossetti to keep some stocks in the game.

That was clear back at Knight early in the morning on July 28. Starbucks, which had closed at $50.35 before the earnings were announced, now was trading above $52.60 at 8 A.M., before regular trading had begun. In the relatively thin trading of the early morning, sometimes the bid and ask spreads grew wide. At one point, Rossetti noted, a buyer was willing to pay $53, but a seller was willing to let go only at $53.25. Slowly the demand to buy pushed up the stock and it climbed to $53.40, then $53.88, and then above $54, before settling back as the official 9:30 A.M. opening approached.

While Starbucks was hot, NutriSystem was crazy. It too had reported earnings after the close of regular trading and the weight-loss business apparently was fat and happy. Net income had jumped nearly sixfold, to $4.3 million, or 12 cents a share, from $758,000, or 2 cents a share, the year before. The day before, despite all Knight's trading in the stock, the shares had barely moved, closing at $16.42, down a nickel.

Now the stock traded as NTRI was up $3.50 and then $4.50, to nearly $21. Rossetti checked in with the salesmen who were sending in buy and sell orders the day before. "You have more to sell or what?" he asked one of them. The response was positive. "Looks like you didn't empty your truck," Rossetti told him.

The big buyer had picked up 150,000 the day before, but its plans for today weren't clear. Meanwhile another stock on Rossetti's screen was up 8 percent and climbing. To prepare for the day Rossetti said he got up at 5 A.M. and checked the news on Bloomberg before driving in from his home on Staten Island. Sometimes he spent Saturday nights reading about his companies to try to catch up. But that helped only a little when the stocks were shooting up or down. Then "a lot of it is managing chaos," he said.

Rossetti stopped to get the phone. It was his young daughter Sophia, calling to tell him that the circus they saw last night was just on the television. He chatted with her about it, spoke briefly to his wife, who was expecting their second child, and returned to the screens flashing in front of him. As the 9:30 official open approached, the NutriSystem (NTRI) trading took off. Some clients were looking to sell— quickly. The action in the stock attracted a new buyer interested in 50,000 shares at no more than a certain price. Knowing how volatile the stock was, Rossetti started small, hoping to get a better price. "To protect the customer, I don't go out and tell the world I'm a buyer. I'll buy a little and let them know I'm in a buying way," he said.

Another customer wanted 12,000 NTRI shares at the market price. Rossetti entered the order in the opening cross, the Nasdaq's first-of-the-day auction.

As 9:30 came closer, one of the West Coast salesmen called: His recent buyer had become a seller. Rossetti called another salesman with NTRI customers. "I've got 10 for sale. What will you pay for 10?" he barked, rushing to get the trade done. They settled on $21.25, and bang, the deal was made. He grabbed the microphone on his console and announced a trade for 10,000 shares of NTRI at $21.25.

NutriSystem shares opened officially at $21.50, up 31 percent from yesterday's close. Now another customer wanted to sell 75,000 shares. There was a buyer for a part of it at

$21.44, and to make the rest of the trade work, Rossetti bought the rest.

Five minutes later, however, the buyers seemed to disappear. The stock drooped back to $21 and kept falling, to $20.75 to $20.37 to $20.19. Rossetti was a glum man. He held several thousand NTRI shares in his account and the ledger was definitely red. But by 9:50, his attitude had recovered, even if his account had not. "We're okay," he said, certain the buyers would return.

While NutriSystem swooned, Starbucks was soaring. It opened at $53.62, up $3.27, or 6.5 percent, from yesterday's closing price and trading was fast and furious. By 9:35, buying was so strong that it was trading above $54 and on its way to its intraday high of $54.40. But unlike the frantic swapping and shouting in NutriSystem, Starbucks' trading was virtually silent. On one of Rossetti's screens, the trades flew by as they were matched electronically, many of them small 100-, 300-, or 500-share exchanges, with larger ones floating by as well. It was like watching a ball zoom through a pinball machine while providing your own sound effects: ping, ping, ping, ping, bumpbumpbumpbumpbumpbumpbumpbump, buuzzzz, ping, ping, ping.

A few short sales—bets that the stock would go down— passed by as well. To sell short, as mentioned earlier, the individual or fund borrowed shares and sold them with the belief that they could buy the stock back at a cheaper price later. Like so many of the trades, most of the sales were small— 300, 200, or 400 shares. Whether they came from small investors or big ones, however, was impossible to tell. With electronic trading the largest buyers and sellers could break their trades into dozens of tiny pieces and send them through looking like any trade you or I might make.

By noon Starbucks stock had calmed down. It was still up about 5 percent, trading at $53 a share, when Jim Donald, the CEO, appeared on CNBC's *Power Lunch* to talk about the company and its earnings. The message highlighted some new projections and repeated others that were familiar and comforting: In fiscal 2006, Donald said, Starbucks planned to open 1,800 new stores, up from 1,500 in 2005. It still believed that "for the long haul," it could have 30,000 stores. Internationally "China will ultimately be our largest market outside the U.S.," he said.

A host asked if the coffee wasn't "a little bit pricey," especially considering rising costs for necessities like gasoline. Donald noted that people come to Starbucks for the atmosphere and to take a break. "We like to think that coffee is just a little bit of what we sell at Starbucks," he said.

Upbeat, but offering nothing beyond the press release, Donald made a good showing. The stock didn't budge. The market apparently had heard it already.

After the frenzied early hours, trading slowed later in the day. NutriSystem, which had fallen a buck or two off its high, rose back to almost where it started, at $21.80 a share, on unusually heavy volume. Starbucks, by contrast, had slid under $53. As D'Amato had predicted the day before, it tested the highs above its 200-day moving average, but couldn't hold on to the gains. It would close at $52.68, up $2.33 a share or about 5 percent. The Dow Jones Industrial Average finished the day above 10700 for the first time in four months, and the Nasdaq and the S&P 500 Index both hit four-year highs. *The Wall Street Journal* credited Starbucks' impressive profits as one factor that helped lift the market's spirits.

By Nasdaq standards it was a so-so day in terms of stock volume traded. But it was a huge day for Starbucks, with almost 13 million shares changing hands, making it the third busiest day of 2005, behind two lousy days early in the year when investors grew disenchanted and pushed the stock down. Merrill Lynch had been the biggest trader, according to the computer screens at Knight. Lime's records show its customers accounted for about 6 percent of the volume.

Rossetti, in his role as market maker, only rarely actually pushed a button to execute a Starbucks trade. Yet Knight traded more than 700,000 Starbucks shares—ping ping ping, bumpbumpbumpbump—nearly all without human intervention.

8

August

★ THE COFFEE MOAT ★

It's all about the brand

On August 3 Starbucks told investors that its July same-store sales grew 7 percent, just about what analysts were expecting. On the same day Starbucks rolled out a different message for its customers. In a press release and in an exclusive story in *USA Today*, it announced its stores were now selling its own brand of bottled water, called Ethos.

What was significant about the new water wasn't its $1.80 a bottle price tag, more than the Crystal Geyser it replaced, or its sleek postmodern logo design. Rather Starbucks wanted customers to know that this was a brand with a social conscience and that it would be donating 5 cents from the sale of each bottle to help provide clean water in some of the world's poorest countries. In fact it hoped to donate up to $10 million over the next five years. *USA Today* turned the announcement into a story about the hot business of "cause-related marketing."

A story on the *Fortune* Web site was catchier. Ethos "sells to the rich to help the poor," the headline read. "This is shrewd marketing," added the story, noting that the brand could garner attention in a business dominated by PepsiCo, Coca-Cola, and Nestlé.

On the surface, the water news seemed, at best, marginally significant to the stock price, which was still stuck in the low $50s. The company had purchased Ethos in the spring for a mere $8 million. While Starbucks rang up billions of dollars in annual sales from coffee-based beverages, the company sold an estimated $25 million a year in bottled water. Of course now Starbucks would get the full $1.80 of revenue from the sale of each Ethos bottle, rather than paying wholesale prices for its old brand. And it would promote Ethos, boosting water sales, though they would still remain relatively small.

But Ethos was noteworthy nonetheless in that fuzzy netherworld of top brands and pristine reputations. As I toured the workings behind the stock, I kept coming back to two very basic, though seemingly unrelated, questions: Why, beyond the stellar store growth, did Starbucks' stock command such a premium price? And why did customers come back again and again to plop down such big sums for coffee and milk combinations? The two questions, I discovered, were related, and the answers had a lot to do with the kinds of strategies that Ethos represented.

As we heard from investors who owned Starbucks stock, only some of the reasons for buying or holding shares were quantified on a spreadsheet. In *Common Stocks and Uncom-*

mon Profits, the 1957 classic guide to growth-stock investing, Philip A. Fisher listed fifteen questions for investors to ask before buying a stock, and about half of them focused on the kinds of mushy areas that were impossible to calculate. He urged investors to consider the company's research and development, its labor relations, its management's integrity and especially the quality of its sales force. "It is the making of repeat sales to satisfied customers that is the first benchmark of success," he wrote decades before anyone had the urge for a daily venti nonfat vanilla latte.

Warren Buffett used a more romantic term, looking for companies with impenetrable "moats" to protect the investor's economic castle. The casual Starbucks observer might have a hard time seeing such a moat, arguing that anyone could hire outgoing clerks to sell a decent cup of coffee. But that failed to explain how Starbucks could shine in a declining industry and why some 35 million people a week were passing by McDonald's, 7-Eleven, Dunkin' Donuts, and who knows how many Mr. Coffees to stop at a Starbucks.

What became clear was that Starbucks had built its moat on multiple levels: It had a reputation as a top corporate citizen that set it apart from other fast-food retailers and retailing stocks, a sparkling brand that made customers from all walks of life feel special just for buying it, and a dominant market share that kept any serious direct competition at bay. Like many icons and idols, Starbucks didn't always live up to the hype. But consumers buy reputations and brands, and ultimately investors do too. Starbucks' manicured image brought customers back day after day—and contributed to that smoking price-to-earnings ratio.

(True, the addictive nature of caffeine helped too, but not

as much as you might think. Many Starbucks drinks are mostly milk, and a shot of espresso has far less caffeine than a regular drip coffee.)

Trying to quantify how much such a moat contributed was a bit like trying to measure love. A 2004 corporate citizenship survey by Cone Inc., a Boston-based brand-strategy consultant, found that 86 percent of those questioned would switch brands if one company supported a cause with its business, all other things being equal. And 70 percent said a company's social responsibility was important in deciding which stocks to buy.

Interbrand, a brand consulting firm, and *BusinessWeek* magazine tried to value brands in the same way financial analysts tallied up other assets. They estimated a company's sales and profits for the next five years and stripped out costs, taxes, and some investment expenses. They then discounted the future earnings to come up with a present value of the brand. By that measure Coca-Cola led the 2005 list with a brand value of $67.5 billion, an amount equal to about two-thirds of its stock-market value. As a relative newcomer, Starbucks' estimated brand value was a more modest $2.58 billion; still that was more than 10 percent of its summertime stock-market value.

Just as Starbucks built its thousands of physically inviting stores with careful attention to site selection and decor, it built its moat step by step, involving employees in the mission, using clever and unorthodox marketing, and meticulously managing and massaging its message. There was no slogan and no jingle, only a curvy green siren, but she represented a company with huge ambitions. As early as the mid-1990s, when the chain had all of one store in Japan, top executives set a goal of creating a global brand "that would be of the power and strength of the greatest brands in the world, the Pepsi-Colas, the Coca-Colas, the McDonald's, the Disneys, the Nikes," said Orin Smith, the CEO who retired in March. And the twenty-five-year ambition? "We were going to become effectively the number one brand in the world," Smith said. But it sounded so grandiose, so over the top, that when he and Schultz discussed it publicly, he added, chuckling, they more modestly talked about becoming "*one* of the most recognized and respected brands in the world, rather than *the* most respected brand."

The first and most crucial building block of the brand was the barista, the entry-level employee who made the coffee drinks and served the customers. "We're in the people business," Schultz said during one of our interviews. "If we forget that, we'd end up being . . ." He searched for an example, and then looked up, "Taco Bell."

Taco Bell?

"A fast-food purveyor without any soul," he explained.

To be a company with soul, Starbucks had to position itself as a good employer, one that could attract the top-notch workers who would take pride in delivering high-quality service. The chain didn't pay much more than McDonald's. Starbucks' baristas start at about $8.75 an hour in New York and $7 an hour in Indianapolis, and they all receive a pound of coffee a week. What sets Starbucks apart from McDonald's as an employer is its reputation for treating employees well.

In the late 1980s, well before the company turned a profit, Schultz pushed for health-care benefits for all employees, making Starbucks possibly the first American retailer or restaurant company to extend health insurance to its part-time workers. Over the years Schultz said many times that he was moved to offer such generous benefits by the rotten treatment his father faced as an unskilled worker. Once his dad broke his ankle and was out of work for a month without insurance. The family had to borrow money to get by.

Initially Schultz's board was leery. Schultz, who sincerely believed the move was the right thing to do, argued that it would help reduce turnover and save on training costs. The board ultimately gave in, but it had one other reason to do so. When Schultz bought Starbucks, the small chain's workers were represented by a union and employee relations were strained at best. One request the employees had made before unionizing was for more equitable benefits, particularly for part-timers. The most powerful benefits Starbucks could offer were decent pay, medical and dental insurance for everyone, and stock options—and by 1991 it offered them all to employees who worked at least twenty hours a week.

Before the company went public in 1992, the union disbanded.

The company frequently publicized and was cited for its health benefits. President Bill Clinton recognized Starbucks and Schultz for their leadership on the issue, and when the company concluded in 2004 that it needed more visibility in Washington, Schultz and his lobbyist chose health care for all as their defining issue.

Starbucks picked up about 75 percent of the cost of health insurance for its partners and less for their dependents after the employee had been on the job three months. Sometimes it was reported that it spent more for health care than for coffee—though that was an exaggeration. The company paid more for health insurance for its U.S. employees than it spent on the coffee beans it used in its U.S. retail stores, not including coffee sold in grocery stores. In total it spent $400 million a year on raw beans, known as green coffee, and about $200 million on health insurance.

The benefits gave the company's reputation a certain glow, even though there was slightly less than met the eye. About 80 percent of the company's employees were part-time, mostly young, single workers or those working a second job. While turnover was far lower than at many fast-food restaurants, 80 percent of the store staff still came and went each year. That meant most employees weren't there long enough to receive benefits, or at least to receive them for very long. In all about 65 percent of the company's workforce of more than 100,000 qualified for health benefits and 42 percent of the total workforce signed up. By comparison about 46 percent of all retail employees signed up for health care. (Many retailers, however, limited the benefits to full-time workers—but they also offered many more full-time jobs.)

The Bean Stock plan awarded stock options valued at about 14 percent of an employee's annual pay to those who had worked at the company since the previous April 1. But a worker had to stay four years to be able to exercise all the options and reap the full bonanza—again unlikely with a retail staff with 80 percent turnover. In contrast to the Bean Stock, most executives' options vested over three years.

From the earliest days Schultz also saw baristas and the stores as the front lines of the company's marketing efforts, in part because the fledgling chain couldn't afford much advertising, especially not on television. Lon LaFlamme, a former Seattle advertising executive, remembered Schultz coming to speak to his firm in the early 1990s around year-end. More than a hundred employees of Evans Group crowded into the conference room, and almost immediately, Schultz challenged them.

"Throw a stone in the water," LaFlamme remembered him saying. "What is it? And what are all those ripples?"

The staff looked back at the Starbucks leader with confusion. What was he talking about?

Schultz repeated his questions. "Throw a stone in the water. What is it? Where does it hit?"

Still no answer.

Finally he answered his own questions. "The stone is the store," he explained. And where it hits is where it touches the customer, the moments when it sells and delivers a cup of coffee. The farthest ripples, he went on, were the television commercials. Though Evans Group made its money off advertising for television, radio, and print, Schultz believed that a shotgun approach was a lousy way to reach Starbucks customers. Instead their loyalty and their business would be built sale by sale and by the inevitable word of mouth that followed a warm experience. People would come back for the great service, the great coffee, and the inviting atmosphere of what he came to call the "third place," the relaxing spot between work and home.

To keep the experience just right, store executives, marketing teams, and "customer-care" employees spent a lot of time conveying what was, in internal terms, "Starbuckian." That is, Starbucks employees would give you advice or information about an espresso maker or coffee grinder, but wouldn't push you to buy it. Starbucks never gave out cents-off coupons, but it would offer 100 samples a day of its newest beverage. Starbucks wouldn't pass out one of those loyalty cards that rewards you with a free drink after so many purchases—too déclassé. But it would sell you a very groovy plastic gift card that you could refill at the store or online and use to speed up your purchase. By the middle of 2005 Americans were carrying around more than $150 million on their Starbucks gifts cards, essentially an interest-free loan to their favorite coffee peddler. (There was a reward of sorts. If you registered your card online and used it enough, Starbucks would occasionally send you a coupon for a free drink or other free stuff. But it wouldn't tell you that; if you knew, it couldn't, to use one of the company's favorite terms, "surprise and delight" you.)

The company still spent well under 2 percent of its sales on advertising, and its only television advertising was through its PepsiCo joint venture, which sold bottled Frappuccinos and canned coffee drinks. As a result much of its marketing took place in the field, with local promotions that made stores feel like they were part of the neighborhood rather than part of a faceless worldwide chain. On the Thursday night before a new store opened on Friday, Starbucks often hosted a "friends and family" night that typically benefited a local charity. Baristas got to practice in a live setting and the store started to build community support right off the bat. Local Starbucks marketers have purchased a whole night of movie tickets for lucky theatergoers in Los Angeles and paid for parking in downtown areas for a day during the holidays. "Eighty percent of my dollars are spent either in our stores with collateral or in that kind of activity," said Anne Saunders, Starbucks senior vice president, global brand strategy and communications.

One particular advantage of local marketing was that clever gimmicks may get noted in the local press. Schultz and Starbucks learned early on that upbeat stories in local newspapers and on local radio and television gave it more credibility and attention than it could ever have purchased. Or as Saunders put it, "We have found non-paid media to be a really effective way to get our message out. People are interested in us."

The chain got plenty of other attention, especially from comedians and late-night talk show hosts. After oil executives testified before Congress about sky-high energy prices, Jay Leno told *The Tonight Show* audience that "the only way the oil companies could make more money is if they were drilling for oil and struck Starbucks coffee." After Starbucks began putting quotations on its cups, Conan O'Brien took a jab: "Starbucks says they are going to start putting religious quotes on cups. The very first one will say, 'Jesus, this cup is expensive!'"

When the message was just right, Starbucks played along. During a ratings "sweeps" week, David Letterman of *The Late Show* decided he needed his Starbucks faster—and at his own desk. The Starbucks at 54th Street and Broadway was linked to a spout on Letterman's desk with the help of 550 feet of clear plastic tubing and a nitrogen tank for power. Someday, the talk-show host predicted, every house in America would have a direct Starbucks spigot.

After a barista turned on the power to send decaf Sumatra shooting through the tubing, cameras followed the coffee out of the store, across 54th Street, across Broadway, into the lobby, through the theater and out the spigot. A clearly delighted Letterman took a big gulp. "It's ice cold!" he said. "But still, in all, I'm happy to have it."

The company wasn't willing, however, to play ball with the rookie *Late, Late Show* host Craig Ferguson, who complained in several monologues that the Starbucks on Melrose Avenue in Los Angeles didn't have a bathroom. "How can you sell a diuretic beverage and not have a bathroom?" he griped. The store did have one once, he was told, but it had been closed because prostitutes used it. (Starbucks, in an e-mail, said that there had been "numerous misuses of the facilities" at the Melrose store and it closed the restrooms to the public "to mitigate the unwanted behaviors.") Ferguson began a campaign to bring Howard Schultz on the show. But the request never made it past the public relations team. Potty humor was definitely not Starbuckian.

Keeping the message upbeat was part of the company's carefully groomed marketing plan. It played out in the company's six "guiding principles" (which included "Provide a great work environment" and "Contribute positively to our communities and our environment"), as well as in often-repeated aphorisms like, "We're not a coffee company serving people; we're a people company serving coffee," and the company's goal to "stay small while growing big." Starbucks frequently tied a charitable donation to its business initiatives. In August Schultz was preparing for a September trip to China, his first in several years. As the date approached, he asked what special program Starbucks would announce for the growing market. Marketers and operations executives had to scramble to pull one together. During the trip, he announced a $5 million fund to support education there; details would have to come later.

As the world's largest buyer of green coffee, Starbucks touted—and won recognition for—its Coffee and Farmer Equity or C.A.F.E. practices, which offered premium prices to suppliers who met its standards for economic, social, and environmental processes. The program helped farmers—and Starbucks. With the chain already buying close to 20 percent of all the high-quality coffee grown and still expanding quickly, it needed to ensure an adequate supply of top-notch arabica coffee, the fussier and more flavorful beans grown at higher altitudes around the equator. By encouraging more farmers and cooperatives to meet its requirements, it ideally would increase the supply available to it. It also reached agreements to buy Fair Trade coffee, coffee bought from participating cooperatives at above-market prices. But it still was criticized for failing to buy enough.

Sometimes the message spun out of control. After the September 11, 2001, terrorist attacks, an employee at a New York store near the disaster site charged rescue workers $130 cash for three cases of bottled water. A call to the company to complain allegedly was ignored, and the story quickly began to circulate on the Internet.

Within two weeks Smith, then CEO, had reimbursed the ambulance company and apologized, and provided free coffee and other gifts. "We thought we had taken care of it," said Audrey Lincoff, Starbucks' media relations director. But with the word continuing to travel via e-mail and the Internet, the damage continued, and Starbucks looked like every other greedy, profit-mongering corporation. "What occurred was this influx of interest that was out of our control because, you know, the Internet is [out of control]. It has a life of its own," Lincoff said. "That was something that was new to us." The company spent months answering questions about the incident.

But it learned its lesson. After the invasion of Iraq, e-mails began circulating that Starbucks refused to donate coffee to the military. Lincoff said Starbucks contacted the writer of the original e-mail to ask for the letter that supposedly stated Starbucks' position. She said the writer admitted to jumping to conclusions and apologized. But as the war escalated, the e-mail continued to make the rounds. The company provided a letter that its employees could share with customers and posted a statement on its Web site saying that it had donated 50,000 pounds of coffee to troops through the American Red Cross and that its employees were collecting and sending their weekly free coffee as well.

As the company expanded, Starbucks increasingly encountered the sorts of backlash that could tarnish its image and the enthusiasm for its stock, including health concerns, the financial bite it took from customers' wallets, and how it handled union activism. In late August the company's daily media report picked up a story about a new list of "ten foods you should never eat" from the Center for Science in the Public Interest, a consumer advocacy group that has scathing words for fast food. Among the delicacies on the elite list: Strawberries and Crème Frappuccino, with the 16-ounce version weighing in at 570 calories with whipped cream and 440 without.

While McDonald's was under fire for contributing to the nation's obesity, Starbucks largely escaped criticism about the calories and fat it served up—though it could be hefty. A McDonald's quarter-pounder with cheese had 510 calories and 25 grams of fat—but those killer Starbucks cinnamon scones had 510 to 580 calories and 25 to 27 grams of fat, depending on where you bought them. A 16-ounce mocha latte topped with whipped cream delivered 400 calories, half from fat, and the company's Chantico "drinking chocolate" carried 390 calories in the little 6-ounce cup, both just slightly less than a 12-ounce McDonald's vanilla shake. Aware that customers were caring more about the calorie count, Starbucks hired a nutritionist in 2005 and began to introduce more low-fat and reduced-fat offerings.

Other consumer advocates began to worry that too many Americans were frittering away their futures on Frappuccinos. The heaviest Starbucks users—nearly a quarter of all customers—averaged sixteen visits a month. With the average customer spending about $4.25 a visit, that could add up to more than $800 a year. *The Washington Post* reported that college financial aid officers were trying to convince students that using their student loans to buy daily lattes was lunacy—and dangerous to their financial health. Using borrowed money to buy a $3 latte five times a week for four years would cost a total of $4,154 if it was paid back over ten years at 6 percent interest.

Even the Internal Revenue Service weighed in. With my refund for my 2004 taxes, the nation's tax collector included a card promoting Treasury securities that showed a row of steaming hot paper cups of coffee. The tagline: "Why not start a savings habit instead?" The IRS didn't mention Starbucks, but the reference (and the nondescript round logo on the cups) was impossible to miss.

The company also faced an effort to unionize a few New York City stores. The movement by the Industrial Workers of the World was small, but it garnered national media coverage after the National Labor Relations Board issued a complaint charging that the company had tried to stop employees at three stores from participating in union activities. Starbucks later settled the charges by agreeing to rehire two terminated workers, paying less than $2,000 in back pay and changing some policies, including one that banned union pins at work.

To keep the brand-machine chugging along, Starbucks continually nurtured its reputation. The Ethos purchase put all the pieces in action, with offbeat marketing, careful con-

struction of the message, and close attention to the social responsibility résumé.

The little company had been founded by Peter Thum, a
former McKinsey & Co. consultant whose work took him to
South Africa, where he saw up close the price of severe
poverty and the simple needs in underdeveloped countries.
"Probably the most serious problem that I encountered was
the lack of clean water," he said. He recruited a pal from business school, Jonathan Greenblatt, to help him build a company that would donate half its profits to providing clean
water to children in underdeveloped countries.

Their philanthropic mission made a lot of sense. Unfortunately their business plan didn't. They looked to other models, like Paul Newman's Newman's Own brands, but they
didn't have a movie star's name, or bank account, to go with
their product. Instead they were asking investors to put
money into a company that would sell a commodity, bottled
water, compete against multinational giants, and then give
away half the profits—half the *investors'* profits. And they
were doing it in 2002 and 2003, as the technology industry
and the stock market were scraping modern-day lows. "We
were talking to investors, and again and again and again, they
said to us, 'This is just not interesting,'" Greenblatt said.

Finally Greenblatt saw a parallel in technology companies. Those firms produced a prototype and let potential customers play with it. If they wanted to sell a special kind of
water, they needed to show investors what it would look like.
They designed a bottle with a snappy logo, a world map, and
explanation of Ethos' goals. Then, with a borrowed Volvo station wagon, they began to search for potential customers. To
show that the nonprofit side of their concept also worked,

they helped fund a water project in Ethiopia and another in Honduras. The cost? Less than $500 in places where a little can go a long way.

A couple of other technology entrepreneurs invested enough that they could buy the plastic for their bottles and get going. By early 2004 Thum and Greenblatt started to find takers: natural food stores, yoga studios, cafés, and later a Whole Foods grocery in the Westwood neighborhood of Los Angeles. They also tried creative marketing. Knowing that a big brand name had paid for the rights to pass out water on the red carpet at the Academy Awards, they managed to get their water into Toyota Priuses that were delivering environmentally conscious stars to the big event. Tom Hanks and Will Farrell carried their bottles out of the cars. A Greenblatt acquaintance who had been a White House speechwriter became a scriptwriter for *The West Wing* and got a bottle on an episode. Another supporter helped win it a cameo on *Without a Trace*.

Still they were desperate for more investment. They took a gamble on the 2004 TED conference, an annual gathering in Monterey, California, of big thinkers in technology, entertainment, and design. Attending was costly, several thousand dollars from a shrinking treasury. But there they met Pierre Omidyar, the founder and chairman of eBay, who was beginning to put some of his enormous wealth to work funding projects with a mission. A few weeks later an Omidyar representative contacted them about an investment, which was completed in June 2004, giving them enough to move out of Greenblatt's spare bedroom and to begin receiving paychecks.

All the while Thum and Greenblatt had been trying to make contacts at Starbucks, which seemed like a perfect fit for their water. But months of door-knocking hadn't yielded much progress. Omidyar, though, had the key. He knew Schultz, a former eBay director, and was willing to ask him to hear the Ethos fellows out.

A meeting was scheduled for July 2004 and Thum and Greenblatt worked for weeks on their presentation, a Power-Point to end all PowerPoints. Schultz bounded in and almost immediately waved off the formal show, asking instead for them to just tell him about Ethos. He was instantly enthusiastic. "He said, 'This is great. I love it. Let's go. Let's do this,'" Greenblatt remembered.

Schultz began calling in other executives to hear the spiel. Before long talks began to bring Ethos bottles into Starbucks stores. The water company was still embryonic, with sales of just a few hundred thousand dollars. Since there were no profits yet, it had invested in international water projects by treating the donations as something like a marketing expense, a cost of doing business. To serve Starbucks' more than 4,000 company-owned U.S. stores, Ethos needed to put its distribution system on steroids and find another water supplier on the East Coast. Sometime during the talks in 2004, the discussion turned from adding Ethos Water to the stores to acquiring the business.

The Ethos deal fit as well in Starbucks' business as it did in its social responsibility portfolio. Nationwide sales of bottled water were growing 7 to 9 percent a year, faster than sales of soft drinks. Company officials had talked from time to time about a proprietary water brand, but had never made the leap. As with coffee, owning the whole production chain could improve margins. The driving force behind the deal, however, was the do-good angle and its almost irresistible sound bite: Water for water.

Starbucks announced the purchase in early April 2005, focusing not on the water business, but on its role in providing clean water in developing countries. "Starbucks and Ethos share a deep passion to improve global communities," CEO Jim Donald said in the press release. What did the coffee company get for its $8 million? Mostly the value of the trade name of a brand available in some West Coast Whole Foods stores and yoga studios. Virtually all the purchase price was treated as goodwill, the accounting term for the price paid above and beyond real assets like cash and equipment. Schultz's friend Omidyar made a quick profit on his investment.

To prepare for an August launch in U.S. stores, the PR machine geared up. While Ethos originally planned to give up half its profits for clean-water projects, Starbucks would donate a nickel from the retail sales price to the clean-water cause, promising a minimum of $250,000 in 2005 and $1 million in 2006, far more than Ethos could have spent alone. Later Starbucks announced a heftier "goal" of providing $10 million to clean-water projects over five years.

Rather than create an ad campaign to launch the water in stores in August, Thum and Greenblatt agreed to drive a recreational vehicle (running on biodiesel) across the country, keeping a blog, stopping at stores, and organizing "Walks for Water" with Starbucks partners. The primary goal was to excite employees, who then would extol Ethos Water's virtues to customers. Though the daily diary hardly made for riveting reading ("Milwaukee is really a terrific city." "After my first-ever visit, I can now say that I like Cleveland."), the visits and the water walks got a fair bit of coverage in the local newspapers and television.

There was a little backlash as well. Leno took a shot at the price and the nickel for charity on *The Tonight Show*. "Why don't you drink the water out of a fountain and give $1.80 to the poor country?" he said. Greenblatt noted in a blog entry that some folks had questioned the retail price, which, he explained, represented the higher cost of a fully recyclable bottle and a smaller distribution system, as well as being consistent with "our premium co-hort." (My translation: Everything at Starbucks costs more.)

To bring attention to the new water, stores displayed it in baskets and bins in prime spots directly in front of the cash registers, a surefire way to improve sales, and printed up small brochures with the "Ethos story." In the first months after the launch, Starbucks boasted, water sales were up more than 30 percent over the previous year.

There was one major hitch: Late in the year Starbucks' own quality assurance tests found the level of bromates in the water bottled at the Ethos California supplier to be above the maximum allowed by U.S. Food and Drug Administration standards. (Bromates are formed from the mineral bromide during the purification process.) Quietly Starbucks pulled the water from shelves in fourteen states, from Texas and Oklahoma west to Washington and California. For months water was trucked at a steep price to the western states from the Pennsylvania supplier, except in California and Nevada, where another brand was sold.

No press release announced the news. Rather Starbucks posted a notice on the Ethos and Starbucks Web sites for a week and alerted the FDA, but otherwise was silent about the problem. Not a single media outlet reported on it. Lining up a new California distributor took months, and Ethos didn't reappear in California until early March 2006. Despite the hitch, Ethos almost immediately added to the corporate aura.

That kind of careful image building was a key reason that Starbucks continued to stand out in a business that others had been unable to master. Once Starbucks demonstrated for the world the same eye-popping profit potential that captivated Schultz, thousands of entrepreneurs took a stab at their own coffeehouses. On the surface, at least, the business appeared to be a license to print money. The ingredients in a cup of coffee or caffè latte cost probably 20 to 30 cents, including the coffee, the milk, the cup and lid, and the water, sugar, and stirrer. If you sold your 12-ounce creations for $1.50 for straight coffee or $2.50 or more for a latte, your gross margin, or the profit after your cost for the goods, could total a tasty 85 percent.

Labor, rent, and other costs added to expenses. But a store in a good location with the right mix of coffee and regular customers could be impressively profitable, with profit margins around 20 percent, said Bruce Milletto, a coffee consultant. No wonder, then, that as Starbucks grew, the number of U.S. coffeehouses exploded to an estimated 18,600 in 2004 from just 3,600 in 1994. About 12,000 of those stores or kiosks were named something other than Starbucks.

Some of them even sold better-tasting coffee. At the end of 2004 *Consumer Reports* ranked the Colombian coffee from Caribou Coffee of Brooklyn Center, Minnesota, as the best on the market. Dunkin' Donuts ground Colombian was ranked "very good," and Folgers whole bean coffee came in fifth, as "good." And Starbucks? It ranked eleventh. Two *Consumer Reports* expert tasters noted the coffee tasted astringent and burnt.

The explosion in coffeehouses explained why "specialty" coffee, higher quality beans carefully roasted, was the only bright spot in a declining industry. Only about half of U.S.

adults drank coffee every day, down from 78 percent in 1954. And in 2005, according to the trade publication *Beverage Digest,* each American on average consumed about 16.4 gallons a year, per person, down a third from the mid-1980s, as soft drinks, fruit juices, teas, and bottled waters gained market share. But in 2005 15 percent of Americans had a cup of specialty coffee every day, up from just 9 percent five years earlier. Sixty percent enjoyed a specialty blend occasionally.

Still none of Starbucks' competitors could achieve anywhere near the size or scale of Starbucks. Peet's Coffee and Tea, which had spawned Starbucks so many years ago, still specialized in whole beans and expanded slowly, with only about 100 stores open. Caribou Coffee, with 337 outlets, was a big hit in the Twin Cities. When it expanded into the Midwest and mid-Atlantic states, it located its stores near Starbucks in hope of drawing in its competitor's customers. But its sales volume per store was far less than Starbucks' and it struggled to turn solidly profitable. Similarly a northwest chain called Tully's, with about 100 stores, matched Starbucks drink for drink, but this August it was selling assets to straighten out its balance sheet, despite more than a decade in business.

McDonald's and Dunkin' Donuts, feeling the heat from Starbucks, both took steps to improve their coffees. But while analysts and much of the business press characterized the shifts as battles between the big players, the chains actually appealed to different kinds of customers. Dunkin' Donuts discovered that firsthand when it tried an experiment.

Dunkin' paid Starbucks customers in Phoenix, Chicago, and Charlotte, North Carolina, to go to Dunkin' Donuts instead, and paid its own customers to switch to Starbucks. Neither group was happy about the assignment. The Starbucks loyalists were appalled when Dunkin' employees put milk and sugar in their coffee for them. "The Starbucks people couldn't bear that they weren't special anymore," an ad-agency executive who helped with the research told *The Wall Street Journal.* In equal measure the Dunkin' devotees were put off by the fancy names, fat prices, and big couches of a Starbucks store. One complained that hanging out in a Starbucks felt like "celebrating Christmas with people you don't know."

The existence of such different kinds of consumers explained how millions of cups of coffee could be sold each day by thousands of varying outlets. But within that Starbucks had carved a high-end niche where it didn't yet have a major challenger—no Pepsi to the Coke, no Burger King to the McDonald's. Starbucks might offer 55,000 different ways to customize a drink, but its real secret recipe was its ability to bring regular customers back again and again, and to entice new customers to try the product—and then come back again and again.

As with Coca-Cola, someone—in fact, almost anyone—could try to copy Starbucks exactly, down to the roasting, the drinks, the training, and the comfy chairs. And the copycat still wouldn't have what Starbucks had, because it wouldn't have the number of outlets, the efficiencies, or the brand recognition that had been roughly twenty years in the making. At the same time, there was no patent to protect it or special technology to block an astute marketer from coming along with something newer and hipper. In that sense Starbucks was forever vulnerable to the fickle nature of consumer tastes and desires, making its brand and image as important as its locations and coffee.

9

September

★ THE STOCK SPLIT ★

Nobody rings a bell at the top or bottom of the market

A t the very end of August, Hurricane Katrina roared through the Gulf of Mexico and wreaked devastation along the coast, flooding New Orleans and displacing hundreds of thousands of people. Scores of stores and businesses closed. Gasoline prices soared to record levels above $3 a gallon as oil and gas production and distribution were disrupted.

While dazed survivors struggled to dig out and dry out from the mess and find shelter, Wall Street traders and investors kept their singular focus on business and the economy. Would higher energy prices finally slow consumer spending, prompting Americans to curtail their shopping and eating out? Would the impact of the natural disaster convince the Federal Reserve to take a break from a year-long hike in interest rates? Would higher interest rates slow the housing boom, further discouraging consumers? Or would all the rebuilding and investment ultimately help the economy?

The broader market couldn't decide. Initially stock indexes fell in the aftermath of Katrina. But they recovered and then moved in a narrow range, even as Hurricane Rita approached Florida and then Texas and Louisiana later in the month. Restaurant and retail stocks weren't so lucky. Many in the groups were buffeted during the summer amid worries of higher energy prices and higher interest rates, and the beating intensified after Katrina.

Caribou Coffee went public in late September, selling more than 5 million shares at $14 each. But its stock began to slip the first day on investor concerns about consumers and its potential to make consistent profits. Within a few weeks the new stock was down almost 40 percent, trading below $9.

Starbucks, too, was singled out. Since early summer, clouds had been gathering over how Starbucks would weather October and beyond, after it hit the one-year anniversary of its 3 percent price increase. Without the price increase in the mix, same-store sales growth could sink to a paltry 4 percent or less. Meanwhile same-store sales in August, reported at the very end of the month, rose 7 percent, the same increase as in May, June, and July. But analysts had been hoping for a smidge better, more like an 8 percent increase. After reaching an August high above $52 in the middle of the month, still down 16 percent from the end of 2004, the stock began another downward slide. On the first day of September, a day after August sales were reported, it dropped to $48.69. Then it fell some more. Between mid-August and September 20, the stock lost about 10 percent of its value, going down more days than it went up, even though the broader market stayed mostly flat. On September 20 Starbucks stock closed at $46.16, within 50 cents of its low for the year.

The specific hit to Starbucks from Katrina was relatively mild. The company had fewer than a hundred stores in the hardest-hit region and fewer than twenty in the New Orleans areas. Though New Orleans was a crucial coffee port and much of the nation's coffee imports were stored in warehouses there, Starbucks' coffee was stored far away, on the east and west coasts. Even if coffee prices rose in the aftermath, Starbucks bought nearly all its green coffee directly from the source or from exporters, much of it under long-term supply agreements, allowing it to avoid the ups and downs of the commodities markets. Because it was buying a certain quality of coffee, Starbucks paid an average of $1.28 a pound for the approximately 300 million pounds of beans it bought a year, 23 percent more than the average commodity price. The bigger concern was whether customers would kick their coffee habit to pay for gasoline and whether the company could be clever enough to make up for the lost benefit of higher prices.

What was most surprising about the shares and price, though, was how much seemed to be in the company's own hands. Oil and natural gas companies logically trade higher when oil and gas prices rise, since their sales are tied to those commodities. Conversely the stocks of heavy energy consumers like airlines and trucking companies fall when oil prices take off. Homebuilders and banks are sensitive to interest rates. Big-company stocks—industry bellwethers—tend to trade almost in concert with the big indexes, like the Dow Jones Industrial Average or the S&P 500. Occasionally Starbucks would join the dance, trading in sync for a few weeks or a month or two with an index or the restaurant group.

But just as often as not, it would go hurtling in another direction, propelled by its monthly sales numbers or earnings results or, occasionally, an analyst's upgrade or downgrade. In the first nine months of the year, the stock had climbed or fallen 3 percent or more on roughly a dozen trading days. More than half those big moves came in January, after December sales disappointed investors and others cashed out their gains from late 2004. Another cluster of big drops followed the disappointing March sales—reversed a few weeks later by an analyst upgrade and second-quarter earnings.

With the stock now in a steady downward march, Starbucks management seemed eager to convince investors that the company's stock deserved a bit more respect. On September 19, during his trip to China, Schultz tried to address the anxiety over same-store sales beginning in October. In an interview with Reuters, he said that the company wouldn't be raising prices again any time soon and that the chain's same-store sales growth would be "more than acceptable" even after it lapped the year-ago price increase.

Then two days after Schultz talked with Reuters, Starbucks executives offered its stockholders a sweet surprise. Though the company usually announced financial news after the close of regular stock trading, this press release went out as the morning lines were forming in Starbucks stores. The company would pay a two-for-one stock split on October 21, the fifth stock split since it went public and the first since April 2001.

The next day, September 22, the company put out yet another press release, this time saying its board authorized it to buy five million more shares, even though more than seven million shares were still available under the previous autho-rization. Clearly it still believed its shares were undervalued and it was still buying. In fact by the end of the month, the company would have borrowed $277 million from its new bank credit line so that it could purchase more of its own shares.

A week after the two announcements, the stock was back near $50, up more than 8 percent from the month's low.

The timing of the stock split was, well, weird. In November 2004, after the stock began its end-of-the-year tear, an analyst asked executives on the fourth-quarter earnings conference call if a stock split might be coming, since the price was in the mid-$50s at the time. He was told there weren't any plans for a split. The stock then soared past $60 in late 2004, and still no split. At the annual meeting in February, even though the price had pulled back, it was still above $50 and some shareholders and employees remained hopeful. But there was no announcement.

Inquiries about a stock split were one of the most frequent questions put to Starbucks' investor relations staff in 2004 and 2005, but those who asked got a vague answer. "What we tell investors is that it really is up to the board of directors when and if a stock split takes place," said Mary Ekman, Starbucks vice president, corporate development and investor relations. Nearly the entire fiscal year passed before Starbucks finally took the step.

So why September?

"It's not a science," CFO Michael Casey said. "We have a history of splitting the stock somewhere around $50 a share and it was trading in that general range. It just seemed like a good time."

Why shareholders cared so much about stock splits was a

bit of a mystery—but they did. At its core a split merely re-arranged the furniture. If you owned 100 shares trading at $50 before a split, or $5,000 in stock, you would own 200 shares trading at $25 after a two-for-one split, or $5,000 in stock. But the action ignited a psychic boost for little inves-tors. One reason may be that owning more seemed to look better than owning less, the same logic small children apply when, given the choice, they take five pennies instead of a quarter.

Another was that a lower price felt like a better deal than a higher price—and there was a little bit of logic there. For years purchasing fewer than 100 shares, known as an "odd lot," cost more in commissions than buying in blocks of 100. Though that wasn't the case anymore, small investors still might lean toward stocks that were cheaper and more afford-able in blocks of 100, shying away from $75 or $100 stocks. And for reasons that are a bit illogical, it just seemed easier for a stock to go from $20 to $40 than from $50 to $100, even though both represent a 100 percent increase.

"It's kind of a Goldilocks-type story, not too hot, not too cold, looking for what feels just right," said David Ikenberry, a finance professor at the University of Illinois at Urbana-Champaign who has studied the subject extensively. Perhaps because of that, he said, the typical stock on the New York Stock Exchange trades between $25 and $50, a range that has been stable for a hundred years, regardless of inflation or other factors.

Companies were more comfortable in that $25 to $50 range, too, because it encouraged ownership by employees and small investors, who tended to be loyal buy-and-hold types. At Starbucks and other companies where employees might make $8 or $9 an hour, workers could, through payroll deductions, buy a $25 share more quickly than a $50 share. (Warren Buffett took a completely oppositional view, however, refusing to split the stock of his Berkshire Hathaway. His theory: He wanted only "high-quality" shareholders, not the low-life speculators who could afford a cheaper stock. On the day Starbucks announced its stock split, Berkshire Hathaway closed at $80,500. A share.)

None of those small attractions, however, explained why academic research found that stocks that split were, on average, 9 percentage points higher a year later than similar stocks that hadn't split. To Ikenberry there was only one truly meaningful reason that splits were enticing: Even more than stock buybacks or optimistic projections, a stock split was management's declaration of faith in the company's prospects. (It helped, too, that fast-growing companies with rising stock prices tended to be the ones most likely to declare a split.) Executives might be tempted to split a stock just for appearances, but few of them wanted to execute a split and then watch their stock decline.

"Stock splits are the after-effect," Ikenberry said. "They are not the causal effect."

Starbucks believed that, too. The main reason the company split the stock was to make the shares more affordable. But there was a secondary reason as well: "It sends a signal to the marketplace that the management and directors that declared the split are confident in the future," Casey said.

An intuitive sense of that promise drew in the Greenbills Investment Club of Seattle, a group of Boeing retirees who met monthly to talk about investing and add $30 to $100 each to the investment pot. One of the group's first investments was a 1998 purchase of 50 shares of Starbucks at between $43 and $44 a share. The stock split in 1999 and again in 2001, giving the club 200 shares. When the 2005 split was announced, the group eagerly voted to buy 50 more shares before the split. It did so at $50.43 a share.

The purchase "represented our confidence in Starbucks," said Diane Ellison, a retired buyer and the group's treasurer. "It's been our best holding." In fact by the end of 2005, after the split, the group had about $78,400 invested in fifteen stocks, but its 500 shares of Starbucks made up 20 percent of its portfolio.

As the end of Starbucks' fiscal year neared, the company's achievements looked strong, even if its stock price was down for the year. On September 30, the last trading day before the fourth quarter ended, the shares closed at just over $50— progress but still 20 percent below the last trading price in 2004. Altogether the company had plowed $1.1 billion into buying its own stock, purchasing 22.55 million shares at a cost of about $50.52 a share.

For those who were looking for smoke signals about where Starbucks was headed, company executives might as well have been shooting off fireworks. Though none of the individual executives were putting their own money into buying shares, they were doing virtually everything else possible to show their enthusiasm. They projected earnings growth of 20 percent to 25 percent for the next fiscal year. They opened more stores in fiscal 2005 than the 1,500 they had promised, and pledged to open 1,800 more new stores in fiscal 2006. They were investing huge sums of the company's money in the stock and splitting a stock that they hoped would only go up. Intentionally or not they were sending a loud and clear message: They believed the stock price had room to grow.

10

October

★ SAME-STORE SALES ★

Retail is detail

In early October, Stan, the last major hurricane of the season, rammed into Central America, causing flooding and mudslides. How much it damaged the delicate high-altitude coffee-growing regions in Guatemala and El Salvador wouldn't be known for some time. Meanwhile the stock market, as nearly always seemed to be the case, was focused on the moment.

The next day, October 5, Starbucks would announce same-store sales for September, the last month when it would benefit from the price increase. After seeing several months of 7 percent growth in existing stores, analysts were expecting more of the same. If they were close, the stock likely would hold steady. But if they were wrong, as they had been with January, March, and August sales, the price could move sharply. And with so many analysts and investors obsessing over how Starbucks would fare without the impact of the price hike, October's sales promised to be the most volatile of all. Several analysts were predicting October comparable store-sales growth would fall to as low as 3 or 4 percent. That would be the smallest increase in several years—and perhaps would signal that Starbucks' rapid growth was slowing down.

Even by Wall Street's standards, this monthly guess-and-gamble game seemed like a bizarre ritual. Clearly this was a sport for short-term investors—the computers, short sellers, day traders, and others looking to make a quick buck on a sharp move. But, I wondered, what, if anything, did it mean for long-term investors? And if we dug more deeply into what was behind the sales numbers, as we had with the company's growth and its brand, would we also better understand the stock's movements on these days? With so much at stake this month, it was time to find out.

While many numbers that companies reported were proscribed by accounting rules and checked by auditors, same-store sales were unofficial and unregulated statistics. They first were developed about thirty years ago by Jerry Gallagher, then a new retail analyst for Donaldson, Lufkin & Jenrette in New York who was concerned about W. T. Grant, a well-known mass merchant that was rapidly opening stores and reporting increasing sales. Gallagher wondered how much of Grant's sales came from new outlets and how much came from the existing business.

The company refused to say. "I was told by the chief financial officer that they didn't have that number and if they did have it, they didn't believe it would be useful to me," Gallagher said in an interview. Determined, he began to develop his own method for sorting out how existing stores were faring without the obvious benefit from brand-new stores. He built into his models a recognition that new stores tend to grow faster than old ones, with mall-based stores maturing in about three years and large department stores maturing only after seven or eight years. His conclusion: Same-store sales at Grant were actually declining. He didn't recommend the stock.

By about the middle 1970s retailers began to report their own monthly same-store sales growth numbers, along with their overall monthly sales. Though a few retailers balk at playing the game, most retailers still do it, often on the first Thursday of the month. Many restaurant chains do the same, though Starbucks and McDonald's might make their announcements on different days. Since the numbers are voluntary, one company may calculate the sales differently than another. Starbucks, for instance, reported sales increases at stores open at least thirteen months, adding the extra month to essentially eliminate the very first month a store is open, when promotions or a short month might skew the numbers. When a Starbucks store was closed for more than three weeks, as some stores were after Hurricane Katrina, it was dropped from the numbers. Wal-Mart, until early 2006, only included stores in its calculation if they had been open at least a year on February 1, the first day of its fiscal year, meaning some stores might be open nearly two years before they were included in the mix.

Gallagher left the analyst business in 1977 to become a retail executive and then a venture capital investor specializing in retail. He said he was sometimes dismayed at how closely investors followed the volatile same-store sales numbers, which can misrepresent how well a company is doing. For instance Starbucks and others regularly open new stores near old stores. The new stores cannibalize sales from existing stores, but the company ends up with more sales overall.

If the market share grows, that's a good thing, even if same-store sales suffer a little—but investors may not think so. Another worry was that retailers might get a little too frisky marking down items to improve sales numbers, even if that hurts profits later.

Gallagher believed investors shouldn't put too much weight on any one monthly number. But he saw his creation as a useful tool, since the monthly numbers, over time, ultimately reflected how well a company operated and innovated, as well as what customers thought of it. "On average," he said, "it's probably as good a sign as there is of the overall health of a business."

Starbucks began reporting its monthly sales early on to help win attention to its success, and it had an impressive record to boast about. Every year since it had been a public company, it had reported annual same-store sales growth of at least 5 percent, meaning it was constantly finding new ways to generate more sales within a single store, a task that got more challenging each year. Yet month after month, Starbucks reported sales increases; it had never reported a monthly sales decline at existing stores.

To keep the growth train chugging forward, the company kept close tabs on where its future sales would come from. For starters it knew exactly how many customers had come into its stores the year before and the year before that. It also knew more than a year in advance what new beverages and treats it would be introducing, when its annual brewing equipment sale or whole bean promotion would launch and what regions were in line to add lunch sandwiches to the refrigerator case. In early October, just a few days into the 2006 fiscal year, CEO Jim Donald was already working on monthly comparable store sales numbers for the 2007 fiscal year.

"This weekend I turned my first glimpse at FY '07 in to my vice president of strategy," he said in an interview. "I told him where our comps are going to be, but I said, don't take it from me, get it built from the ground up."

To the public and to investors, however, Starbucks was unusually reserved about its projections. While it predicted its quarterly earnings down to one or two pennies a share, it offered only a wide estimate for its comparable sales, saying it expected same-store sales to grow on average 3 percent to 7 percent, with "monthly anomalies." Occasionally it hinted that results might perk up a bit more or gently warned that last month's levels might not be "sustainable," but it didn't go into detail.

While it put out several effusive press releases a month about new drinks, new coffees, and community contributions, it offered very little detail or insight about why sales growth might be 6 percent one month and 9 percent another. The company never made excuses or blamed factors outside its control. Rain, cold, heat, and hurricanes never made cameo appearances. Nor did Starbucks mention the $3 a gallon gasoline in late summer 2005 that crimped consumer spending at some retailers and beat down the stocks of many consumer-driven companies.

Of February's 9 percent growth, Donald said in a press release only that the "particularly strong February comparable store sales reflect our customers' continuing enthusiasm for our handcrafted beverages and the passion our partners have for flawlessly executing the Starbucks experience each day." When June comps grew 7 percent, Donald said, "Sales of our core handcrafted beverages, delivered with consistency and commitment by our partners, generated these results." Occasionally the press releases mentioned something specific—the timing of the annual brewing equipment sale hurt March sales growth but helped April's—or he cited a particular beverage, like the green tea offerings in July and August. But mostly "handcrafted beverages" got all the glory, without any elaboration.

With little specific information to work with, analysts built forecasts after visiting stores and chatting up baristas, looking at last year's numbers—or combining the trend over two or three years—and infusing a little bit of research pixie dust. But ultimately their predictions were a guesstimate. Larry Miller, the Prudential Equity Group restaurant analyst, was able to forecast same-store sales with some accuracy for McDonald's and Wendy's through a series of "channel checks"—analyst lingo for visiting stores or calling up insiders who could tell him how things were shaping up. But his efforts to tease out that kind of information about Starbucks had so far been unsuccessful, especially since the company didn't have big franchisees who might drop hints about how sales were faring. "We've had a harder time," he said.

Occasionally the company's reticence meant it left out crucial information. The first hint of its 2004 price increase came in July that year, during the hour-long earnings conference call with the investment community. According to a transcript from CallStreet.com, Michael Casey, the chief financial officer, told the approximately 130 investors, analysts, and reporters listening in that he wanted to comment on a commonly asked question about the possibility of a price increase. "We are not announcing a price increase today," he said. "However, as prudent managers, we have included the likelihood of a beverage price increase in North America as part of our planning for fiscal 2005." It was too soon, he added, to discuss how big the increase might be or when it might happen. The comment got little public attention.

The next hint came in early September, when Howard Schultz told *The Wall Street Journal* that Starbucks was planning to raise prices for the first time in four years. He cited higher milk and commodity costs, along with higher rent and health insurance expenses as the reasons behind the hike, which would take place before the end of calendar 2004. However he declined to say exactly how much the increase would be.

The actual details seemed to dribble out like a Frappuccino melting on a summer day. Sometime in late September, Starbucks told partners that they could alert their customers to a price increase averaging about 11 cents a drink, which would go into effect October 6, 2004. Someone from the Seattle brokerage company McAdams Wright Ragen heard the news from a barista at one of a half-dozen Starbucks within two blocks of the company's office tower. Tim Bueneman, a managing director who runs the institutional trading desk at McAdams Wright Ragen, sent an e-mail on September 27 to institutional clients and a few reporters. Dow Jones Newswires confirmed the price increase with Starbucks and reported it. Over the next few days, newspapers around the country passed along the news.

Dan Geiman, the McAdams Wright research analyst who follows the stock, didn't put out a note to all the firm's clients until October 5. More notable, Starbucks didn't formally disclose the price increase at all—not in its October 6, 2004, press release about September 2004 sales, not in three press releases detailing the highlights of the October 2004 meeting with analysts and institutional investors, and not even in the

November 3, 2004, press release announcing that October same-store sales growth had shot up 11 percent, after the prices were raised. The analysts and institutional investors who tuned in to the quarterly conference calls or attended the big analysts' meeting knew, of course, and factored it into their models, but the year-long boost to sales and profit may well have been lost on many small investors.

Though price increases usually are taken to cover higher expenses, the danger is that retailers and restaurants will use them to hide deeper operational problems that will eventually reveal themselves in shabby same-store sales. Starbucks may have been guilty of that in the late 1990s. As the company continued to expand its stores rapidly, it also tried to move into a number of different businesses away from its core business. Over a couple of years, training and customer service began to slide, but promotional drinks and price increases in 1997, 1999, and 2000 propped up sales at stores open more than a year.

In the late 1990s Starbucks experimented, unsuccessfully, with a sit-down restaurant in Seattle and an offbeat bohemian coffee shop in San Francisco. A venture with Time Warner to publish an artsy literary magazine called *Joe* fell apart after three issues. But probably the most boneheaded move was jumping feetfirst into the Internet craze just as the dot-com boom was peaking.

In spring 1999 Schultz, with a bit of hyperbole, told analysts that the company was studying an Internet strategy that would make it the "undisputed leader" in a new Internet e-commerce business, leveraging the company's upscale customers and its trusted name. He suggested that the company might even someday sell part of what he called "Starbucks X" to the public. He was passionate but vague with details—

though he did have an Internet résumé. A venture fund he helped start had invested $2.5 million in a fledgling auction business called eBay that had ballooned to $100 million in value. He was on the board of eBay as well as Drugstore.com.

But at the end of June that year, Starbucks disclosed terrible news: Its fiscal 1999 earnings would be 10 percent lower than Wall Street's estimates. It said labor costs had been higher than expected and a price increase hadn't boosted results as much as projected, resulting in a revenue shortfall. In addition, $4 million in costs related to launching the Internet business had crimped the bottom line.

Investors reacted as if caffeine caused hair loss. The next day, in a skittish and volatile stock market response, Starbucks' shares plunged in value. Roughly 40 percent of all the company's stock outstanding changed hands that day, the highest volume trading day in the company's history. When the dust settled, the stock price had fallen 28 percent, slashing $1.9 billion from the company's market value.

"Earth to Howard Schultz," *The Wall Street Journal* wrote a day later. "Return from cyberspace. Your coffee needs you."

A few weeks later Schultz scaled back his plans, saying the company wouldn't go whole hog into cyber-retailing. But the company did make more Internet investments over several months, putting $20 million in Living.com, a nascent online furniture retailer that had some of the same investors as eBay, $25 million in Kozmo.com, a high-flying home delivery service, and smaller amounts in Cooking.com and a business called Talk City.

Within a few short months, the whole strategy crumbled. In August 2000, barely a year after Starbucks made its Living.com investment, the online furniture retailer ceased operations. When Starbucks' fiscal year ended October 1, 2000, it reviewed all its Internet investments and decided to write nearly all of them off. In the fourth quarter, it recorded a $59 million charge to reduce the total value of its Internet investments to less than $5 million. The move just about wiped out its fourth quarter profit. (Schultz, by the way, fared much better with Internet investments: According to Securities and Exchange Commission filings, he personally sold about $31.6 million in eBay stock between 1999 and 2001.)

Orin Smith, the company's president, became the company's chief executive officer in June 2000, in the midst of the debacle. He said Starbucks resisted the dot-com siren for years, and then, like so many individual investors, joined the parade too late. "We had analysts and commentators and business magazines all talking about 'That's the future,'" he said. "It can cause you to start wondering, are you missing the train?" On top of that, he added, "All the examples of companies that failed to adapt and that ultimately were crushed by the change caused you to be a bit paranoid about those kinds of opportunities. So we looked at it, and said, hey, there may be a big opportunity for us in some of these categories."

"We were, in hindsight, clearly in very dangerous territory."

Chastened, "we went back to our core with a frenzy," Smith said. But the distractions left some lingering problems that showed up in slumping same-store sales. Growth in customer transactions fell off, and in the spring of 2001, same-store sales growth cratered, falling to 2 and 3 percent. In August 2001, when the 2000 price increase had run its course, Starbucks' same-store sales gain fell to just 1 percent, the lowest ever. Operations officials blamed cannibalization from opening too many stores close together. But a team that took a closer look concluded that staffing, hiring and retention, and speed of service were to blame.

Howard Behar, one of the company's earliest executives, came out of retirement in September 2001 to run the U.S. stores, and officials redoubled efforts to improve customer service. One result was to redefine the culture, which later became a little pamphlet called the "Green Apron Book" that articulated the company's approach in simple terms:

WHY WE'RE HERE: To provide an uplifting experience that enriches people's daily lives.

HOW WE DO IT: Together, in legendary ways, big and small.

Be welcoming . . . Be Genuine . . . Be Knowledgeable . . . Be Considerate . . . Be Involved.

In spring 2002 same-store sales began to pick up again.

Beyond the 2004 price increase, much of the same-store sales growth at company-owned stores in 2005 came from layer upon layer of tweaks, improvements, and product offerings, which together helped Starbucks maintain its stellar sales growth record. In most years, the bulk of the sales growth came from additional traffic—that is, more transactions—as opposed to customers spending more on each purchase. So keeping the lines from growing too long was crucial, and a constant challenge. A few years before, the chain waived signatures on credit or debit card purchases of less than $25 and encouraged customers to use their Starbucks card, both of which sped up the time spent at the cash register. To deliver drinks more quickly, Starbucks rolled out a series of automated espresso machines, which grind, tamp, and brew at the push of a button, freeing up human hands for steaming milk or adding flavors to a drink. It added employees called floaters to run for more supplies or take orders from customers in line, and assistant managers to deepen its talent pool. In 2005 the company developed new Frappuccino stations to allow two workers to make the iced drinks at the same time, hoping to ease summertime logjams. (Other chains simply dispensed their slushy drinks from a machine, but doing that meant they wouldn't be "handcrafted.")

Starbucks wanted customers to move from line to drink in about three minutes, depending on the store and the time of day, and it succeeded about 60 percent of the time. To see it firsthand, I visited a Washington, DC, store across from a subway stop early one summer morning. Customers came in by the twos and threes, some in shorts and some in suits. A second register opened at 7:40 A.M., and the two lines rarely grew more than four deep. In other big urban stores, the lines can grow longer. But here customers ordered regular coffees, lattes, grande white mochas, venti caramel Frappuccinos with extra caramel, and tall iced caramel macchiatos, and three to four employees nearly stepped on each other in the long, narrow store to keep the drinks moving. Boxes of pastries were stacked on a cart next to the pastry case, the few tables were messy, and the bathrooms were toxic. But most customers hardly had time to even look around; nearly everyone was in and out the door in three or four minutes, even after a stop at the condiment bar for sugar or a napkin.

If faster service was a layer that helped Starbucks add to daily transactions, then additional products were the icing, building the average sales ticket without really adding to costs. Consider the chain's music sales. For years it sold a handful of CDs through small displays on its counters, typically compilations put together by the Hear Music business that it bought in 1999. More recently it branched out, coproducing the Grammy-winning album of Ray Charles duets,

Genius Loves Company, in 2004. In 2005 it launched the first album of a group called Antigone Rising and supported the little-known Amos Lee. Starbucks promoted itself as an "editor" of musical taste for its customers, giving them appealing music that was convenient to buy, and it boasted that it was becoming an influential and innovative new leader in the struggling music business.

Indeed the chain could move an impressive number of CDs—it sold 3.5 million of them in fiscal 2005—but its power was as much from its girth as its good taste. The company said in May that Antigone Rising sold more than 21,000 copies in its first twelve days in Starbucks stores. Had it been available at retail music stores, those sales, Starbucks bragged, would have ranked it 93rd on the Billboard 200 Albums Chart, ahead of new releases from Queens of the Stone Age and Lisa Marie Presley. But the chain also noted that it was selling the CD in more than 4,400 Starbucks, meaning that each store sold an average of about five albums in the first two weeks.

In pure dollar terms the music sales were almost insignificant, maybe 1 percent of sales, or less than $100 million of its $6.4 billion in annual revenue. A test of CD-burning stations in Seattle and Austin, Texas, launched with much fanfare in fall 2004, seemed to be a washout, with customers using the stations more to listen to music for free than to burn custom CDs. (Though the company insisted it was pleased with the results, it didn't expand the test.)

The impact the music could have on same-store sales growth, however, was significant. In summer 2005 Starbucks added rotating racks that could hold up to twenty different albums to its U.S. stores, bringing in far more albums than could fit on the countertop next to the cash register. With a typical CD priced around $15, selling just two additional CDs a day would add more than $10,000 a year to a single store's sales. Given that the average company-owned U.S. store recorded about $1 million in sales in fiscal 2005, those additional CD sales system-wide could add a full percentage point to same-store sales growth—often the difference between meeting and exceeding investors' expectations.

Sales of sandwiches made an even bigger splash. To build traffic and sales in the middle part of the day, the company introduced and then removed lunch offerings several times over the years, never quite satisfied with the quality or results. It experimented again in 200 stores in 1999. Finally, in fiscal 2004, it aggressively expanded its lunch program, adding sandwiches like tuna, Southwestern turkey, and dilled egg salad and havarti to more than 1,300 stores. In fiscal 2005 it stocked another 758 U.S. stores with lunch items. With a price tag around $5 to $6 a sandwich and a small selection of salads, the company said the additions contributed about $30,000 a year to a store's sales, increasing an average store's sales about 3 percent. As the products rolled out and caught on with customers, they would also give an extra pop to overall same-store sales growth, with the contribution depending on how many stores added sandwiches in the last year or two.

Right behind the sandwich rollout was a breakfast experiment that started in 2005 in about eighty Seattle stores. The company sold a fancier and tastier version of the Egg McMuffin: English muffins with egg, ham, and cheese, eggs Florentine with spinach and havarti, and other combinations for about $3. This test was more complicated. Like lunch sandwiches, these arrived at the stores prepared. But the breakfast offerings needed heating, forcing Starbucks to find an oven that could warm food without ruining the crucial smell of morning coffee. In addition heating food took longer than dropping a muffin into a bag, which threatened to slow down those fast-moving lines.

The company compensated by adding more employees so that lattes would keep flowing, and in spring 2005 the experiment was expanded to Washington, DC. Starbucks found this new meal, too, added about $30,000 in annual sales to a store, and in the fall it announced that it would expand warm breakfast food to about 600 stores in fiscal 2006 from about 200 in mid-2005. The move gave analysts hope that breakfast sales could stack upon lunch sales, bumping up overall store growth for several years.

Joe Kernen, the stocks editor on the financial cable network CNBC, underscored how all the pieces add up when he helped present Schultz with a CNBC–Wall Street Journal executive leadership award for entrepreneurial excellence in late fall. "Every weekend, rain or shine, sleet or snow, the whole family and I head off to Starbucks," he told the black-tie crowd. And every time, he said, "I utter those famous thirteen words: venti, 2 percent, no-foam latte; venti skim, no-foam iced latte, please.

"I don't even know what language that is in," he told the laughing crowd.

"But that's not all I say. I also say, oh and a slice of marble loaf. Oh, oh, wait a minute—and a cinnamon scone. Oh, one more thing: can I get that Miles Davis CD I hear playing?

"And then," Kernen added, "Howard hears those four words that he loves so much: $24 dollars, please." The audience roared.

As Starbucks added new lines, its core business continued to expand, stoked from season to season by promotional drinks, like Peppermint Mochas at the holidays and Mint

Mocha Chip Frappuccinos in the spring. The most popular innovations brought customers back for extra visits, nudging up transactions and sales growth. The duds, however, disappeared almost without a whimper.

Remember Chantico? The company announced the thick "drinking chocolate" in October 2004 through a story in *USA Today*. Named for the Aztec goddess of the hearth, the new $3 drink was like a chocolate bar in a 6-ounce cup and was supposed to bring in more customers for an afternoon or nighttime indulgence. "This is Starbucks at its savviest: concocting a new product, then creating consumer demand by making it hip," the newspaper said, bubbling about the potential of the drink to change hot chocolate forever.

Launched with magazine print ads, billboards, and samples in January, the new drink spurred a flurry of media coverage and taste tests. In talking about earnings for the quarter ended April 3, Donald effusively told investors that Chantico, along with decadent new desserts, had excited customers, driven transactions, and helped build business later in the day.

But on a Web site devoted to Starbucks news called Starbucks Gossip, baristas said sales of the fattening drink had been slim after the first few weeks. "We definitely throw out more than we make," one barista wrote, and the sentiment was echoed by several others. At year-end the company confirmed that it was taking the drink off the menu in January.

While those who followed the company concluded that sales simply weren't up to snuff, a Starbucks spokesman tried to spin it differently to Reuters. "It was something customers did like, but they wanted to be able to do something else with it," in the same way they customize other drinks, the spokesman said. He didn't offer up what exactly customers wanted to change, only that "we wanted to go back and give customers what they are looking for."

More successful specialty drinks, like the summer Green Tea Frappuccino and the fall's Pumpkin Spice Latte, had the potential to add up to a couple percentage points in same-store sales growth, though the biggest push came during the winter holidays, the biggest season of the year for retailers overall and for Starbucks, both in drink and merchandise sales. To get ready, the company began planning seventy-two weeks in advance, working on theme, colors, merchandise, and products. By midsummer a mock 2005 holiday store was already set up behind a locked door in the headquarters building, with a working menu, the annual Christmas Blend coffee beans on the shelves, and fake cranberry bliss bars, gingerbread, and mini peppermint cookies in the pastry case.

The theme: "It Only Happens Once A Year." The palette: red and silver. (In the mid-90s, the company tried to break away from traditional colors with a pastel palette. The resulting bomb became known as "the Easter Christmas.") Red trim covered displays and all the packaging featured whimsical cartoonlike drawings.

Janet Parks, vice president of merchandise, who had joined the company about a year before from Disney, began working on the holiday gifts almost from her first day on the job. The stores would carry a French press dressed in a red handle, three-tiered gift packs mixing coffee and chocolate, colorful shot glasses, red and silver polka-dot mugs, and even a tiny Starbucks mug ornament. The popular gift cards came with a free red-felt bag for wrapping.

But the real draw to the store would be the holiday drinks: the traditional Eggnog Latte, Gingerbread Latte, and Peppermint Mocha, as well as a new line featuring the spicy

Chai tea, including a Chai Eggnog Latte. To make a bigger impact and get off to a quick start, the company also plotted out what it called a "hard launch" of the holiday season. In previous years, stores had stocked merchandise as it arrived, converting to red paper cups and adding drinks and Christmas Blend over several days and weeks. But on November 9, 2005, all the stores would turn the calendar at once. Employees would stay after work and staple trim to displays, change out mugs and tumblers, and set up holiday drinks. The next day samples and promotions would launch in high gear.

How much would all that add to same-store sales? Starbucks wanted a good showing, and it needed a terrific month to show real growth over the 8 percent same-store sales growth it reported for December 2004. But even when the numbers were extraordinary, Michael Casey found it hard to pinpoint for investors exactly what was behind them, which was one reason, he said, that Starbucks didn't offer too much explanation. Month after month analysts and investors wanted a sound bite. They wanted something simple and clear to explain the results. From Casey's vantage point, though, there were too many factors in the monthly sales to single out just one—especially when drink sales truly drove the business week after week.

To make his point in an interview after the fact, Casey pulled out the December sales of the new Chai Eggnog Latte. The drink had brought in $2.5 million to $2.6 million at company-owned stores, just a tiny fraction of the $791 million in total sales that stores rang up that month. But that little number was enough to add half a percentage point of growth to the comparable store sales.

When investors asked what was behind the December number, "I could tell them that five-tenths of a percent of the comp came from the Chai Eggnog Latte, and five-tenths came from Peppermint Mocha and three-tenths from Gingerbread Latte, three-tenths from Pumpkin," he said, reading off the numbers from a chart. But to Casey those statistics didn't begin to capture what really happened in the stores. They didn't reflect the traffic, the extra return visits or maybe the decision to go "grande" instead of "tall." "They're all little tiny things," he said of the drink sales. "The reason we're continuing to generate more business is because we're building more loyal customers. And we're building more loyal customers because we're continuing to surprise and delight them, not just with Chai Eggnog but with Green Tea Frappuccino, with cinnamon swirl coffee cake, with WiFi, with a CD from an artist they've never heard of but they liked, with warmed breakfast sandwiches. . . ."

Together, he noted, special drinks added 2.4 percentage points to the same-store sales for December. "But more importantly than that," he added, "most of that 2.4 percent is cannibalization. We don't do that much advertising outside the store. The person that walks in the store and has Chai Eggnog decides the second before they were going to have a vanilla latte because they saw it on the board. . . . It isn't as if all the eggnog fans, you know, are leaving Jack in the Box and coming to us. They were coming to us anyway."

So when the company said over and over that "handcrafted beverages" were behind same-store sales increases, he insisted, that was about as close as Starbucks could get to summing up the numbers in a few words. "That's true . . . I shouldn't make something up because they're searching," he said. Holiday sales might be good because of the drinks. Or the colorful mugs. Or maybe just because the promotion was executed well. "If I had to answer, 'Why did we have such a good holiday?'" he said, "I would say because the partners were more excited about it, they smiled at more customers—and (investors) are not going to like that any better."

Casey also dismissed investor worries in the summer and early fall that Starbucks' comps would slide to their lowest levels in several years when October rolled around. "There is so much success in this story, so many things that are happening right, that people search for something negative to think about, to worry about, to talk about," he said. "So they hunt for stuff like, 'Ohmigod, what happens when they lap the price increase? Are comps going to go negative?'" The company was reporting same-store sales gains all summer of 7 percent, "so you subtract 3, you're at 3 or 4 or 5. There was no hand-wringing necessary even in the worst situation," he said.

But while the company's stock rallied a bit in September on the announcement of the stock split and plans to buy more of its own shares, it was still stuck at about $50 and below. Starbucks, naturally, found a new way to surprise and delight. With little fuss it brought back its Pumpkin Spice Latte and a new Pumpkin Spice Frappuccino in September, a month earlier than the flavor had debuted the year before.

It also changed the packaging on its whole beans, replacing the busy paisley designs with a white bag with a distinctive colorful stripe around the bottom third of the bag. As Jim Donald knew from his grocery-store days, that kind of change always helps sales. "It just creates awareness that wasn't there before," he said. "We used to say when you changed packaging, particularly private-label packaging, that you'd see a 10 to a 15 percent spike just off the packaging change," and the bump would last for about six months. How much Starbucks' new design helped whole-bean sales wasn't clear, he said, "but I'm sure there was a lift from the packaging." Beyond that the stores were pushing whole bean sales in September like never before, motivating employees with a sales contest. The prizes hardly seemed remarkable, but partners hustled to win T-shirts, dinners with Donald or other executives, or a trip to the Starbucks' roasting plant.

The roasting plant?

"That's huge, that's like going back to the Holy Land," Donald said of the trip.

Some stores gave away a free drink with a whole bean purchase, others handed out samples. In Dallas a store offered its own "Lake Highlands Blend," a mix of Breakfast Blend and French Roast named for a local neighborhood. Between the design change and the contest, Donald reported that in September the company "had probably the best week in the history of the company in whole bean sales," which on average ran about 4 percent of store sales.

The combination of efforts more than did the trick. In early October Starbucks reported that same-stores sales for September had been spectacular, up a stellar 10 percent over the year before, the first double-digit gain in nearly a year. The next day the stock jumped nearly 4 percent, to $51.67. Over the next couple of weeks, it climbed steadily day by day as some investors grew more confident that their fears about October were overblown. The two-for-one stock split was paid, doubling the number of shares and halving the price, and giving some investors more reassurance.

The company, in addition to coffee beans, breakfasts, sandwiches, and Pumpkin Spice, had one other little-noticed weapon to bulk up the crucial October sales: year-old stores. Newer stores tended to grow faster than older outlets, and while the company opened stores all year long, real-estate and operations people, like many of us, apparently were deadline-driven. The biggest months for store openings were usually the last month in each quarter, and the biggest month of all was September, the last month of the fiscal year. In 2004 Starbucks decided that half or more of its new U.S. stores should be drive-through outlets. Those stores brought in significantly more revenue, but the switch required more time to develop sites, get permits, construct the stores, and build up a backlog. At least partly because of the change, in September 2004 Starbucks opened 144 company-owned U.S. stores, 28 percent of the company-owned stores it opened on its home turf that fiscal year.

In October 2005 those fast-growing new stores stepped into the same-store sales parade, joining several thousand stores. Their actual contribution to the same-store sales number was probably very small, just another increment, but in the layer upon layer of extras, it was likely the crowning decoration. On November 3 the company reported that those frightful October sales at existing stores had grown 7 percent, a more-than-solid number at the top of Starbucks' projections.

The market breathed a huge sigh of relief. Long-term investors could be assured that the Starbucks growth-machine was still finely tuned. The next day investors bid up the stock another 3 percent, to a split-adjusted $30.36, within $1 of its end-of-2004 price.

Between the sales numbers and the stock split, the shares had soared more than 30 percent in the six weeks since their September low. Suddenly there was hope that the stock had turned the corner. There were still a couple of stomach-churning issues to be addressed: The company would soon start expensing executives' stock options, reducing reported net income, and the crucial holiday season was just ahead. But to the market optimists, the last major storm of the season had blown through and everything was intact. Sales were back on track, profits should follow, and the price of Starbucks' shares were rocketing upward once again.

11

November

★ THE ANALYST ★

The trend is your friend

O n November 17, two weeks after the October sales worries abated, the S&P 500 Index settled at 1243, up 2.6 percent for the year. By comparison Starbucks' stock closed at $31.22, almost exactly where it ended in 2004. But that afternoon, just after regular trading ended, the company reported results for its fiscal year ended October 2 that were anything but flat.

Over twelve months Starbucks had opened 1,672 new stores—an average of more than four a day—including 735 that were company owned. Revenue had soared to $6.4 billion from $5.3 billion in 2004 (which, by a fluke of the calendar, was a 53-week year), awesome growth for a company that was approaching twenty years old. Net income climbed to $494 million, or 61 cents a share, from $389 million, or 47 cents a share. Earnings for the fourth quarter alone had come in at 16 cents a share, up from 12 cents a share the year before.

More important, the quarterly results were a penny higher than analysts had predicted—again—helped by those months of heavy stock buybacks. To see how the numbers would play in Stockland, I traveled to Chicago to spend a few days with Sharon Zackfia, the research analyst who follows Starbucks for William Blair & Company, a regional brokerage that specializes in growth stocks. After watching analysts make predictions all year, I wanted to see how they did their jobs and what roles they played in moving the stock and how. What did the pros know that little investors didn't, and how big was their advantage?

Zackfia had followed the company for five years, and William Blair had recommended it to clients the whole time. She saw it as a consistent and reliable performer that had more potential than nearly any other stock its size. "The nice thing about the Starbucks story is, it just doesn't change that much. It continues to meet or to exceed expectations," she said. "That's why it's such a great growth stock."

Zackfia had spent November 17 at the hospital with a sick aunt, but she hustled after hours to get her assessment out on the earnings. Her company's salesmen would want to know what she thought so they could pass her insights on to the various investors who did business with them. She listened to the company's conference call from her cell phone in the car and followed up with a call to Michael Casey at about 6 P.M. At about 6:30 she recorded a voice mail to be sent to the firm's institutional sales traders and money managers who wanted her take on the news. Already they would have seen the headlines as they moved across financial wires, and if they were especially interested, they could have read the company's lengthy press release. Her job was to highlight the key points that the salesmen and traders and their clients needed to focus on.

Starbucks' release, it turned out, also had a tidbit of news on another company she covered, a small maker of industrial convection ovens with a volatile stock that happened to sell some of its ovens to Starbucks.

"Hi, I'm Sharon Zackfia on Starbucks, with some commentary that is relevant to TurboChef," her voice mail began. Her headline: She was keeping her long-running "outperform" rating on the stock and raising her earnings estimate for the next fiscal year by a penny. One good turn deserved another: She now believed the company would earn 65 cents a share, after including expenses for stock options for the first time, moving her to the high end of the company's projection that it would earn 63 to 65 cents a share in the coming year.

She reviewed the main numbers, adding, "This marked an excellent finish to a year in which the company grew sales by 20 percent and earnings by 28 percent despite one less week, and aggressive growth that pushed the company to over 10,000 global locations." Then, in the three-minute call, she went on to note three main points that might affect the stock over the coming weeks: "First, as expected, given easy dairy costs comparisons and strong sales, the domestic business grew operating margins by 200 basis points to 17.3 percent. But the real surprise came from the international division, where operating margins broke into the double digits for the first time," she said. Second, she said, the company planned to expand its hot breakfast test to approximately 600 locations in the next year. Though the move added roughly $30,000 to a store's sales, it wouldn't be in enough stores overall to add even a percentage point to comp store sales, she noted. But the expansion made her optimistic that warm breakfasts would eventually expand to all stores. Because she also followed TurboChef, the provider of convection ovens, her listeners knew that the expansion might also promise additional oven sales for that growing company.

Finally, she told listeners, the company had added cash register scanners to all its U.S. company-owned stores in time for the holidays, "which should bolster throughput during this merchandise-intensive selling season and therefore potentially also bolster comps."

Zackfia had some credibility riding on these numbers because back in mid-July, she had nominated Starbucks for her firm's "Current Better Values List," a bimonthly list of analyst picks that were expected to perform well over the next twenty-four months. "It was a pretty compelling entry point to get into Starbucks," she said later.

With her voice mail recorded, Zackfia turned her attention to updating her Starbucks spreadsheet and writing up a longer report that would go out by e-mail and on a service called First Call the next morning. Her assistant, Tania Bykkonen, typed up a summary of the numbers and took a crack at a first draft, e-mailing it to Zackfia at about 9 P.M. Zackfia added analysis and made sure the report rolled through the relevant numbers again, reiterated her highlights and updated her future forecasts in a couple of single-spaced pages. She sent off the report to a supervisor at 11:29 P.M. The next morning she would be on the hot seat at the firm's daily 7:30 A.M. sales call, reviewing the numbers again and answering questions for salesmen and money managers who would be talking to institutional investors or making investment decisions for wealthy clients.

Such detail work was hardly the image of analysts during the tech boom of the late 1990s. Then a small cadre of technology and telecommunications analysts emerged as the human face of Wall Street, endlessly bullish investment cheerleaders and media darlings, predicting vast stock-market profits from nascent companies with business plans still damp from the kitchen table. In the bust investors discovered that some analysts had inflated their stock ratings and issued overly optimistic reports to win the companies' lucrative investment banking business, not to help the little guys or major institutions find a good stock buy. At the peak, some of the top analysts took home as much as $20 million a year, lush compensation for bringing their firms investment-banking riches.

That ended quickly with the market slide between 2000 and 2002. The resulting dot-com disasters laid bare the flimsy and sometimes fraudulent analysis that had been issued. In a couple of particularly egregious examples, some analysts disparaged stocks to colleagues that they recommended to investors. Many of the calls turned out to be rotten, and many of the allegedly promising companies ended up in the dust heap. In 2003 ten major securities firms agreed to pay $1.4 billion in fines and penalties to settle civil charges that they issued overly optimistic and sometimes misleading research and other misdeeds. They also agreed to clearly separate the research business from the investment bankers.

The euphoria and heady financial windfalls of the boom masked other dramatic changes taking place that were already changing the investment research business. While some analysts were helping investment bankers bring in new clients in the 1990s, the original source of income for analysts—stock trading commissions—was shrinking, forcing the industry to find new and better ways to serve their most valuable institutional clients.

Trading commissions had paid for research since late

1959, when the securities firm Donaldson, Lufkin and Jenrette began offering in-depth stock assessments. Rather than charge directly for research, the firm asked customers to buy their stocks through its trading desk, paying commissions that at the time were fixed at high rates by the New York Stock Exchange. The decision proved lucrative, and the rest of Wall Street quickly followed. Fixed commission rates disappeared in the mid-1970s, but institutional money managers, for the most part, still paid inflated trading commissions in exchange for research, what the industry called "soft dollars." In 2005 that added up to about $1 billion, or about 9 percent of the total institutional commissions paid.

In recent years, shrinking trading commissions, combined with fallout from the scandals, led firms to cut back their analyst teams and sent some senior analysts looking for better jobs with hedge funds and mutual funds. The National Research Exchange, which works to provide independent stock analysis for smaller companies, estimated that the number of Wall Street research analysts dropped nearly 30 percent between 2001 and 2005. Pay fell sharply too. The average analyst at a big New York brokerage made in the high $300,000 range in 2005, about half of the $600,000 to $700,000 earned in the boom years, according to Johnson Associates, a New York compensation consulting firm. Analysts at regional firms earned a bit less, in the low $300s, on average.

The other radical change in the research business affected the flow of information. In 2000 the SEC adopted a rule known as Regulation Fair Disclosure, or "Reg FD," which dramatically changed the rules for what companies could say privately to investors and analysts. Before the rule companies frequently slipped bits of important information to analysts that had yet to make it into a press release or financial disclosure. They would tell them, for instance, that sales were looking strong or weak, that a specific product was selling well, or that earnings were going to be higher or lower than originally thought. With juicy information the fuel that makes Wall Street run, analysts who were particularly close to a company could provide a steady stream of inside insight to clients, who could trade well before the rest of the world knew what was going on.

After Reg FD took effect, however, companies were required to issue press releases or publicly disclose any details that were material to its stock price so that everyone had a chance to know at the same time. The rule change made information harder to get—and more desirable than ever. Now, though, instead of analysts providing the scoop, mutual funds and money managers began to look more and more to analysts to provide something else: access to top company management. "Everybody is looking for unique, proprietary information and that's one easy way to do it," said John Feng, a principal consultant at Greenwich Associates, a financial services consulting firm.

At the 2005 William Blair Annual Growth Stock Conference in June, for instance, Blair invited its top clients to a Chicago hotel to hear presentations from more than 180 companies it covered, including Starbucks, Apollo Group, First Data, and CarMax. No reporters were allowed at the sessions; in fact reporters weren't even welcome to meet up with an analyst at the meeting hotel.

The thirty-minute presentations before the whole group of invitees were Webcast, meeting public disclosure requirements. In the Starbucks segment, Donald and Casey gave a rundown of the company's growth, its goals, and some new products. Afterward shareholders and money managers with a particular interest in Starbucks adjourned to a different room, away from the microphones, where they could ask questions in private. Then some investors had a chance to meet one-on-one with the executives. Under Reg FD, company executives weren't allowed to divulge any new material information, but they could go into more detail about already disclosed issues, talk about competitors, and offer more insight into their thinking. In a cozier environment, investors could get a much better sense of an executive's mood—the enthusiasm of a Jim Donald, for instance, or the resolute confidence of a Michael Casey—than they would ever get from the highly scripted conference calls or annual meetings.

Exactly what executives could say legally in private was less than clear. In a widely followed case, the SEC sued Siebel Systems in 2004, charging that it violated Reg FD by saying in one meeting that business activity was "good" and by telling big investors that it had about $5 million in deals in the pipeline. After a meeting with one big investor and a dinner with other investors, both sponsored by Morgan Stanley, at least two investors bought the company's stock and another ended a short position and bought the stock outright.

Siebel fought the SEC charges, saying it had stayed within the rules and had only repeated previous public statements. In September 2005 a federal judge in Manhattan agreed, dismissing the SEC's suit.

In addition to investment conferences, analysts frequently organized "marketing trips," where they escorted a company's top executives to an investment hot spot like New York, Boston, Denver, or Los Angeles to meet with funds and portfolio managers, or they led pilgrimages of big investors to headquarters to see the operation up close and in person.

While the biggest investors could talk with management without an analyst in the middle, both sides often preferred the arranged meetings. Even so they created an intrinsically intertwined relationship. The analysts were supposed to prepare independent analyses of a company's financial and business performance, but they also needed the CEOs and the CFOs to attend their investor conferences and travel to meet their clients. It wouldn't take much—a strained relationship or a neutral rating on a stock—for executives to decide to spend their precious time with someone else.

In addition to wooing Starbucks executives to the William Blair conference, in October Zackfia led about ten investors to Seattle for a tour that included stores with the new hot breakfasts and a visit with Donald and Casey. She later published a report with some newsy highlights, noting that the cost to build new stores was climbing and that the breakfast experiment likely would be expanded to a few new markets.

Dan Geiman, the analyst with Seattle's McAdams Wright Ragen, in late 2004 set up appointments for Donald and Casey in Denver with major money managers there. But he spent much of his time chilling in waiting rooms. Because he was required to publish any relevant insights—and because investors want the good stuff for themselves—he wasn't invited in to hear some of the discussions. Geiman headed to Spain shortly after the trip and didn't publish a report.

On September 29, 2005, before the Starbucks stock split took effect and before the crucial October same-store sales numbers were reported, he rounded up a small group of investors and a few of his salespeople for a two-hour visit to Starbucks headquarters. "In the case of Starbucks and others, you just get so much by talking one-on-one. You get an awful lot more information when you do talk to management," he said. "That's something Joe Investor is not going to have the opportunity to do."

When Geiman and other brokerage-firm stock analysts published a report, they had to disclose any investment banking relationships with the company and explain their buy, hold, or sell ratings. Since the reports were official firm publications, they were carefully edited and vetted. Within certain limits, traders and salespeople could also pass along to customers factual information they gleaned, with less oversight. After the Starbucks meeting, two of the McAdams Wright salespeople sent out their own e-mails about the visit, revealing the level of detail that may be shared behind closed doors.

"These are my own impressions and my own quick personal notes, not a research report," wrote Tim Bueneman, who ran the firm's institutional trading desk, in a detailed, two-page, single-spaced e-mail to customers. In talking about earnings, he noted, "Management (Casey) went out of his way (my opinion) to say the company was comfortable with 20–25% earnings growth over the next 3–5 years."

Music, he went on, was a small part of the business, but profitable, "and is never likely to exceed 3 percent. Casey believes music CDs, while they provide incremental revenue, really don't drive traffic as much as many analysts believe." Chantico, the rich chocolate drink, he reported, "probably wasn't sampled and tested correctly before introduction, according to Jim Donald. . . . SBUX is not sure if it will be reintroduced this winter."

If there was any "news" in the meeting, it was about Starbucks' soaring possibilities in China. "Management sounds *even more upbeat about China than we had heard them before,*" Bueneman wrote, adding emphasis as he went along.

"For the first time, we heard Casey say that China could eventually be as big as the U.S. and possibly even bigger (we've always heard China would be #2 before). Casey said, **'China may be bigger than the U.S. over time.'** He hinted at **a possible number of 10K stores in China** whereas we've heard numbers in the 1–2,000 range before (about 300 now). Casey said that when he got a request for $1 mil spending in China, **he actually authorized twice that amount to send the signal that China should be ramped up as fast as possible.**" And while Starbucks' international executives had been coy about saying publicly how many stores would open there in the next year, the salesman reported that "Casey will be 'delighted' if SBUX can open 100 stores in China next year."

The CFO also offered hope that the stock would soon bounce back, the salesman wrote: "Paraphrasing Casey: We are just coming off our best quarter ever. Our P/E has contracted substantially. When the Street gets over the fear of lapping the October price increase, our outlook for steady 20–25% earnings growth could take over in investors' minds."

Between the upbeat demeanor and pure good news, the salesman left excited and ready to tout the stock. **"We came away feeling better about our Buy rating and $63 price target"** (or $31.50 post-split), he wrote.

His colleague was just as pleased, though more restrained. In a much shorter e-mail summary to clients, she offered a few more nuggets, including the little morsel that Starbucks didn't see a need for a roasting plant in China. "Very economical to send beans West from here, as most of the ships are empty when sailing back to China," she noted. She quoted Donald as saying, "This holiday season will be the best ever." And, she added, "To sum up the meeting, Jim

Donald said: **'All the metrics are better now than they were at the end of '04. I'm damn excited about '06!'** "

Geiman's note, which was published October 6 for a broader audience, covered fewer subjects in less detail—and without an exclamation point or boldface. He skipped the fine points on Chantico or the stock price, but noted the new wrinkle in the China story: "We were somewhat surprised to learn that management envisions perhaps as many as 10,000 or more locations in that market over time," he wrote. Without offering any numbers on the company's current stores at the time, he wrote only that "Near-term expansion will continue to ramp."

Geiman, too, was optimistic, but he was far more tempered. "We remain favorably disposed toward SBUX and its operations," he wrote. While same-store sales may be lower in fiscal 2006 than in previous years, he believed the company's earnings could grow 20 to 25 percent, "in the near-to-mid-term—and long-term as well, particularly as China becomes a more material piece of the company's operations. As such, we remain comfortable with our Buy rating."

The morning after Starbucks reported year-end results, Zackfia was recommending the stock again at the 7:30 A.M. sales meeting. A native of northern Indiana who attended Yale, she intended to become a clinical psychologist. But during a summer internship in public relations, a colleague told her that Wall Street would value her writing and math skills. After college she worked for a New York investment firm, and then for the Nasdaq in the new listings area before returning to Chicago five years previously to join William Blair. When the analyst she worked for left in 2002, she took over coverage of an eclectic group of consumer, retail, and food-related companies, including CarMax, Guitar Center, P. F. Chang's

China Bistro, Life Time Fitness, Sonic, and Starbucks. Unlike other brokerage firms, William Blair specialized in growth stocks in just five areas—technology, consumer products, business services, financial services, and health care—and Zackfia's list was such an odd mix that she almost certainly would never fit into any of the industry categories where analysts were ranked.

Fortified by her venti Starbucks coffee, Zackfia headed down to a lower floor through a maze of offices and past a small trading floor to talk more about the company before stock-market trading opened at 8:30 A.M. Chicago time. More than twenty salespeople lined the conference table and chairs around the wall, while others listened on the phone as she again ran through the earnings' highlights, the aggressive stock buybacks for the year, and improvement in the international business. She noted the breakfast program and the new scanners, but mentioning both, she warned, "Don't get too excited. Remember, we are up against tough comps in November," which could mean modest same-store sales growth in the next month.

After her quick review, the sales trading people fired questions her way. What was her comp estimate for the next three quarters? Did the international results prompt her to change her model? Starbucks doesn't talk about gasoline prices or moves by competitors, but what problems out there could hurt it?

Answering the questions as they came, she told the group she was looking for 4 to 5 percent same-store sales growth in the holiday quarter, rising slightly during the year, when comparisons to the year-ago would be easier. "They just reported an absolutely stellar comp for the month of October," and for the holidays, she added, "I do think merchandise looks good. Also, Christmas falls on Sunday, which is beneficial for all retailers."

On the international business, she told them, "I did increase international margins, but not as much as you might think." The margins will go up over time, but not in a straight line, she said. "The way they get there will be lumpy." As for understanding the external pressures on the business, McDonald's and the other competition usually plug their speed and price, while "Starbucks has positioned themselves on image," she said. "You never hear them talk about hurricanes. They didn't even talk about them in September when it happened." Instead they focus on what they could do in each store—or what they've done wrong. "It gives them control over their own destiny," she added. "Their kryptonite would be generated internally."

The questions for Zackfia over, the group moved on to a maker of dental equipment. She returned to her small office to catch up. Settled back in, with one wall lined with signed baseballs and other tchotchkes, a giant, colorful vintage McGovern poster from her birth year, 1972, on another wall and a speaker for her iPod on her desk, she returned a call to an investor. He was concerned about P. F. Chang's, the Asian-food restaurant chain that had reported rocky sales numbers after a big disappointment in the summer. Then a salesman called to ask, "Shouldn't the Starbucks news be super bullish for OVEN?" the stock symbol for TurboChef.

TurboChef's shares had peaked in the mid-$20s at the end of 2004, but nearly a year later, it was trading at about $14 and struggling to show regular profits. The salesman clearly was looking for something to sell, but Zackfia tried to cool him down. By her projections, spelled out in a research note sent out this day as well, TurboChef was expected to record $70 million in revenue in the next year; the 400 potential ovens from Starbucks would add all of $2 million. The bigger expectations, she told the caller, were the two major announcements TurboChef was supposed to make before year-end and the rollout of its first residential ovens, which wouldn't make an impact for a year or two.

She took another call about OVEN, and then a salesman patched her into one of his clients to talk about Guitar Center, a retail and online seller of music equipment that was one of her hottest picks at the moment. She was optimistic that the company would have a big Christmas, but, at the same time, she couldn't commit. "Everyone shops at the last minute," she said. "I won't know til the morning of December 26."

There was another call about OVEN, and then another. In this office Starbucks had made news all right, but not about Starbucks. One salesman wanted to know more about how the hot breakfast worked. "Can you outline it for me? I worry about throughput. You get down there and the lines are so ridiculously long," he said.

"That's the worry—that they trade high-margin beverage sales for low-margin food sales," Zackfia told him. In the Washington, DC, test, she said, one person manned the oven to keep the lines moving, and "now you get your sandwich before you get your coffee." The conversation then veered quickly back to TurboChef.

By now it was just after 9 A.M., and the calls were still coming, still mostly about whether the sales team should be pumping up the TurboChef news to clients. Zackfia was a research analyst, but it was hard to see when she had a chance to actually do research. "When you're in, you spend all day on the phone," she said during a short break in the calls.

Individual investors can make a decision and let it ride for a while, shrugging off the usual zigs and zags of the stock. While Zackfia made recommendations that were intended for a stock investment of at least a year or two, she had to be ready to give an opinion at any time, or respond to any development. When she wasn't taking calls, she was expected to call some clients on her own to discuss her companies and to stay on top of her stocks. At the end of the year, she would be evaluated partly on how well she served both her colleagues and her clients; in fact some of the biggest clients would be surveyed on which analysts had been most valuable. She also would be assessed on whether her picks made money for clients and how well her work contributed to the firm's overall reputation. The results would be reflected in her annual bonus, which was the majority of her compensation.

Because William Blair analysts specialized in growth companies, most of the companies that its analysts followed were small to mid-size by market value. So while McDonald's was one of Chicago's premier companies, it wasn't on the list (though, oddly, Wal-Mart Stores, the world's largest retailer, was). Starbucks, a large-cap company, was among the biggest in the crowd, but the firm had stayed with it because the spectacular growth had continued.

Despite its track record, Starbucks, with a market value north of $20 billion, was followed by relatively few analysts. Early in 2005 Starbucks listed between fifteen and seventeen analysts who followed the shares. That grew to nineteen during the year, but was still well below the twenty-six analysts who followed Brinker International, the owner of the Chili's chain, which had a market value of less than $4 billion. One theory was that the coffee company, as part retailer, part restaurant, part fast-food, simply didn't have a real competitor, making it somewhat of a corporate orphan.

As part of her job, Zackfia was expected to travel several weeks a year to see both clients and companies. To get to know Starbucks better, she also pulled off something of a research coup: a trip around the world. She went to Bob Newman, the research director, in fall 2003, when Starbucks was coming out of an international tailspin, and proposed the adventure. "She said her investment thesis on Starbucks really hinged on their ability to grow internationally," Newman said. What was remarkable wasn't that William Blair agreed to spend roughly $25,000 on the effort—they are supposed to do research, after all—but that such extensive projects are extremely rare.

Over about two weeks, Zackfia worked her way from England through continental Europe to China and Japan, talking to store managers and competitors. Producing the thirty-seven-page report took more than six months, mostly because she was sidetracked by other work. The result, "Around the World in 80 Lattes," was chock-full of insights and statistics on the overseas markets, from turnaround efforts in Japan to competitive pressures in the United Kingdom. The firm was so proud of the research that it featured the report in its own annual review for clients.

The report made Zackfia something of an expert on the overseas businesses, but there was little appreciation of that expertise today, despite Starbucks' big improvement in international profits. The interest was in TurboChef, whose stock climbed almost 50 cents, to $13.80, a gain of 3.7 percent for the day. Starbucks, despite its good news, dropped 24 cents, to close at $30.98, apparently reflecting its healthy price and continued discomfort with its sales prospects.

Two weeks later, when Starbucks announced November sales, Zackfia was at her desk waiting for the release to cross. The holiday season was in full swing, and Starbucks, as expected, had converted its stores to seas of red and silver the night of November 9, followed by a series of clever, high-profile promotions. In eight markets large painted walls started with a giant white Starbucks cup that was gradually painted red over several days. Special billboards were decorated with Christmas lights. Snow was even trucked into central spots in Miami, Phoenix, San Francisco, and, of all places, Chicago, to get customers in a holiday spirit. Today there was another promotion: The small Starbucks in her building was offering free drinks from 2 to 4 P.M.

The markets were in a cheerful mood, too: On December 1 the S&P 500 was now up 4.4 percent for the year, and the Dow, after surging 106 points that day, was up slightly for 2005. Starbucks, though, had hardly budged. At $31.14, it was in the same place it had been before the earnings announcement and at year-end. Analysts still fretted that same-store sales would grow a modest 4 to 5 percent in coming months.

Just after the market closed, the unexpected news crossed the wires. Same-store sales were up 7 percent.

"Bye, bye shorts," Zackfia said, mocking the naysayers. Immediately she turned to her spreadsheet of financial projections. She updated the November number and then increased her estimate for December sales to 6 percent from 5.

"I was looking for 3 to 5 [percent]," she said. With the price increase since September, "the fear was the stock had run its course. They had to do 5 to maintain the price. On 7, there's no doubt in my mind the stock's going up."

As usual the press release lacked illumination: "Starbucks handcrafted espresso beverages, including both core and holiday offerings, were the leading contributors to our strong November results," the company said.

The phone rang. The salesman on the other skipped the "hello" for another word: "Wow!"

"Are you worrying about Starbucks now?" Zackfia asked. She told him that she would have to talk to Michael Casey to "see what drove the sales. But it's a good name to hold." The salesman engaged, she went on to review a recent note out on P. F. Chang's, and her confidence that Guitar Center would have a good holiday.

When the call was over, she turned back to her financial model. She was increasing sales projections across all four quarters, and when she increased the fiscal fourth-quarter 2006 comp-store sales estimate to 7.6 percent from 6.3 percent, the fourth quarter profit estimate climbed too. But with that quarter nearly a year away, she wasn't ready to commit to higher earnings.

She was still skeptical about this current month because the stores sell much more merchandise in December than in other months of the year. "You can increase sales of coffee when you open a store," she explained, "but you don't necessarily increase sales of mugs." In other words, sales of holiday gift merchandise could act as a bit of a drag on same-store sales.

While she typed, the computer emitted a steady stream of pings. "I'm getting e-mails from clients saying, 'Great Starbucks sales,'" she said. Clearly she was pleased, but she resisted being smug. "In this business, you can be wrong as easily as you're right," she added.

While customers e-mailed, the phone was relatively quiet. "There won't be a lot of calls," she added. "Usually when things are good, you don't get as many calls as when they aren't."

She looked over the numbers again. In November 2004 Starbucks had reported a 13 percent gain in same-store sales and this jump was, impressively, on top of that. And she noted that Starbucks' store openings had been on a tear. In two months the company had opened 354 stores, up from 249 in October and November 2004.

From memory she dialed Casey's direct number and he answered right away.

"It was obviously a very, very good November—the highest two-year comp ever," she told him. "Congrats!" She eased into her questions, asking whether the new launch of the holiday merchandise and drinks had made a difference. Had the new beverages made an impact? And was her instinct correct that merchandise could hold back the comps?

She moved to her future comp-store estimates. "You've been right at the high end," she said, referring to the company's 3 percent to 7 percent range. "Aside from September, you've been at 7 for months." She paused to listen. "So you're telling me 7 for December? . . . Oh, you're feeling good with 3 to 7. . . ."

She asked a question about the hot breakfast program and then told Casey that everyone in her office was heading downstairs for a free beverage. She knew because they had all e-mailed her to tell her about it. "We're trying to destroy your margins," she joked. "If you miss the quarter, you can blame William Blair."

When she hung up, she turned to her model again and raised the December same-store growth estimate to 7 percent. That increased the full fiscal-year estimate to 6 percent from 5.

Then a colleague stuck his head into her office to tell her to hurry before she missed her free drink. Heading down to stand in line with twenty others for a free nonfat Peppermint Mocha, she compared notes with the other analyst, who followed retailers like Wal-Mart and Target, which were having a tougher time maintaining sales growth with higher gasoline prices. Later, she said, some of her colleagues were jealous of Starbucks. "Everyone wants to follow a company that has sustainable, consistent strong earnings with a strong path still ahead of them."

Fortified by the cup of caffeine and a squirt of chocolate and mint, she returned to finish putting together her note for clients and the company-wide voice mail, "for people who don't like to read." By 4:30, she was recording: "Illustrating the robust strength of their business model, Starbucks' November comps rose an impressive 7 percent," she began. "We believe that comps were mostly composed of traffic gains, although the hard launch of the holiday season this year may have accelerated a beneficial mix shift toward seasonal beverages and holiday merchandise." The new drinks, Chai Eggnog Latte and Eggnog Frappuccino "appear to have been very well received by customers."

She was sticking with her current earnings estimates, but she said she believed "good likelihood exists of earnings upside given continued strong sales trends." With the stock at 39 times her calendar 2006 estimate, before subtracting the cost of stock options, she didn't see room for the P/E to grow, but said, "we expect investors will be well rewarded with 20%-plus earnings growth."

Though she planned to skip the 7:30 A.M. sales meeting the next morning, figuring the news wasn't newsworthy enough, she changed her mind at the last minute—not because of Starbucks but because she wanted to remind her team about two of her top picks at the moment, CarMax, the used-car seller, and Guitar Center. She ran through the Starbucks numbers again, then reiterated her confidence in the other stocks. In particular she was finishing a new bullish report on Guitar Center, whose stock had been clobbered after it reported disappointing numbers in October. Its shares had fallen from about $60 to the high $40s, though it had closed yesterday at $53.78.

"I'm trying to keep people up to date on my thoughts," she explained later. "This is the time of year when consumer names are controversial." She was also in the holiday spirit, dressed in a ruffled maroon shirt and tweed jacket for the firm's holiday party that started at 4:30.

Back in her office, she fielded a few congratulatory calls on Starbucks, which was climbing on the impressive sales numbers. "Starbucks is a phenomenal company," one of the salesmen gushed.

Zackfia pushed him. "Did you get anybody to buy it this summer?" when she pounded the table and called it a good buy from July to September.

"I did. I have one large cap growth manager who bought it," he said. "You did a great job of calling the bottom. Another job well done, Ms. Zackfia."

As she expected, however, mostly the callers wanted to talk about CarMax and Guitar Center—and the holiday party. She told a London caller that he should have flown in, though the party tended to be crowded and overly warm.

"Is there dancing?" he asked.

"There's only dancing if you stay long enough," she told him. "Sooner or later, someone does the Electric Slide."

Between calls she checked stock prices. Guitar Center was rallying. "I see my sales guys are driving up the stock this morning," she said.

By year-end, both of the stocks would slip some. But today things were clearly going in Zackfia's direction. The broader market was mostly flat, but November sales propelled Starbucks stock up 2.5 percent to $31.93, near its all-time high. Guitar Center gained 2.6 percent, to close at $55.17. And the holiday party—and the Electric Slide—were still to come.

12

December

★ THE EARNINGS ★

A penny here, a penny there

Once the fourth-quarter earnings for Starbucks were revealed in mid-November, the stock once again settled into a rut, trading in a very narrow range between $30 and $32 for weeks on end. The shares had recovered from the disappointments of the winter and the worries of late summer, the stores were in full holiday swing, and baristas were moving those Peppermint Mochas and new Chai Eggnog Lattes. But investors wanted more evidence of fast growth and higher earnings to propel the stock to new heights.

In our journey through the months, we have seen many steps in the elaborate dance of expectations between Starbucks and the people who bought and sold, reflected on, and recommended its stock. The company carefully detailed its growth plans and then delivered, motivating investors to buy its shares. It painstakingly built and polished its reputation and the Starbucks brand, adding comfort to the buy-and-hold decisions and pizzazz to the P/E ratio. We saw the give-and-take over the monthly same-store sales numbers, as Starbucks made broad predictions and analysts tried to home in on the specifics. And we saw analysts process the company's information into earnings estimates that became the basis for the market's hopes and disappointments.

Now there was one last dance step to consider: How did the company itself create and manage its earnings expectations, the most fundamental numbers in the stock market equations? How did it prepare investors for its results, and what did it do to be sure its projections were met? The best clue would come in mid-December, when the company filed its annual 10-K report with the SEC for its year ended October 2, the most comprehensive look available into its business and its numbers.

The stakes in the earnings game were high. Remember back in the summer, when Starbucks reported that its third-quarter earnings beat expectations by a penny a share? At the time, before the stock split, that extra penny a share represented about $4 million in additional after-tax profit. The news was such a pleasant surprise that Starbucks' price jumped $2.33 a share the next day—increasing Starbucks' stock market value by more than $900 million.

The pressure on chief financial officers to hit Wall Street's estimates in legitimate ways was intense, as three professors learned when they surveyed about 400 financial executives. In the study published in 2005 in the *Journal of Accounting and Economics,* the authors found that 80 percent of those executives surveyed believed that they had to meet earnings estimates to maintain or increase the company's stock price, while also building credibility with investors. "In sum," the study's authors wrote, "the dominant reasons to meet or beat earnings benchmarks relate to stock prices." Personal reputations and potential bonuses were also on the line, but executives considered them secondary factors.

Executives told the surveyors that investors had come to expect competent managers to be able to "find the money" to make their earnings targets. If executives couldn't find a penny or two to meet estimates, investors might well assume the company had deeper problems and dump the stock. "If you see one cockroach, you immediately assume that there are hundreds behind the walls," one financial executive said.

The professors also uncovered a disturbing reality: Hitting the numbers was so important that a majority of the executives said that they would postpone a new project, potentially hurting the company in the long run, to meet quarterly earnings projections.

In notorious cases in recent years, the push to make earnings estimates or exceed them by a penny or two led to outright fraud. WorldCom improperly spread out billions of dollars of expenses over several years, rather than taking them all at once, so that it could improve its standing with investors. HealthSouth made up accounting entries to treat operating costs as if they were purchases of real assets. Enron resorted to all kinds of accounting trickery and bogus reserves to fool investors and keep the company's stock price surging.

Similarly in the summer of 2005, a special committee of Krispy Kreme Doughnuts' directors concluded that the once-high-flying chain had repeatedly fudged its accounting to make its profits look better than they were. In more than a dozen little accounting choices, most between $500,000 and $2 million, company officials had bent the rules or simply ignored them in order to meet earnings expectations that bolstered both the stock and their personal bonuses.

As part of the investigation, the company restated its earnings between 2001 and 2005, reducing the reported numbers by about 9 percent. "While some may see the accounting errors . . . as relatively small in magnitude," the committee said, "they were critical in a corporate culture driven by a narrowly focused goal of exceeding projected earnings by a penny each quarter."

These were extreme cases and fairly rare in the universe of all public companies. But the desire to consistently meet targets was human nature, part of doing your job well. The allure wasn't just about hitting the targets; it was also what the numbers said about the companies that reported them. Earnings, after all, were a company's financial box score, the official record of its achievements and shortcomings. They reflected how good the company was and, by extension, how good the management was. Executives who could make their earnings grow in nice smooth upward lines and who could exceed the expectations of investors time and again were rewarded with higher stock prices, fatter price-to-earnings multiples, and shining reputations. (Their personal wealth usually benefited too.) Those with earnings that bounced around—or worse, fell short of their own estimates or those of Wall Street—risked a reputation as unreliable or inept. Wall Street pummeled (or just ignored) their stocks and the executives sometimes lost their jobs.

The rapt attention to estimates and projections, instead of to true performance, began in the late 1970s, when folks like Leonard Zacks, a former investment analyst with a PhD in operations research, began to recognize a relationship between what analysts expected of companies and how the companies' stocks performed. When analysts' estimates for a company's earnings went up, so did the company's stock. When estimates went down, so did the share price. And the impact was far more pronounced when a company did better or worse than what analysts were expecting. Stocks prices might respond for weeks or even months after a big earnings surprise.

Initially Zacks printed a monthly report on analyst estimates that was mailed to institutional investors, getting to them probably two months after the estimates had been made. In the 1980s, when dial-up services became available, the data was sold to institutions, which could access it by dialing into a proprietary database. Zacks and his Zacks Investment Research began to track analysts' quarterly estimates and revisions and helped zero in on "earnings surprises," which seemed to accurately predict stock price increases.

In the 1990s financial information proliferated on the Internet and cable television and the lists of earnings surprises and disappointments from Zacks, First Call, and others became the perfect sound bite. In short order a newswire or an anchor could broadcast a headline that the Big Deal Company earned $1 per share, beating or missing Wall Street's expectations. By the late 1990s investors began to reward companies mostly for meeting Wall Street estimates, routinely shrugging off large losses because they were "expected" but severely punishing huge earnings gains that fell just shy of Wall Street's high hopes. In fact, in 2004 Merrill Lynch asked about 200 money managers what they looked for in picking stocks, and almost half said they looked for companies that routinely beat earnings estimates. Factors like return on equity or dividend yield were less important.

At the same time that investors were paying closer

attention to expectations, regulators were loosening restrictions on what kinds of forecasts companies could make. Legislation in 1995, for instance, allowed companies to make "forward-looking statements" without worrying about being sued if the predictions turned out to be wrong. By 2003 according to surveys by Greenwich Associates and the National Investor Relations Institute, about 75 percent of companies gave out estimates of what they expected their quarterly earnings to be.

In the aftermath of the accounting and stock scandals after the tech debacle, however, many companies began to reconsider, worrying that the quarterly projections or "guidance," as it was called, forced them to focus too much on the short term. Newer rules, such as the Sarbanes-Oxley legislation passed in the aftermath of the bust and the SEC's Reg FD, made some companies skittish about running afoul of the law by saying too much.

Michael Casey didn't see what the fuss was about. To the Starbucks CFO, there was less risk in sharing projections with investors than in keeping them under wraps and dealing with whatever numbers analysts concocted. Then "those expectations in some cases get set by one or two analysts who don't really know very much about what's going on," he said. "Since I feel we know more than any analyst out there, we should contribute our guidance as to what we think the earnings are going to be."

He didn't see a downside. "We don't put expectations out casually, we don't use it to try to drive the stock price up. We try to give a best estimate of what we think is going to happen," Casey said. "If we miss our own expectations, I'm not particularly worried about that either, because they're the best information we have at the time—and we don't miss them very often."

What concerned critics of the earnings guidance practice was that companies might play games with their numbers, intentionally putting out low estimates, for example, so that they could beat them. Or, alternatively, companies would feel so much pressure to make the numbers that they would "manage" their books or their business so that the results came out just right.

The survey of 400 financial executives reinforced that fear, with 80 percent saying they would be willing to take actions to ensure they met their targets. Those steps might include reducing discretionary spending on research and development, advertising, or maintenance; announcing a price increase for the next quarter to increase volume in this current quarter or changing the timing on pension-plan funding. Just over half said they would delay a capital project to meet projections. One CFO characterized such decisions to meet earnings targets as the "screwdriver" effect: "you turn the screws just a little so that it fits," the researchers wrote.

To some degree, the moves made sense. If your football team was down at halftime, you wouldn't want it to stick with a game plan that wasn't working; you'd want it to make adjustments so that it could win the game. Yet you wouldn't want it to do something stupid that could hurt it later.

Orin Smith, the retired CEO who had been Starbucks' CFO in the early days, said the company tried to take care when setting projections. He said the company discouraged overly optimistic estimates, but also made sure that managers "really believe they can meet those expectations and they understand they are going to be held accountable for meeting them." He said Starbucks insisted that managers alert higher-ups to problems early "so that we had some time to find fixes in other parts of the business." For instance, the company might have time to run a promotion to boost sales or hold back on some discretionary spending. "A quarter's 90 days long, and if you don't find out about that until the middle of the quarter, you're darn fortunate to be able to get a fix in that will affect the outcome of that quarter," he said.

When companies do miss, he said, many tended to underestimate the size of their problems and then miss estimates again for two or three quarters in a row. "By the time you've done that, you've eroded trust and confidence in the management so much that it takes a year to regain that kind of confidence. Your stock is hurt for a long period of time," he said. When Starbucks decided to write down its Internet investments in 2000, he said, the company tried to assess the worst-possible scenario and account for that, so that the next quarter wouldn't be disappointing as well.

Generally the penalties for missing estimates were great enough that it was worth making mid-quarter adjustments, he added. In addition to the impact on the stock price, the employees and customers also are affected, he said. "The impact can be felt by your people and by your customers because everything they see and read is, 'The company's got a problem.'"

At the holidays a few years ago, he said, Starbucks realized that its results were going to come up a bit short. "So we cut labor costs. We'd done everything else and we cut labor costs," he said. It seemed like the right move at the time—and the company made the quarter. But it suffered unexpected fallout. Employees were unhappy, and so were customers.

"We failed to meet the service expectations of our customers," Smith said. "In hindsight I think every one of us would have said that was a mistake. It would have been better for us to miss the expectations than cut those labor costs at that time." He said he vowed not to do that again.

Though the company considered itself to be conservative in its accounting, Starbucks and hundreds of other retailers and restaurant companies were caught up in an embarrassing accounting challenge from the SEC in early 2005. The SEC concluded that for years companies had been improperly recording when they actually took possession of a property and how they booked improvements to the space. For instance, before the change, Starbucks began accounting for a lease when the store opened. After the change, it had to begin accounting for the property when it took possession to finish out the store.

The changes to the bottom line were barely noticeable and the stock price didn't move, even though the company had to delay filing its first quarter financial report until it sorted all the issues out. But months later, Casey was still steamed about it. "I didn't agree with it all. The rule-maker interpreted the rules in a way that nobody had interpreted them before," he said. "It was just a lot of to-do about nothing."

The restatement underscored how fuzzy accounting standards can be. On the outside, accounting appeared so cut and dried, so clear-cut and rule-bound. In reality, though, "generally accepted accounting principles" were nothing like our checkbooks, with their simple records of purchases and deposits. Instead corporate accounting required companies to make all kinds of assumptions and estimates, giving them plenty of room to legitimately squeeze a penny—or a few—into their earnings per share. Companies had plenty of leeway to make judgment calls about how long certain equipment might last, whether something was temporary or permanent, and whether a bill needed to be paid right now or a little later. They could legitimately create reserves to cover upcoming expenses, whether it was the cost of selling a division, severance payments for laid-off workers, or funds set aside for inventory that would be marked down. And the requirement that companies expense the value of stock options paid to employees and managers, in place fully in 2006, was based largely on educated guesses about what would happen in the future: The formula called for estimating how long people would hold their options, how volatile the stock would be, and a reasonable assumption of interest rates—all areas where there was room for interpretation.

Sorting out accounting issues wasn't for the numerically squeamish or the impatient. A 10-K report was hardly fine literature, and investors had to root around in the guts of the filings, digging deep into the charts, the lengthy descriptions, and the densely written footnotes to find potential problems hidden there. The most sophisticated analysts and investors built extensive financial models that calculated all manner of percentages, ratios, and year-over-year percentage changes in the hope that unusual developments would jump out from the numbers.

Some of the assumptions that companies made or the actions they took were impossible to excavate from the financial statements. But a fair number of issues were spelled out, or at least hinted at—though they were belated. Big companies usually released their earnings within a few weeks of the quarter's end, but they had up to forty days after the end of the quarter or up to seventy-five days after year-end to file their financial documents. By then the information was gathering dust, especially for growth investors, who were focused on what was ahead, what the company would do the next quarter and the quarter after that. Only those who took the time to go back and do an autopsy on old results would have a shot at spotting festering problems or the roots of aggressive accounting.

By most standards Starbucks' numbers were relatively clean. The company rarely recorded large charges or unusual reserves or made big acquisitions; its income statement showing its revenue and profits was about as plain as a cup of black coffee. But as with virtually any company, its 10-K report for the year ended October 2, 2005, filed with the SEC on December 16, included some unexpected items and a few little secrets.

The company's balance sheet, for instance, showed relatively little debt—basically the $277 million it had borrowed to buy shares during the year. If it owned its stores, its debt would have been far higher because it would have to record the mortgages it owed. But its thousands of leases, real financial commitments to pay for store space over many years, weren't considered debts under accounting rules. An investor had to rummage back to footnote 12 to see that the company was committed to $3 billion in rent payments in the future.

Given that Starbucks so consistently met or exceeded its expectations, the critical question was, Where, if it wanted to, might Starbucks find a penny or two to make sure its results pleased investors? There were a number of perfectly acceptable and legal ways to tinker with the accounting to tease out a little more net profit. Uncomfortable though it might be, let's snap on the rubber gloves and dissect a few of the innards of the 2005 year-end financial statement to see where a cent or two might come from:

* **Warranties.** Among its coffee mugs and cute tumblers, Starbucks sold a small selection of coffeemakers and espresso machines under its own brand, with warranties ranging from one to two years. To cover the warranties, Starbucks set aside reserves based on its sales and historical experience. In fiscal 2005 customers collected $8.8 million in warranty claims, more than twice the claims in fiscal 2004.

In tables in its 10-K filing, Starbucks reported that it had added only $7.5 million to its warranty reserves during the year, less than what it had paid out to unhappy customers. The $7.5 million addition to reserves was included as part of Starbucks' expenses and reduced its profits. The filing didn't offer any further information—and without it, the number stood out like a giant question mark. The reserve seemed to be at least $1.3 million short. After all, shouldn't next year's reserves at least cover this year's costs? Was there a change in the brewing equipment business—or was Starbucks being stingy with the reserves to pad the bottom line?

* **Inventories and inventory reserves.** The bulk of Starbucks' inventory was in coffee, both green and roasted. But in the last part of 2005, its inventory of merchandise held for sale soared by about a third over the year before to $109.1 million from $81.6 million. At the same time, its reserves for inventory that was obsolete, slow moving, broken, or stolen grew 46 percent, to $8.3 million. Some of the growth in both categories may have reflected stocking up and straightening up for the holiday season. Still merchandise inventories were growing much faster than overall sales. Did that mean that goods might be stacking up in the warehouse? Should even more have been marked down, a move that would also pinch earnings?

* **Advertising.** Traditionally Starbucks recorded all of its advertising right away as an expense, which was deducted from revenue and reflected in the bottom line. But in 2005 it revealed that it was capitalizing some direct-mail advertising expenses that primarily went to promoting its "Duetto" credit card. By capitalizing the expenses, it spread them out over three years rather than recording them right away. The amount to be expensed in later years was recorded as an asset on the balance sheet, under "prepaid expenses."

The practice was allowed under accounting rules if Starbucks could directly link the expenses to revenue it would receive later from the credit cards. But some accounting experts said they were surprised that Starbucks used the more aggressive accounting method and noted that three years seemed like a long time to spread out such expenses. Moreover the amount capitalized more than doubled, to $11.8 million in fiscal 2005 from $5.8 million in 2004. That meant $6 million was kept out of the company's expenses.

* **Gift cards.** About three years after Starbucks introduced refillable gift cards, the amount that customers put on the cards continued to explode. At the end of fiscal 2005 more than $150 million in cash had been paid to Starbucks and was sitting on cards waiting to be spent.

Starbucks hadn't touched that money—yet—but some retailers began to see that growing pile of cash as a potential windfall. Home Depot, for one, concluded that some of the approximately $500 million that its customers had put on gift cards would never be spent. In its fiscal first quarter ended May 1, 2005, it recorded $43 million in onetime income from what it euphemistically called "gift card breakage."

Starbucks' expanding gift-card balance was a sign of future

sales and earnings strength, said Charles Mulford, an accounting professor at Georgia Tech. But if the company needed a little extra help with earnings in the future, he said, it might "start to recognize amounts that won't be redeemed."

✷ **Depreciation.** Every company with hard assets, like buildings, property, and equipment, must record depreciation each quarter, to reflect that the assets have a limited life. The number is only an accounting entry—companies don't actually set aside cash to replace the assets later—but it does reduce net income. While accounting rule makers have guidelines for determining how to calculate depreciation, a great deal is left to the companies to decide.

Starbucks said it depreciated its nearly $650 million in store equipment over two to seven years, though it didn't offer an average life span. Any change in that average life span would make a huge difference in earnings. Professor Mulford noted that if the average rose to four and a half years from three and a half years, the company would remove $40 million in depreciation expense from its income statement— and add $40 million in pretax profit.

All these issues were on the up-and-up, yet added together they might have made a difference in whether Starbucks met or beat Wall Street's expectations. Let's add up just a few: Take the $1.3 million that wasn't spent on warranty reserves and throw in the additional $6 million in capitalized advertising expenses. If we assumed that inventories might have been overstated by a modest $5 million or so, we would have identified $12 million to $13 million in potential expenses that didn't show up in operating income. Adjusting that number for taxes left us with about $8 million. With about 800 million shares outstanding—you guessed it—$8 million equaled a penny a share.

Curious about the string of items, I asked Michael Casey to walk through them. The warranty issues, he said, reflected troubles with an espresso machine that had been discontinued. In addition the company was selling fewer such machines in general. "It's not the most successful thing we do," he said of the brewing equipment sales, "but it's part of being the coffee expert. It's an important part of our business." In the future the company didn't need such large warranty reserves because "the ones that were problematic are gone."

The increase in inventory reserves was likely related to the growth in sales of music CDs. Starbucks expanded its offerings in 2005 from a few titles to as many as a dozen per store. While the company had rarely returned goods to the warehouse from the stores, it had sent a few CDs, like *Charlie Brown's Christmas* and the Rolling Stones *Rarities* album, back for a time. Later they might be returned to the stores. The items were written down in value when they went back, however, on the chance that they wouldn't actually be sold in the future. "We're being very conservative about any assumptions about things like that that we bring back," Casey said. "If there are any surprises, the surprises are going to be, 'Hey, we sold it.'"

Direct-response advertising expenses were capitalized, he said, because that's what the accountants said the company should do under accounting rules. (Two big credit card issuers, Capital One Financial and Citigroup, however, didn't capitalize direct-marketing expenses.) While the amount could make a difference of a half a penny of earnings, Casey scoffed at the notion that spreading out the expenses might have helped the bottom line, saying that amount wasn't worth the trouble of matching the costs and the revenue. "It has nothing to do with earnings manipulation, believe me," he said.

Casey said the company hadn't yet recognized any income from the gift cards but he expected that to change as the cards grew older. (In fact, in fiscal 2006 the company recognized about $1 million a quarter in income from the cards.) "Eventually, the accountants will say, you have that balance and it's clear that's not all going to be redeemed," he said. When the gains were taken, he said it would be based on a formula, hypothetically, something along the lines of taking 50 percent of the untouched amount that had been sitting on cards for five years; 25 percent of what hadn't been touched in four years, and 10 percent of a card that hadn't been used in three years. Even if it booked gains, however, Starbucks would honor its cards. "What we really want," he said, "is we want people to come in and spend the card."

Finally, on depreciation, he said the company only infrequently changed its accounting policies. If anything, he said, the company was more likely to shorten the useful life, rather than lengthen it, because as the stores handled more customers, equipment tended to wear out faster. Shortening the life would add to depreciation expenses and reduce earnings, while increasing the useful life would help profits. "We never bring anything up, which is what would improve the earnings," he said. Unfortunately, to find out what was behind the reported numbers, a shareholder would have to be able to ask Casey that question directly, something little investors rarely have the opportunity to do.

In one of our interviews, Casey grew a bit testy with these questions. "To be honest, I thought these were going to be important questions—and these are *not* important questions," he said. "Those are such tiny little things."

True, they were small. But in poking on a few accounting issues, a few business issues were also revealed: The company had been selling a bum espresso maker, and maybe its music sales weren't quite as frothy as they appeared.

I asked Casey if any analysts or big investors or anyone else ever asked him detailed questions about the accounting or the information in the footnotes. "Almost never," he said. Investors didn't ask about the balance sheet, the cash-flow statement, or the details in the filings, he said, because their interest was in "what's going to happen tomorrow, not what happened yesterday."

As long as Starbucks kept delivering on its promises, investors were likely to keep looking forward, potentially missing any trouble that could be brewing under the surface.

"We have a reputation for high-quality accounting so they don't think it's a territory worth mining," Casey said. "This is an income statement, earnings-per-share growth story, not a balance-sheet story. If we were a bank or a finance company or perhaps even a large manufacturer, the balance sheet would be of much greater interest," he added. "But this is a growth story."

13

January

★ THE ANNUAL REVIEW ★

Don't marry your stocks

hen the last trades crossed on December 30, Starbucks closed at $30.01, down 4 percent for the year, only the third down year in its history as a public company. The new year, though, got off to a somewhat better start.

In the first two days of trading in 2006 Starbucks stock climbed more than $1.50 a share. On January 5 Starbucks said its same-store sales for the crucial December holiday had climbed 7 percent over the previous year, a testament to the power of peppermint, eggnog, and gingerbread. The shares held steady at $31.62, completing the round trip to the prices seen oh-so-briefly at the end of 2004. For longer-term stockholders, the stock's recovery posed one of investing's most vexing questions: When do you sell?

It's a difficult problem, especially if the stock just rebounded from recent lows and is back near an all-time high. If you subscribed to the theory that you should sell regularly after a strong climb, then the end of 2005 might have been the time. At $30 a share after the split, the stock was up roughly a third from the lows reached in both April and September. Still a quick calculation showed that the stock was, once again, trading with whipped cream on top, at about 50 times its just-reported fiscal 2005 earnings and about 46 times its projected earnings for next year.

Of course selling just because the stock has a nice gain could mean leaving more than a little money on the table. If you had owned Starbucks stock from the end of 2002 to the end of 2003 and sold, you would have booked an impressive 63 percent gain. But you also would have missed the stock's truly remarkable performance in 2004, when it rose 88 percent. Yet even scarier was the possibility of hanging on too long. Those with a tendency to believe a rising stock will keep going and that a falling stock will turn the corner any minute risk losing all their profits before they finally throw in the towel.

So how do owners—both professional and amateur—make this toughest of investment choices? What questions do they ask, what numbers do they study? And does the professional advantage really matter? The quest for these answers took me to two annual reviews, one late in the calendar year at the Chicago offices of Voyageur Asset Management, owner of $120 million in Starbucks stock, and the other in a Seattle home in January, where the investment club Profit Prophets reviewed its $3,841 investment.

Both groups had been investing together for a while. The Voyageur group had joined RBC Dain Rauscher en masse in 1999 from Chicago Trust Company. Starting with just $325 million, their portfolio has ballooned to more than $8 billion in stock investments managed for state employee retirement funds, union pension funds, individuals, and companies. The research director for the team, Nancy Scinto, a Voyageur managing director and a senior portfolio manager, stumbled into the business after studying biology in college. She intended to become a veterinarian, but landed a bank job after graduating, saw how analysts evaluated companies, and decided she wanted to do it too. She started working as a research associate for Jerold Stodden, now another Voyageur managing director, back in 1985. A petite woman with Midwestern sincerity, she earned a master's in business administration at night to improve her analytical skills.

The group's biggest fund was its large-cap growth fund. To pick the thirty to forty Charles Barkley–like stocks that can be nimble despite their enormous size, she and the firm's other analysts screened stocks for companies whose earnings consistently grew faster than average but that had less debt and a solid return on stockholder's equity. Then, armed with a list of 250 or more companies, they studied the industry, the management's plans, competitors, and the company's specifics. They looked at company financial filings, listened to its conference calls, and read a smattering of analyst reports from brokerage firms like their Chicago neighbor, William Blair. The goal: to pick a stock with staying power, one that will perform for three or four years—or longer. Walgreens had been in the portfolio for well over a decade.

Scinto plucked Starbucks from the investment pile in 2003. At the time Starbucks had a market value of about $10.7 billion, just enough to squeak beyond mid-cap size into the large-cap bracket. She liked its ability to leap over earnings and sales goals and its potential to grow 20 to 30 percent a year, and Voyageur bought more than a million shares starting in July that year. The timing was terrific: Voyageur caught most of the stock's growth wave in 2003 and 2004. By the end of 2004 Voyageur had increased its stake to about 2 million shares, making it one of Starbucks' twenty-five or thirty largest owners.

The stock-picking strategy was also bringing Voyageur new clients. The Texas Employees Retirement System turned over $1.1 billion to the large-cap growth fund in mid-2004, noting that it had outperformed the S&P 500 more than 60 percent of the time over a decade. It helped, too, that the Voyageur team wasn't too squeamish about high price-to-earning ratios, meaning that it might stick with some of the market's highest-flyers when more skittish managers might bail out. To the managers of the $20 billion Texas fund, that strategy meant Voyageur would be a good contrast to the value funds in its portfolio, which looked more for misfits and other bargains. Toward the end of 2004, the Nevada Public Employees Retirement System and the Illinois Teachers' Retirement System also hired Voyageur to manage some of their money.

The first part of 2005 had been rocky. When the stocks of both eBay and Starbucks tumbled in early 2005, some new accounts suddenly were moving sharply in the wrong direction. Scinto said she expected the stocks to pull back some after their enormous run, but she had to spend some time reassuring some of the new investors in the first quarter.

In midsummer, just after hearing Starbucks' executives speak at a William Blair investment conference, she still had faith in the stock despite its decline. Though she dislikes coffee herself, she was visiting stores regularly for her favorite Chai Tea Latte and began to see the business as more of a lifestyle choice than just another retailer. While short-term traders made hay with the uneven monthly comparable store sales, she zeroed in on growth in square-footage. If the company was building its store base by 15 to 20 percent a year in the United States and overseas, and the business was sound, it couldn't help but expand.

By fall, though, she was feeling a little frustrated. The Voyageur team met twice a week to discuss the portfolio and other possibilities. But the large-cap fund was lagging the S&P 500. When she looked at what she considered high-quality companies, they simply weren't doing very well. The fund was light on two of the year's strongest sectors, utilities and energy stocks, industries that trade on commodity prices rather than pure profit growth. The old tech standbys like Dell and Adobe had been downright disappointing. The team had dumped insurer AIG—luckily—when news first broke about accounting irregularities, but had held on to other financial services stocks a tad too long. "Being a patient manager—it has been shown time and again—it does work out in the long run," Scinto said. "But I'm at a time frame right now where it's not working so well."

That could be a problem for clients and, a bit more personally, for the Voyageur employees. While everyone received a base salary, the Voyageur team also got bonuses based on how the clients did, on their stock picking success and whether they were bringing in new business. They also shared in their group's profits, and the top people could earn million-dollar paydays. The bonuses were based on one year and three years of performance, not the latest quarter, but that was only some solace. After all the clients had to give their own investors quarterly updates and were plenty sensitive to underperformance, short-term as well as long-term.

By late fall Scinto, who owned Starbucks in her personal

account as well, was encouraged again. After Hurricane Katrina devastated the Gulf Coast, the stock market seemed to focus again on stocks with more depth, moving to higher-quality stocks from flash-in-the-pans. The Voyageur fund's results were better, too. After Starbucks' fourth-quarter earnings were reported, the team gathered in the narrow conference room to walk through their annual review; there were nine people in all, including the four managing directors who ultimately decide what goes and what stays in the portfolio, the analysts, and the stock traders, who not only execute the trades, but also keep track of the rumors, tips, and scuttlebutt that feed Wall Street. Typically a few others joined by phone.

In front of them were two pages that Scinto put together. One was an "eight-pager," which, actually, was only one page with eight small charts neatly aligned, summarizing basic financial information: a ten-year stock price chart, ten years of earnings, margins, cash flow, earnings per share ("A nice steady line," Scinto pointed out), returns on equity and capital, projected growth and the price-to-earnings ratio over time. Though much of the data could be pulled from Yahoo! Finance or other free Web sites, she guarded the document closely. All together it provided Voyageur's snapshot of how it saw the company.

The other sheet summarized some of the same information, but also offered a few words to describe the business and the investment thesis, why the analyst thought it was a worthy member of the portfolio. In Starbucks' case, that was the store growth, domestically and internationally; sales growth at the stores; product innovation and keeping expenses in check. The sheet listed risks, too, but just a couple: The stock was vulnerable to gyrations in same-store sales and its international expansion could be tricky. (The research team could come up with a longer list of potential setbacks, Scinto said, but it would be counterproductive. The summary was a miniature marketing tool that should make the case for or against the stock. Given that, she said, "If you're recommending a company, you don't want to put a long list of risks here.")

Charlie Henderson, the white-haired chief investment officer, led the meeting, drawing laughs when he deadpanned, "we always have a very tight agenda that we always follow closely." In fact the group was so collegial and had worked together so long, that they sometimes finished each others' sentences. In twenty minutes or so, they worked over a wide range of information, from sales, profit, and growth numbers to international expansion, stock buybacks, Green Tea Frappuccino, and the new Elton John Christmas CD.

The group was feeling pretty chipper with its portfolio up 4 percent for the year. "We're finally making money for our clients and that's a nice thing," Henderson said. "Right now we're probably more comfortable with our portfolio than we have been all year. And Starbucks is treating us well—what is it, outperforming 23 percent so far this quarter? We should have more like that."

With that introduction, Scinto moved into a quick review of the recently ended fiscal year, adding insights gleaned from the company's hour-long conference call and recent analyst reports from brokerage firms. Fourth-quarter earnings gains reflected a tight rein on expenses and "rather aggressive share buybacks." "Even after the turbulent year that we had with them," she explained, "they definitely beat by four or five cents over the original expectations they put out in July '04. So I thought that was pretty good."

Instead of the 1,500 new outlets planned in the fiscal

year, the company opened 1,672 new stores, increasing the number of stores by almost 20 percent. "I thought they did a great job of executing, especially since everybody was concerned about, you know, all the pricing changes," she said. Back in the fall, when she worried about how same-store sales would fare when the company reached the anniversary of its price increase, she teasingly asked her colleagues at every meeting to stop by Starbucks. "Have some coffee this morning, have some tea," she urged them. Then she expected same-store sales to plunge and the stock to get blasted as momentum investors ditched their stock. Instead the company surprised everyone with its strong October sales, and the stock started its rebound.

Now, in fiscal 2006, total sales were expected to climb another 20 to 25 percent as the company opened another 1,800 stores and carefully worked to keep same-store sales growing 3 percent to 7 percent. "Remember that we were joking about Christmas coming early in Starbucks," Scinto asked, reminding them that the stores had turned red in early November. "I think they partially did it to work on that comp for November." Last year the company had a blowout November, reporting a 13 percent jump in comparable store sales. To improve on that, she said, it appeared to have rolled out the holiday goodies a little early, including an exclusive CD of Elton John–selected Christmas tunes, a selection of holiday music with a never-heard-before Barbra Streisand cut, and the customer-favorite "Christmas Blend" coffee. "I think that helps," she said. She also noted the new coffee-free offerings, Chai Eggnog Latte and a new Eggnog Frappuccino.

"Is that like the caramel one?" someone asked.

"Yeah, but it's eggnog. I think it sounds good," Scinto added. And the old favorites, Peppermint Mocha and Eggnog Lattes, were on the menu again, too. "People wait for those to come back every year," she noted.

"Do they add brandy to it?" Henderson asked hopefully.

The talk shifted back to the store openings, and Henderson couldn't help but marvel at the company's ubiquity. On a trip to Canterbury, England, he walked down an alleyway to an old stone arch that was the gate to Canterbury Cathedral. And there, hugging the arch, was a Starbucks store. "I thought, 'What's wrong with this picture?' They're everywhere," he said.

"I'm always asking Nancy, from where we sit, there's five Starbucks within about a block, right here. How do they all make money?"

"It's amazing, even with all the Caribous and everything else," she said.

Inspired by Henderson's brandy question, David Cox, who, like Henderson is a senior managing director, asked about sales and profits outside the stores, like grocery sales and the coffee liqueur introduced early in the year. Scinto told him that business was growing 20 percent—but the really impressive profit improvements were in the international business, where operating profit margins jumped to double digit levels from 8 percent a year ago. "Big jumps," she said, "I just don't think those are sustainable, but it still shows how much they're turning around." Japan has struggled, but it's improving, she explained, and in China, the company is increasing its investment.

"Do the Chinese like coffee?" Henderson asked.

"Starbucks has been doing a very good job of educating them on coffee drinking," Scinto answered, repeating the company's line on the market. "It's also the appeal of the American lifestyle. One of the things they pointed out on the call, most Starbuck stores are bigger than any of their homes. So Starbucks becomes more of a destination place. Instead of going home after work and being crowded by family members, you go to Starbucks because it's bigger.

"I thought that was a very good-feeling story of how Starbucks was being incorporated."

Next year, she continued, the company will be investing more in China, which might pinch profits. From there she moved to other concerns for 2006. The team already separately reviewed the potential impact of expensing stock options on all its stocks, but this one deserved special mention. Starbucks reported earnings per share of 61 cents in 2005. Next year the expenses for stock options would knock an estimated 9 cents a share from earnings. As a result Starbucks' bottom line was projected to be just 65 cents a share. "It will look like it's not growing," Scinto added, even though underlying profits would be up about 20 percent or more. "It's something for us to keep in mind."

Another point, she noted, was the year's stock buybacks, 45 million shares at a cost of $1.1 billion. Normally that wasn't a big deal, but it had a huge impact on one of the favorite numbers investors like to follow, return on equity. The number, which in its simplest form was net profit divided by shareholders' equity, showed how much profit the company was generating with the money shareholders invested in it. A young, fast-growing company may have a relatively low return on equity while it waits for its initial investments to pay off. But a maturing company whose business was doing well will have an ROE in the teens or twenties. Starbucks' return on equity jumped to nearly 22 percent in 2005 from 17 percent in 2004. Impressive, until you realized that some of that was sleight of hand. By purchasing so many of its own shares and taking them out of circulation, it reduced its shareholders equity—and the divisor in the equation. As a result the number appeared to soar. "Normally we don't highlight that, but ROE is one of the metrics that we look at," Scinto said.

Quickly she ran through other issues: Coffee costs may rise 10 percent in the next year. The company may continue to buy back shares. Some expenses will be up, but store opening costs should fall.

"Are you concerned about saturation?" Henderson asked.

"No, there are so many markets where there still are not many," Scinto said, and with new designs, like the drive-through, the company is finding plenty of room to expand.

Jerold Stodden, a managing director and senior portfolio manager, asked about music sales. ("Jerry hates the music business," Scinto said later, because he worried that it was a distraction, a business outside the core.)

"The whole idea is to get more people in the store and expand the customer base," she said. By offering music exclusives, the stores enticed customers to make an impulse purchase with their drinks. "They're going to continue to do that because it brings people in and it brings your average ticket price up."

But, she said, "It is not so meaningful that we worry about it. The bigger item that they're pushing is food," which also pumped up the average sale, she said. (What she didn't say was that she personally fretted more about food than music, worrying that it could slow down the rapid service and that poor quality could give the chain a black eye.)

Stodden, following up, inquired whether the stores can speed up their customer service. Scinto explained that new wands for scanning bar codes were installed at the cash registers just before the holidays, helping move customers through more quickly. Noting that this group's proxy for service was based heavily on the store in their office building, Scinto recalled that she didn't make a purchase the other day because the line was too long. The company continued to work on the logjam, she said.

The questions over, Scinto gave her summary: "I think they're in great shape, quite honestly. They're a company I don't think you have much concern about economically. It's a high-end product. We're all kind of addicted to our specialty coffee. They have consistent low-20 percent growth."

Even with the gold-plated premium in the price, the group was comfortable with the investment. "If they keep growing at 20 to 25 percent, then you obviously have a huge stock," Cox said. "If the P/E comes down a point or two every year, and you're growing 20 to 25 percent, you're still looking at a stock that's going to grow in excess of 15 percent the next several years." But, he added, "if you're looking 10 years down the road, they're not going to be growing 20 percent. They're not going to be at 40 times earnings for some time before that." By then, of course, Voyageur would hope to have already sold.

The meeting ended. Clearly Starbucks was a keeper for now, a stock with a safe home in this portfolio.

But when would Voyageur bail? The most likely reason would be if the investment thesis changed, Scinto said. If the group didn't think the company could sustain its growth, for instance, it might sell. But it might also sell if a better opportunity came along or if the stock didn't meet the basic criteria of its stock screens. On the flip side, if the stock grew to more than 5 percent of the portfolio, it would sell some, since that was the most it would hold of any one company.

For the team, the main focus was making sure the company's sales and profits continued to climb. "You have to watch every little news item for the slightest hint of a crack," Scinto said. "At some point in time, Starbucks is going to be a Microsoft, growing 10 percent and looking for cost cutting to help profits. I know that time will come. I just don't know when." And how will she know when it does happen? "I hate to tell you this," she said, "but it's a gut feeling."

For now, though, Starbucks' consistent fast growth, the talented management, the international opportunities, the healthy balance sheet all were pointing in the right direction. "It's close to the perfect stock," she concluded.

Several weeks later, in early January, the Profit Prophets Investment Club of Seattle took up the same exercise. A small group of forty-something working moms, most with teenagers at home, met monthly to review and discuss their portfolio and kick in $20 to $50 each to the pot. The group bought Starbucks in 2001 at a split-adjusted price of $12 a share and watched with awe as it shot up. Though the women made larger initial investments in four other stocks, Starbucks was by far their biggest gainer. It had also become their biggest investment, 22 percent of their $17,200 portfolio. Several of them owned the stock personally as well.

The club formed in 1997 as tech stocks were taking off. Judy Lear, a soft-spoken and thoughtful mother of two, originally began the club with coworkers of her husband who wanted to know more about stocks, and the group members shifted over time. A chemist by training and a self-taught investor, she had dived into the subject after leaving a job with a medical supply company and coming face-to-face with the challenge of managing her own retirement account. Quickly she got the bug and began regularly reading about and studying stocks. For the last eight years, she and her mom had traveled to Las Vegas for Louis Rukeyser's annual spring investment conference.

She and her husband are cautious about money, paying cash for cars and keeping debt to a minimum. But she had accumulated about 50 stocks in her portfolio and sometimes traded in and out over a few months. She first bought 100 shares of Starbucks in 1994, paying $2,800, and for a while she played the cycle, selling some when it seemed to reach a seasonal peak and buying it back later. She never sold more than half at a time "because I might be wrong." After stock splits and purchases, her Starbucks shares swelled to $45,000. In the fall, partly to supplement her family income and partly because she liked the company so much, she got a job as a barista at her neighborhood store.

On a rainy Monday night, the club gathered in Lear's living room, a small tree with ornaments and candy canes still lit in the window. Though it had already been a long day, the eight women were mostly business as they munched cookies and sipped tea while reviewing their holdings. This kind of get-together, bringing friends or associates to study and make investments, dated back to the 1950s, when the members of the Mutual Investment Club of Detroit decided to share their club idea with others. Forming a nonprofit, now called the National Association of Investors Corporation, they began to sell their investing-by-committee concept and their stock-picking methods.

For many years the organization ambled along, until the mid-1990s, when a group of senior citizens from a tiny Illinois town burst onto the scene. Calling their club the Beardstown Ladies, the sixteen women traded recipes as well as stocks and boasted annual returns of more than 20 percent over a decade. Their message—Even grandmas can beat the

market!—resonated just as more and more companies were
turning responsibility for retirement funds over to the rank-
and-file in the form of 401(k) accounts. Their *Beardstown
Ladies Common-Sense Investment Guide* became a runaway
best seller and four more books followed. The ladies became
national celebrities, featured in magazines, on television, and
as expert speakers.

On the heels of their success, the number of registered
investment clubs jumped to 25,400 in 1996 from just over
7,000 in 1991, as friends, coworkers, and neighbors joined
together to pool $50 or $100 a month and learn how to pick
the right stocks. But like most red-hot investments, this one
didn't last either. In 1998 the ladies' calculations were discred-
ited. A formal audit by Price Waterhouse showed that their
annual return over a decade was actually a mere 9.1 percent,
well behind the 12.1 percent gain of the Dow Jones Industrial
Average over the same period. The number of clubs peaked
that year at just over 37,000.

With the steep decline in stock values after the tech bust,
the number of investment clubs slid sharply, falling by half, to
about 18,000 in 2005. Still the clubs provided the first introduction to investing for tens of thousands of people who
might have shied away from owning stocks on their own. Relying heavily on Value Line investment reviews and insights
into what they know and like, club members have gravitated
to some of the nation's best-known stocks. According to an
annual survey that NAIC conducts each year, Pfizer and
Home Depot were the two most popular stocks that clubs
owned in 2005. General Electric, Harley-Davidson, and Intel
were next, with Starbucks coming in at number 17.

Maury Elvekrog didn't understand why. The Bloomfield
Hills, Michigan, money manager wrote a regular "Repair

Shop" column for the *BetterInvesting* magazine that goes to all NAIC members. In it he offered advice to clubs who were disappointed with their results. Three times in 2005 and early 2006, Elvekrog recommended that clubs sell their Starbucks shares and invest them in something with more potential. "I very much believe in holding on to a stock at a price beyond what an investor would be willing to pay to buy it," he wrote to the Women Investing Profitably club. "There's a limit to this, however . . . A stock selling at a P/E of 50 has more than reached that limit."

Instead, he told them, "Other excellent growth stocks are available at much lower prices."

Similarly he told the MM Investment Club of Longview, Texas, that while Starbucks is an American phenomenon, "I would suggest it's impossible to justify this stock's price."

Did the club listen? Joan Porter, a longtime club member, says the group took some of Elvekrog's advice on other stocks, but stuck with Starbucks. The company was still opening stores and its innovative management was finding new ways to make money in areas such as music, she said. In fact the club liked the stock so much that it bought 10 more shares in January 2006 at a price of $31.14, bringing its total to 50 shares. "We still thought it was a good buy," Porter said.

Lots of other clubs agreed. More than 3,000 clubs owned a total of 1.3 million Starbucks shares in 2005, by NAIC's estimates, though its math was a bit reminiscent of the Beardstown Ladies' calculations. Every year the parent organization asked clubs for their portfolios and about 20 percent respond, says Kenneth S. Janke Sr., chairman of the NAIC's board. Mr. Janke's wife and other investment club members recorded the holdings on three-by-five index cards and tallied them. The number was then multiplied by five to get the estimates, he says.

For the Profit Prophets the pressing issue this rainy evening was figuring out how to best invest their money and improve their return, which in 2005 was essentially zero. The official investment club materials encouraged them to follow four basic principles: Invest regularly, reinvest earnings, buy stocks of companies growing faster than average, and diversify. To assess stocks the NAIC produced a "stock selection guide," or SSG, and, through a for-profit arm, it sold software to make the calculations easier.

The two-page SSG covered some of the same concepts that Voyageur's managers studied, packaged a little differently. On the first page, club members charted earnings, sales, and the high and low stock prices over the last five years. The best charts have a relatively straight earnings line, which the NAIC's *Stock Selection Handbook* says, "indicates capable management." (Or, it might add, management that was good at producing consistent numbers.). Then the club members tried to guesstimate how much sales and earnings will grow over the next five years.

The second page tracked pretax profits, return on equity, and the debt-to-equity ratio. But the real focus was an unusual reliance on the price-to-earnings ratio. Rather than consider whether the stock was expensive or cheap relative to its future prospects, the chart looked firmly in the rearview mirror. It asked the club stock analyst to use the stock's average high P/E and the average low P/E over the last five years to estimate where it should trade in the future, and left it to the club member to evaluate whether those P/E ratios were realistic.

Laurakay Vernon, a serious-minded single mom whose real job was handling the accounting for a few small businesses, was responsible for the Starbucks review. "This looks really good," she told the group as she passed out color charts showing lines in a nearly perfect incline. The graphics showed that Starbucks' stock had roughly the same highs and lows in 2005 as in 2004, but they didn't show how low the shares were for most of 2005. Nor did anyone mention that the stock ended 2005 down a little bit from 2004.

Instead the attention was on growth. Though the company was projecting 20 percent earnings and sales increases, those estimates felt too plush to Vernon. Relying largely on her intuition, she went with 18 percent increases instead.

The company's stock had traded at P/Es between 29 and 67 times over the last five years, but she threw out the highest number as too extreme. With the adjustment, she came up with an average high P/E of 51 and an average low of about 33. Then using the SSG chart, she combined those estimates with her earnings projections over five years. By this measure Starbucks could trade as high as $72 in 2011. The downside? If Starbucks earnings were again at last year's 61 cents a share, and it traded at its average low P/E of 33, the stock would fall to about $20 from $30 currently.

And what if the market decides Starbucks' shine is diminished and its P/E premium ratcheted down over time, as happened with onetime stars like Microsoft, Wal-Mart, and Costco?

Unfortunately the stock-selection guide didn't account for that.

The last step was to evaluate whether to buy, sell, or hold the stock. The investment club formula simply divided the potential stock price range of $20 to $72 into equal parts. The lowest range was a buy, the middle a hold, the highest a sell. By this measure, Starbucks' current $30 price was a clear "buy." By this assessment, the stock had to rise if the earnings went up.

"For a while, we couldn't believe what we were getting. It looks too good," Vernon told the group. But Lear did the calculations on her own and their numbers were almost the same.

Laura Wharton, a county supervisor, wanted to know what big things will drive the growth.

"When I go to the news, it's China," Vernon answered. "Next is music. It seems to me like they're counting on a lot of their stuff from international. I'm not sure how profitable music is, it's just that Howard Schultz and their people are really excited about it."

While the women liked some of the music, they—like the Voyageur team—were skeptical about whether the CDs or the company's CD-burning stations in a handful of stores were significant. One of them got an Apple iPod for Christmas, and nearly all of them had iPods in the family. They wondered aloud if Starbucks was missing the point here with CDs instead of digital downloads. But it wasn't a big enough concern to change their view of the stock.

The one-page Value Line review that Vernon included with the stock-selection guide was crammed with numbers and analysis, including an italicized warning that the earnings projections "include stock-based compensation"—the new stock-option expenses that would appear in financial results in the 2006 fiscal year. That impact was lost on the group. It also skipped over the Value Line commentary that the stock market already appeared to have accounted for the company's "measurable earnings potential to the decade's end," a vague reference to the fact that the stock price was so high that it already reflected the profits the company might earn for the next several years.

But Vernon did have another issue. "I'm thinking, what incoming can change this picture?" she said. "What if a coffee blight occurred?"

It was a great question, especially considering how fast the company is growing. But she couldn't find an answer. She tried searching for Starbucks' coffee supply and found nothing. And when she typed "coffee bean supply" into a search engine, all she got were dozens of hits on coffee beans for sale.

Kathy Berd, a local potter who had attended several Starbucks annual meetings, remembered that the company made a point of highlighting how it tried to deal fairly with its coffee growers, and that it built schools in some areas where it buys coffee. "They seem to be ethical about it," she said. Others chimed in with the company's philanthropic efforts and how it treated its employees. Clearly the company's commitment made them feel better about owning the stock.

While the conversation wandered, Lear studied the company's numbers. "They have a 23 percent return on equity," she piped up, using Value Line's number. "Twenty-three percent is really huge." Other numbers were up, too: "Profit has increased. Leverage went up quite a bit. They have more debt—but I don't know where the debt came in."

No one else did either. The debt was taken on to help finance the stock buybacks, but how could they know that? The purchases were mentioned only in the middle of a financial statement deep in the company's fourteen-page year-end-earnings news release and near the end of the company's analyst conference call. To know that, someone would have to read the company's financial filings or listen to its entire conference call.

Do any of them do that?

The group looked back blankly. A couple stifled snickers. Between jobs and families, it seemed absurd that they could find the time to prowl the Starbucks investor relations Web site or curl up with SEC filings. Most of them do pick up headlines from the news or the Internet. Berd offered that she watches a nightly business report when she can—though her family teases her about it. Only Lear admitted to trying to dig into the filings.

The talk moved on to the next stock. At the end of the reviews, the members returned to whether they should make a purchase. The group pondered buying more Starbucks—until Berd pointed out that it was already their largest holding. "In the interest of balance, I'd lean away from Starbucks," she said. They settled on buying another stock.

When to sell has been the group's toughest call. The club ditched its Hewlett-Packard stock after Carly Fiorina got the boot as chief executive, believing the stock would rise only temporarily after her departure. (They were wrong.) It sold Hasbro after a decline, when a turnaround didn't look likely. Sometimes the group sold because they found something else they'd rather own. "A lot of it, unfortunately, is an emotional decision," Lear said.

It was there, in the gap between the intuition and the details, where the Profit Prophets and the Voyageur team probably differed most. The Voyageur crew had experience, access to analysts and executives, and an understanding of the significant behind-the-scenes numbers. Armed with all that, the team was far better equipped to identify the early signs of trouble and far more nimble in deciding when to get out. But there were no guarantees. Either group could miss the warning signs and either could get lucky and trade out of Starbucks before the storms ultimately appeared.

In this case, it didn't really matter. One group may have operated far more on feelings than facts, but they both looked at many of the same numbers, made similar projections, and relied on many of the same gut instincts. And they came to the exact same conclusion, the same conclusion that thousands of other investors had made: This was a great stock, one they definitely wanted to own.

For the Prophet Profits, there was one other matter to address. The biggest business extravaganza in Seattle, the Starbucks annual meeting, was coming up. The group counted up available tickets, compared the free goodies from previous years, and excitedly made plans to attend. A few even planned to take the day off from work to check on their investment.

Epilogue

★ ANOTHER NEW YEAR ★

"One of the funny things about the stock market is that every time
one person buys, another sells, and both think they are astute."
—William Feather

T his new year, there would be no touchy issues to tiptoe around, no unexpected disappointments just ahead of the annual meeting. On February 1 Starbucks reported that it earned 22 cents a share in the first quarter, smoking analysts' projections—and the company's own previous estimate—that it would earn 20 cents. The profits from the holiday season were far higher than the 17 cents a share reported a year ago (after adjusting for the split), even after recording first-time stock-option expenses of 2 cents a share. Altogether, for the quarter ended January 1, the company's top line grew 22 percent, to $1.9 billion, and net income jumped 20 percent, to $174.2 million.

Same-store sales for January, announced at the same time, were just as impressive, jumping 10 percent over the year ago, far above even the rosiest guesses. One huge and unexpected reason: The Starbucks gift card. In December alone the chain sold $165 million in plastic cards, and by the end of the quarter, close to $300 million in customer cash sat on cards and on the balance sheet waiting to be used—and to be recorded as revenue.

In January many of those stocking stuffers came walking back into the stores. Starbucks said customers redeemed $93 million off the cards after New Year's, or 22 percent of the sales at its company stores in the United States and Canada.

On the conference call with analysts, Jim Donald brimmed with optimism about the upcoming year. The company was looking at entering Brazil, Russia, and, eventually, India, as well as expanding in mainland China, where it had 221 stores at the end of calendar 2005. He gushed about the new Cinnamon Dolce Latte drink, which, he noted, would pair well with the new reduced-fat cinnamon swirl coffee cake, for those who wanted to make "more healthy choices" in the new year. (For the record, the grande version of the drink had 340 calories without the whipped cream; the new cake about 330.)

Then Schultz took several minutes to sell investors and analysts on the company's new entertainment strategy. In January, Starbucks announced that it would be an equity partner in and coproducer of a feel-good family film called *Akeelah and the Bee*, about an inner-city girl gunning for spelling-bee glory. Without investing any money, Starbucks would earn its share by promoting the movie extensively in its stores. The stores also would sell the soundtrack and, later, the DVD.

That wasn't all. The company also would begin selling selected books sometime in the year, completing a three-pronged entertainment foray into music, film, and literature. "This isn't a one-off," Schultz said in an interview in early January, just before the venture was unveiled. "This is the beginning of a broader entertainment strategy that we think is complementary to what our customers have come to expect of us."

In Schultz's vision Starbucks could drive customers to the movie by intriguing and exciting them, much like it enticed them to try a CD of a new artist. But this had some of the odor of the Internet experiments of 2000, and the image of the Voyageur money manager who so disliked the distraction of the music business came to mind. As we had seen back in April and again in October, successful financial growth usually emanated from an almost obsessive focus on the core business—and veering too far off course could spell trouble. "Do you think this is going to be received well by Wall Street?" I asked.

Schultz looked surprised. "I haven't even asked myself that question," he said. He paused—but only for a second. "We're going to do what we think is right for the business. And we think this is not only right for the business, but so creative and thoughtful and such a unique way to monetize the equity of the brand."

If anything, our journey through Stockland underscored that public companies like Starbucks worked diligently to attract long-term investors and keep them happy, from carefully managing earnings expectations to delivering on expansion promises to keeping the financial reputation pristine. The payoff came when the many players on Wall Street—the analysts, the people who managed the money of little investors and big ones, and those who sold the stock to them— bought into the big ideas and expectations of management and relayed them to customers.

Schultz, though, seemed almost defensive about including

those folks in his equation. Toward the end of the interview, he came back to the issue. "When you asked earlier, 'What do you think the Street is going to think of the announcement tomorrow,' I suspect there will be a mixed reaction," he said. "There's always people who will doubt and be cynical. If those people don't like what we do, they can sell the stock. . . .

"We're in business to satisfy our customers. They're in a different business than we are."

As it turned out, however, the reaction was less mixed than nonexistent. The stock barely moved over the next few days—either on the belief that management wouldn't be distracted by Hollywood or the inherent understanding that this was a minuscule financial gamble.

But now, on the earnings conference call, Schultz wanted to explain to Wall Street how the entertainment business fit in. Starbucks aimed to "change the model of how new films reach the public," Schultz said, while deliberately avoiding the way other fast-food restaurants used movie tie-ins to sell more food. "What we are doing is leveraging our vast retail store footprint and the cultural relevancy of the Starbucks brand to bring film to the public in a new way during a time when the film industry has been challenged," he told them.

And, he promised, shareholders would benefit. "It all gets back to the basics, the foundation upon which we have built our company," he said. "It's around the human connection and our passion to innovate and grow with new offerings, new sounds and new experiences, while seeking unique opportunities to monetize our assets and, in doing so, increase shareholder value."

Analysts and investors may have heard him. But truth be told, there was a much more exciting crescendo to this symphony of good news: On top of the stellar earnings and January sales, Starbucks raised its estimate for its full-year profits by a full nickel a share, or roughly $40 million. Instead of earning 63 cents to 65 cents a share after including those stock option expenses, Starbucks now expected to earn 68 cents to 70 cents a share. Once again it had underpromised and overdelivered—and investors loved it.

The next day the stock jumped 10 percent to an all-time high on the surprising and delightful new estimate. The shares closed at $34.40, up $3.04, on a day when the Dow Jones Industrial Average slid more than 100 points and the broader market was down. More than 20 million Starbucks shares changed hands, four to five times the usual daily volume. With the annual meeting just a week away, Schultz would have a real treat to deliver to his staunchest and most loyal shareholders.

The financial clues of the previous year had generally been effective in foreshadowing the stock's movement. After Schultz sold some of his Starbucks shares in late 2004, he didn't sell the company's stock again during the year. He did exercise some stock options, but he held on to the shares. Other executives bought and sold over the year without any obvious pattern, but Schultz, as the spiritual leader and chairman, turned out to be a good barometer for gauging when the stock was lofty or near a peak.

Over twelve months, the company itself bought nearly 50 million of its own shares, taking on just a little bit of debt, and the substantial spending hadn't slowed the growth one iota. The fundamentals of the business were still strong, indicating the company hadn't mortgaged its future or merely tried to pump up results with its more than $1.2 billion in stock purchases. In fact the stock buybacks and the stock split turned out to be exactly what the academics predicted they would be: strong indicators of the company's optimism about the months ahead.

I made plans to go back to the annual meeting to take stock of the year. But first I checked back with some of the players to see where they had ended up. Morningstar, the Chicago mutual fund and stock research firm, it turned out, had been going through a fair bit of soul-searching. With a philosophy based on Benjamin Graham's work, it had long leaned toward value stocks and been skeptical of high price-to-earnings multiples and rich stock prices. But in doing so, its customers had missed out on some star-studded opportunities, Starbucks included. Then, quite suddenly, at the very end of 2005, the rating on Starbucks jumped to four stars from one, without any significant change in the business or the stock price.

Carl Sibilski, the analyst who followed the stock, said the Morningstar team finally concluded that its model worked well for value stocks but was failing on the hottest growth companies. As we had seen back in the early months of the year, relative value, or the price-to-earnings ratio, was one measure of a stock, but it didn't always capture the expectations that investors had and the premiums they were willing to pay for rapid, profitable growth. "It was intellectually dishonest not to try to figure out what you can do to improve," he said.

The firm already had reevaluated Whole Foods, recognizing that Americans didn't have to be organic-obsessed to shop there. Just after Christmas a small group of Morningstar senior analysts got together to discuss Starbucks, and it became clear that many of the most negative arguments about the fast-growing chain weren't holding up either.

"Every point we ever threw at the stock over the last five years I've been proven wrong on," Sibilski said. Initially he thought the product would appeal only to premium coffee connoisseurs. "Well, that got shot down."

And then, he thought, "As soon as the economy turns down, that's it. Well, that theory didn't work out."

With the company adding more than 1,000 stores a year, he figured that "growth will have to taper down." But then "they started opening more stores every year."

The more he studied the potential, the more convinced he became that Starbucks could have more stores than Mc-Donald's. "When you start talking like that, you realize this really isn't a concept or a coffeehouse, this is a real-estate developer," he said. "They know how to put a Starbucks into any real-estate opportunity." As we had seen in April, the company's true business, that it was a store-opening machine, was its most telling feature. Looking at where the growth really came from, along with the competition and the industry, prompted Morningstar to reassess Starbucks' value.

With the stock trading at $30, the group raised the "fair value" estimate of the stock's worth to $36 a share, far higher than the previous estimate of $26, and higher than the stock had ever traded. Still the Morningstar brain trust decided that even with good management and a strong reputation, the company's economic moat wasn't wide enough and the stock wasn't cheap enough to justify its top five-star rating. They settled on four stars. For the first time in memory, Morningstar was essentially recommending the stock.

As before investment professionals looked at the same numbers, listened to the same conference calls, read similar analyst reports—and reached different conclusions. Robert Stimpson continued building his Rock Oak Core Growth

Fund, which had seen its assets grow about 10 percent, to about $11 million, still a piddling amount in the investment world. His fund had climbed 4.6 percent in 2005, about the same as the Russell 1000 Growth Index, a large-cap growth index, but slightly below the 4.9 percent total return of the S&P 500 Index, including dividends.

Because he had bought more Starbucks shares as the stock fell, that investment was now up 36 percent and the stock was now more than 4 percent of his total fund. "I made it a top ten holding and its performance made it a top three holding," he said.

With the price up, he was ready to take some profits. Early in February one of his investors pulled out a sizable amount, and he chose to sell some Starbucks to cover the withdrawal. "All the good news is baked into the stock from here," he said. With the stock up, he didn't see as much room for future appreciation in coming months, a factor that other investors said they weighed when they considered whether to sell. A long-term investor might weather the ups and downs without worrying about mutual-fund ratings or portfolio-manager rankings, but the mutual fund manager might be better off locking in profits and then buying back the shares later. Though he was still wowed by the company's growth prospects domestically and internationally, he wasn't wed to it. "I'm definitely not going to add to it here, and I might trim a little," he said, especially if another attractive stock came along.

At the same time Nancy Scinto at Voyageur went the other way: She was buying a little more.

Starbucks had been her fund's fourth-quarter star, the best performer in the portfolio in that period. Voyageur had done well in the fourth quarter too, but it wasn't enough to catch up for the year. The fund was too light on energy and a little too heavy on traditional growth stocks. It finished 2005 up 4.3 percent, slightly below the total return for both the Russell 1000 Growth Index and the S&P 500.

When Scinto took a look at Starbucks in the light of the new year, a few things jumped out. The company didn't just beat expectations for its December quarter; it did so at a time when many big names, including Google, Outback Steakhouse, Wal-Mart, and Amazon.com, missed expectations or warned that they would fall short. "It was one of the few companies that gave guidance and didn't bring anything down," she said.

She was also intrigued by the company's rapid store openings late in the calendar year, which continued into January. With so many stores open already, more stores would move into the comp-store sales numbers the following winter. "That gave us more visibility to next year. Most people weren't talking about that," she said. Given that trend and her confidence in the company's ability to maintain its store expansion, keep costs in line, and to come up with enticing new drinks, she was willing to add to the portfolio even as the price climbed. Many small investors might think about buying only when a stock price was low or selling only when it was at a recent high. But as we saw with the trading at Knight in July, professionals like Scinto kept their eye on the reasons for buying or selling, not on the price itself.

The film venture didn't move her one way or the other—though, as predicted, her colleague Jerry Stodden fussed that it would be too volatile and was off-point. Her own nightmare? The fallout if Starbucks' comparable-store sales growth took a dive. As we saw in October, the monthly results have a sharp impact on the stock short-term—and raise long-term fears.

"Zero comps for a month or two, and this thing is underwater for a while. It's going to be down 40 percent in the opening for the day," she said. "It's a risk to the price."

She wasn't expecting that anytime soon. Like most investment professionals, she only hoped that she was right more than she was wrong, the most basic goal for those who made their living trying to outsmart the market. "In this business, if you're right 55 percent of the time, you're a genius," she said.

While the pros took another look at their Starbucks holdings, the company itself was planning for another big show, built around this year's theme, "It all starts over a cup of coffee."

As always Starbucks was carefully cultivating investors' expectations. The day before the February 8, 2006, meeting, as workers hurried to finish setting up the Seattle opera hall, more than 100 headquarters and store employees gathered in a nearby lecture hall to get their marching orders. "Last year was a good show, but this year will be a better show," said Kevin Carothers, a member of the public affairs team responsible for the affair. The annual meeting, he explained, "is a time when we come together and review fiscal 2005 results and talk about what is happening in the next year—and basically pump up our shareholders."

Warning that as many as 6,000 people might show up, he had a specific request. "Please come with a great attitude," he added, "because this is a crazy day. These shareholders are very passionate. It's a free-for-all."

Once the show finally started at 10 A.M., Carothers continued, employees could watch from the main auditorium or the lecture hall. But they were to gather back in the lobby at 11 A.M. to move 5,500 gift bags, 6,000 bags of Seattle's Best

Coffee, and another 6,000 Tazo tea bags from their storage
area to the front doors. The goodies, including a can of iced
coffee, a tumbler, and coffee samples, would be distributed
in two waves—to the shareholders who left after the big entertainment and the ones who stayed through the actual business. In case of problems, greeters would be armed with a
handful of Starbucks gift cards to placate any shareholders
who felt upset or slighted.

The volunteers were divided into groups for more specific
instructions. The greeters and the ushers followed Carothers
back to the lobby, where he explained how to move latecomers
to the Exhibition Hall next door when the main auditorium
was full. Out on the plaza, he described how the early-
morning lines would be arranged. Then he lowered his voice.
"There's a potential that we're going to have protesters," he
added. If so, and shareholders ask what's going on, "just say,
they are here to express their opinion," he said. Last year one
lone protestor showed up—and "we gave him coffee."

Back inside he pointed out that emergency medical tech-
nicians would be stationed by the coatroom in case of medical problems. "We have had one or two heart attacks over the
years, and I'm not kidding," he said. "We have lots of excited,
excited shareholders."

All the planning paid off. The annual meeting day was
damp and only modestly chilly, nothing like the deeper cold
of a year ago. By 8 A.M. more than 300 shareholders were in
line to assure a seat inside the hall. Once the doors opened,
shareholders huddled around tables bulging with stacks of
muffins, doughnuts, and pastries the size of ballpark hot dogs.
They lined up ten deep at espresso bars. Emergency medical
personnel actually tended to an older man who appeared to

be having heart problems. And when the auditorium doors finally opened around 9 A.M., the roughly 5,000 attendees filled the hall.

At 10:05 the sparkling red curtain rose to the Seattle Choral Company singing "Oh Fortuna" and scenes of Starbucks stores and people, interspersed with quotes from its coffee cups. Schultz was introduced, and immediately he cut to the chase.

"As I was coming out I was handed a note that with our stock price at its all-time high . . ." he said, and the rest of the thought was lost to the thundering applause and cheers that followed. "What an absolutely wonderful way to introduce this year's annual meeting!" he added. The room exploded in applause again.

During trading the stock had touched $35, 9 percent higher than the previous peak in 2004, a more than 6,500 percent gain from where it started in 1992. A person who had bought a single share on that day for $17 would now have 32 shares, valued at about $1,120.

The rest of the meeting was purely Starbuckian—a little sentimental, a little offbeat, a little geeky, and absolutely, positively in line with its image expectations: Starbucks was a dedicated corporate citizen, a powerful growth machine, and one of the world's most recognized and respected brands, the company told its owners. Moreover it was an entity overflowing with big dreams for the future, all of which would continue to reward these dedicated followers with a climbing stock priced at a fat premium.

Mixed in, of course, were some drama, the famous "culture" video, speeches, and, naturally, some surprises. They started with the video of David Letterman's effort to get Starbucks coffee delivered through a spigot on his desk. (Letterman's exclamation that the coffee had arrived cold, however, was edited out.) Then, to one-up the talk-show host, the company tried its own trick. It launched coffee flowing through 3,000 feet of tubing from the top of the Seattle Space Needle to the opera hall, cameras following it all the way, to the absolute joy of the audience. Schultz grinned widely when the coffee flowed into his cup. Wisely, though, he didn't drink it. "Thank you all very much for allowing us to indulge ourselves," he said, chuckling.

In his opening speech, Schultz rolled off the statistics: More than 100,000 partners, more than 11,000 stores in thirty-seven countries, some 40 million customers a week. "We are probably the most frequented retailer now in the world," he said.

He recalled the difficulty of starting up his first Il Giornale store in spring 1986, nearly twenty years ago. "It not only was not an overnight success, but I laugh sometimes when I hear Starbucks partners talk about the good old days, the glory days. I gotta tell you they weren't that good," he said. He related how much difficulty he had raising money and how tight things were the first few years.

Like a preacher launching into the heart of his sermon, alternately direct and dramatic, Schultz outlined what he called three transformational periods, starting with the decision in fiscal 1991 to offer stock options and benefits to employees, even though the move ate into shareholder returns. "I honestly do not believe we would be here today if those benefits and that transformation did not take place," he said. The second transformation came in 1996, when the company went overseas for the first time, discovering that the experience translated in many spots around the world (and giving it new growth potential). And, finally, he said, the company was moving into the third period, apparently referring in part to the music and entertainment efforts, which he called "The Starbucks Effect."

"The transformational period that we're in right now is leveraging and monetizing the assets we have beyond the four walls of our stores," while also achieving a balance between profitability and social conscience, he said.

To more loud applause, he moved into another popular segment, reviewing the stock's performance. A year ago Schultz had focused on the 2004 calendar results. This time, he highlighted the last twelve months, including Starbucks' surge in early 2006, noting the Nasdaq was up about 9 percent between February 2005 and 2006. The S&P was up about 5 percent. And Starbucks? Up 36 percent. The audience cheered again.

Jim Donald reviewed some of the year's touchy-feely highlights, including donations to support victims of Hurricane Katrina. He noted the acquisition of Ethos Water and the company's commitment to support water projects in Ethiopia, Honduras, and Kenya, funded by a nickel from the sale of each bottle. And, he said, after eight years of effort, the company had finally begun using a cup with some post-consumer recycled content.

Almost secondarily the company discussed the core of its success, its plans to expand both in the United States and internationally.

China, naturally, got special attention. Christine Day, the head of the Asia-Pacific business, was introduced by a colorful "lion dance," featuring a red dragon, the Chinese symbol of energy, courage, and good luck. Appearing in a long Chinese dress, Day told the audience that Starbucks saw 200 million potential customers in a country of 1.3 billion, including a growing population of affluent young people between the ages of eighteen and twenty-four and a middle class that was growing by 8 million people a year. "In China," she added, "you can be a yuppie on just $10,000 a year." There were no details on how Starbucks would leap from a couple hundred stores to thousands, but yet another video stoked enthusiasm for its future there.

Finally, the speeches ended. The *Akeelah and the Bee* trailer was played, along with music from Sergio Mendez and a new Hear Music artist, Sonya Kitchell. Just after noon, the curtain pulled back to reveal the surprise entertainer: Tony Bennett, dapper in a tuxedo and still crooning. Two CDs would be coming out in honor of his eightieth birthday and would be sold at Starbucks. To an adoring crowd, he sang a medley of three songs, including "The Best Is Yet to Come" and "I Left My Heart in San Francisco."

The show over, the crowd thinned. Directors were elected, and the question-and-answer session, the little investors' one opportunity all year to quiz executives, lasted all of eleven minutes. Five people lined up to ask about environmental issues, the role of food sales, and why Starbucks sponsors rodeos. (The answer: As a corporation, it doesn't, but its stores could, a practice that was under review.)

Beyond Tony Bennett and the Space Needle shenanigans, there were few headlines. The biggest revelation came between the lines, in a small change in how executives described the number of stores Starbucks ultimately expected to open. Now, in press releases and interviews, officials were saying the company believed it could open *at least* 30,000 stores, including *at least* 15,000 internationally. It was subtle, but clearly the P/E pump was being primed again. The number that so effectively drove the expectations and hopes of investors appeared on the verge of another increase.

Theresa Collier, attending again with her son, remained as committed a shareholder as ever. In January she used her dividend from her Whole Foods stock to help buy 100 more Starbucks shares, bringing her Starbucks holding to 200 shares. In the course of the year, her investing philosophy had matured. In the coming months, she would trade some, but not frequently, and she would hold on, in particular, to her best growth stocks, Starbucks and Whole Foods.

After rereading Philip Fisher's book about growth stocks and a book about risk by the noted investor Peter Bernstein, she concluded that she needed to stay in stocks, but in a measured way. Fisher convinced her that there are only a few really top-notch companies, and when you find them, you should invest heavily in them. "I don't see any alternative to stocks. The market could go down, but I can't think where else I could put my money," she said.

Her experience had taught her a lesson that the pros already followed, as we saw with investors in June and Zackfia in November: Pick a strategy and stick with it. Many small investors tend to get frustrated and impatient when their stocks are down or their strategy isn't working, so they ditch that idea and jump to another. In the process they end up buying high and selling low—exactly the opposite of what they want to do. But the investing experts decide which four or five or six key factors are most important, whether they are earnings growth, management, sales potential, or cash flow, and zero in. They buy when the stocks meet their criteria and sell when the story changes or a better opportunity comes along. To balance her risk, Collier decided to build a portfolio with some solid slower-growing companies that paid nice dividends, like PepsiCo, Puget Energy, and Anheuser-Busch, to add to her high-growth companies. She stuck with Whole Foods and Starbucks because she believed their managements had exceptional vision for seeing opportunities and that they adjusted when they ran into challenges. "They made mistakes, learned from them and moved on," she said.

Though the pros had far more access to company information and management than she ever would, smaller investors like Collier could even out the differences by investing time in some homework. Collier leaned on Morningstar's research, but she could just as easily have listened to Starbucks' quarterly conference calls or downloaded the transcripts from its Web sites. She could have read the company's press releases and delved into Starbucks' annual and quarterly financial filings, also posted on the company site, for insight into the earnings that even the pros might have overlooked. At the least then she would know what analysts and big investors were expecting Starbucks to do and when it flew over expectations or fell short.

Altogether Collier's investing last year had worked out well. In the summer her earnings helped pay for a month-long family trip to Europe. Trading online, but keeping her records by hand in a spiral notebook, her page after page of transactions showed that she took some losses in the fall to reduce her taxes. Still she recorded a net return of more than $50,000 in 2005, a more than 10 percent return on a portfolio that was now well over $500,000. Her dividends alone were $17,000.

"My husband works for the city utility. He'll get a pension," she said. "I never worked anywhere long enough. This is my pension." Her passion for the market also might prompt a career change. She recently began taking an online course to become a certified financial planner and was especially looking forward to a segment on how to value stocks.

On the afternoon of the annual meeting, I caught up with Jack Rodgers, Schultz's longtime coach-on-the-bench, at a comfortable suburban Seattle Starbucks, which was literally across the street from another Starbucks. Now in his seventies and truly white-haired, he used his employee discount to buy coffee, and then apologized for it. Recently he had looked back at Schultz's biography and read that Howard always paid full price.

"That was quite a lovefest this morning, wasn't it?" he said, almost understating the crowd's enthusiasm.

With the twentieth anniversary of that very first Il Giornale coffee bar just two months away, he was a little nostalgic. We talked about the early days and the role he played as an ombudsman for customers and potential business partners, as well as employees. He used to visit with the rank-and-file and was a sympathetic shoulder for early managers stressed out by the pressure and demands of a high-growth company. Some of them still talked about going to Rodgers for career advice or to iron out internal issues. "There were some tearful sessions," he remembered. "I tried to be a listener." Since he didn't have a specific title and wasn't even full-time, "I could be there in a very non-threatening way."

The size of the company today and its far-flung operations now awe him. He knew it would be successful—but this? And the stock?

I asked him if he had ever done the math. Early on he had owned stock and "worthless options" equal to about 200,000 shares. I counted out the five stock splits on my fingers. Had he held on to all that stock, he would have more than 6 million shares today.

He shook his head. It was a stunning number. Had he wanted to calculate it at today's brief price of $35 a share, it would add up to something more than $200 million, a testament to the power of stock ownership for those who have enormous patience, deep faith in their convictions, a tolerance for risk, and the good luck to select the right company to invest in. It was the one significant advantage the individual investor had, to hang on through the ups and downs when you still believed the business had a promising future.

Of course Rodgers sold some shares when he exercised options. He had sold shares over the years to diversify his personal investments and shared stock with his children, grandchildren, and a family entity. Altogether the real number held by his family today was much smaller, something "well north of one million shares," he said, but probably less than 2 million.

In his calm and measured way, he stopped for a minute to reflect on that. Then he shared a recent decision.

"As of this day," he said, "I have told my children that I am not selling any more of my stock. I have diversified enough." Starbucks was more than a big corporation. It was more than a four-letter symbol on a stock exchange, more than money in the bank, more than a big cup of strong coffee. It was part of his family.

"I'm not a seller, and I do mean that," he said. "I have confidence and belief it will keep going the way it has."

Just to make clear which way that was, he gave an emphatic thumbs-up.

Notes

While each note starts at the beginning of a paragraph, it may not end there. Because the same sources are repeated within a section, the sources listed generally extend to the next note. Some articles accessed from newspaper Web sites or from the Factiva database do not list the page number where the article appeared. And in a few cases, I absentmindedly neglected to record the date of an interview. In those instances, the approximate date is given.

1. JANUARY ✴ A NEW YEAR

p. 9, **The pause seemed like:** Starbucks Corporation Fiscal 2004 Annual Report, pp. 11, 19, 40. Starbucks Corporation, "Starbucks Continues Successful Expansion of Music Experience," news release, Feb. 9, 2005, p. 2.

p. 10, **With everything clicking:** Starbucks, "Starbucks Delivers Outstanding Revenue Results in January," news release, Jan. 28, 2004; "Starbucks Reports Strong February Revenues," news release, Feb. 25, 2004; "Starbucks Reports March Revenues," news release, Mar. 31, 2004; "Starbucks Reports April Revenues," news release, Apr. 28, 2004; "Starbucks Reports Strong August Revenues," news release, Aug. 25, 2004; "Starbucks Reports Strong September Comparable Store Sales of 7%," news release, Oct. 6, 2004. Starbucks, "Starbucks Reports Strong Third Quarter Fiscal 2003 Results," news release, July 24, 2003. Starbucks, "Starbucks Announces Outstanding November Revenues," news release, Dec. 1, 2004.

p. 11, **During the trading day:** Jonathan Fuerbringer, "Late Stock

Market Rally Makes 2004 a Winning Year," *The New York Times,* Jan. 1, 2004. David Wighton, "US high-technology brews up a mixed performance in 2004," *Financial Times,* Dec. 30, 2004, p. 16.

p. 11, **Those who hadn't:** William Blair Funds Annual Report, Dec. 31, 2004, pp. 4–5

p. 13, **In Akron, Ohio:** Interviews with Robert Stimpson, June 22, 2005, June 27, 2005, and Feb. 16, 2006.

p. 14, **By contrast Don Hodges:** Interview with Don Hodges, Jan. 24, 2005. David Grainger, "Don't Mess with this Texan: Donald Hodges manages his market-beating fund with a strict eye on ethics," *Fortune,* June 28, 2004, p. 200. Stephanie N. Mehta, "Grading our picks," *Fortune,* Dec. 13, 2004, p. 253.

p. 15, **His hunch paid off:** Starbucks, "Starbucks Announces Strong December Revenues," news release, Jan. 5, 2005; "Starbucks Announces Record First Quarter Fiscal 2005 Results & Raises Full Year EPS Target Range," news release, Jan. 26, 2005.

p. 16, **Beyond the company's comments:** SEC Form 4 filings, 2005 proxy. Interviews with Howard Schultz, Jan. 8 and Jan. 11, 2006.

2. FEBRUARY ✴ THE ANNUAL MEETING

p. 19, **The year's rough start:** Starbucks, "Starbucks Reports Continued Strong Revenue Growth in January," news release, Feb. 2, 2005. Mark Kalinowski, "SBUX: Downgrading from Buy (1M) to Hold (2M); Cutting Target Price," Citigroup: Smith Barney research report, Feb. 2, 2005.

p. 21, **A team of Starbucks staffers:** Interview with Peter Tremblay, Dec. 13, 2005, and e-mail, Mar. 13, 2006.

p. 22, **All this was for a tradition:** Lewis D. Gilbert, *Dividends and Democracy* (Larchmont, N.Y.: American Research Council, 1956), pp. 28–31. Robert E. Wright, *The Wealth of Nations Rediscovered: Integration and Expansion in American Financial Markets, 1780–1850* (Cambridge, U.K.: Cambridge University Press, 2002), pp. 38–41.

p. 23, **The meeting reached:** Allison Linn, "Starbucks lays out aggressive growth plans," Associated Press, March 30, 2004. Jake Batsell, "Stock split, growth attract discussion at annual Starbucks meeting," *Seattle Times,* March 31, 2004. Interview with Kathy Berd, Jan. 9, 2006.

p. 24, **Given last year's highlights:** Tremblay interview. Dan Richman, "Some left out in cold for Starbucks meeting," *Seattle Post-Intelligencer,* Jan. 21, 2005. Interviews with Theresa Collier, Feb. 9 and Feb. 15, 2005.

p. 26, **Soon, though, it was clear:** FactSet Research data. Tremblay interview. Schultz interview, Jan. 8, 2006.

p. 27, **In other words:** Brian K. Bucks, Arthur B. Kennickell, and Kevin B. Moore, "Recent Changes in U.S. Family Finances: Evidence from the 2001 and 2004 Survey of Consumer Finances," *Federal Reserve Bulletin,* Mar. 22, 2006, p. A19.

p. 30, **Shareholders dabbed their eyes:** Monica Soto Ouchi, "No Roast, just thanks to can-do coffee man," *Seattle Times,* Feb. 10, 2005, p. A1.

p. 32, **The reporters:** Allison Linn, "Starbucks chairman lashes out at investors who traded shares down," Associated Press, Feb. 10, 2005. OsterDowJones Commodity Wire, "DJ Market Talk: Reaction to Jan Sales Miffs SBUX's Schultz," edited by John Shipman, Feb. 9, 2005. Kristen Millares Bolt, "Analysts chided for stock dip," *Seattle Post-Intelligencer,* Feb. 10, 2005, p. E1.

3. MARCH ✳ THE STOCK

p. 35, **Following the annual meeting:** Starbucks, "Starbucks Announces Strong Feb. Revenues," news release, Mar. 2, 2005.

p. 36, **As it turned out:** Interview with Ron Margolis, Jan. 24, 2006. Howard Schultz and Dori Jones Yang, *Pour Your Heart Into It: How Starbucks Built a Company One Cup at a Time* (New York: Hyperion, 1997), pp. 69–71.

p. 38, **For those who:** Schultz and Yang, pp. 12, 17–18, 21–22, 25, 40–45. Also Howard Schultz speech to the Young Presidents' Organization in Hong Kong, fall 2005.

p. 39, **Starbucks had been founded:** Interview with Jerry Baldwin, Jan. 13, 2006. Mark Pendergrast, *Uncommon Grounds: The History of Coffee and How It Transformed Our World* (New York: Basic Books, 1999), pp. 308–309. Schultz and Yang, pp. 29–34.

p. 40, **Schultz's autobiography:** Schultz and Yang, pp. 49–53. Starbucks, "Company Profile," June 2005. Interview with Scott Greenburg, Feb. 8, 2005. Schultz interview, Jan. 8, 2006. Schultz and Yang, pp. 55–69.

p. 42, **Almost instinctively:** Kathleen Deveny, "Reality of the '90s Hits Yuppie Brands," *The Wall Street Journal,* Dec. 20, 1990, p. B1.

p. 42, **When the first:** Schultz and Yang, pp. 86, 73–75. Howard Schultz, "When It Comes to 'Establishing the Il Giornale Difference . . . ,' " letter to employees, May 19, 1986.

p. 43, **Dawn Pinaud:** Interview with Dawn Pinaud, fall 2005. Pendergrast, p. 369. Interview with Jennifer Ames-Karreman, Jan. 11, 2006. Schultz and Yang, pp. 86–89.

p. 44, **While the new employees:** Schultz's opening remarks at Starbucks' annual meeting, Feb. 8, 2006. Interview with Christine Day, Feb. 28, 2006. Schultz and Yang, p. 73.

p. 45, **The money came in slowly:** Interview with Herman Sarkowsky, July 22, 2005. Schultz, Starbucks annual meeting, Feb. 8, 2006, Schultz and Yang, pp. 78–79, 89, 90–94, 104, 111–114. Interviews with Greenburg, Baldwin.

p. 47, **After the 1987 purchase:** "Starbucks' logo falls to sirens of correctness," *The Globe and Mail,* Jan. 5, 1993. Starbucks, Private placement offering document, 1991, pp. 18–19.

p. 48, **Craig Foley worked:** Interviews with Craig Foley, Sept. 19 and Sept. 20, 2005; Interview with Jeff Brotman, Oct. 18, 2005. Starbucks, prospectus, May 15, 1992, pp. 28–29, F-9.

p. 49, **To expand beyond:** Starbucks, "Stock Partners in Growth: Stock and Option Plans" and "My Brew" employee newsletter, winter 2005. Schultz and Yang, pp. 133–136. Interview with Dan Levitan, Apr. 14, 2005. Interview with Peter Breck, May 23, 2006. Interview with David DiPietro, Oct. 9, 2006. Schultz and Yang, pp. 180–185.

p. 52, **In preparation for:** Interviews with Levitan, Greenburg, Breck, DiPietro. Samuel Perry, "Wall Street Perks up to Seattle Coffee Maker," Reuters News, June 27, 1992. Interview with Howard Behar, July 20, 2005.

p. 54, **Dan Levitan still:** Interviews with Levitan, Foley, Day, Ames-Karreman. Because Starbucks pays stock options in its first fiscal quarter, Schultz received his 2005 fiscal year options in the last months of 2004. The numbers here are based on the proxy statement filed Dec. 16, 2005. Interviews with Schultz, Oct. 17, 2005; Jan. 8 and Jan. 11, 2006. Schultz remarks at the annual meeting, Feb. 8, 2006. Interviews with Jack Rodgers, Oct. 18, 2005 and Feb. 8, 2006. Margolis interview.

4. APRIL ★ THE GROWTH

p. 61, **To see how:** Interviews with Doug Satzman, Oct. 24, 2005, and March 24, 2006. Interview with Orin Smith, Mar. 30, 2006. Interview with Launi Skinner, July 21, 2005. Dina ElBoghdady, "Pouring It On: The Starbucks Strategy? Locations, Locations, Locations," *Washington Post,* Aug. 25, 2002.

p. 63, **The hotel store:** Michael Casey, Bear Stearns 12th Annual Retail, Restaurant & Consumer Conference, slide titled "Key Drivers of Future Growth," Mar. 9, 2006. Casey, Oct. 2004 analysts meeting, slide titled, "Daypart Utilization (2002–2004). Jim Donald, Bear Stearns conference, Mar. 9, 2006.

p. 64, **Once Starbucks knew:** "Highest Coffee Quotients," ePodunk. com, Mar. 2005. NPD Group, "Anchorage Alaska Tops the List of Most Coffee Shops Per Capita in the U.S.," news release, Mar. 14, 2005.

p. 65, **Research showed:** Interviews with Skinner, Satzman. Jim Donald presentation, Oct. 2004 analysts conference, slide titled "Expanding our Customer Base: Shift in Starbucks Demographics." Also slide titled "Off-Highway Opportunities."

p. 69, **To make this one work:** Arthur Rubinfeld and Collins Hemingway, *Built for Growth: Expanding your Business Around the Corner or Across the Globe* (Upper Saddle River, N.J.: Wharton School Publishing, 2005), pp. 73, 88–89. Satzman, Skinner interviews.

p. 70, **That was somewhat less true:** Andy Serwer, "Hot Starbucks To Go: It's a New American Institution," *Fortune*, Jan. 26, 2004, p. 60. Rodgers interview, Feb. 8, 2006. Smith interview, Jan. 9, 2006. Donald presentation at Oct. 2004 analysts' meeting, slide, "U.S. Average Licensed Store Unit Volume. Ernest Beck, "Starbucks to Acquire Coffee Retailer in Britain," The Wall Street Journal Europe, Apr. 30, 1998, p. 5.

p. 71, **Starbucks needed international:** Interview with Scott Svenson, July 20, 2005. Sharon Zackfia, "Starbucks Corporation: Around the World in 80 Lattes," research report from William Blair & Co., Sept. 29, 2004. Day interview. Interview with Martin Coles, Jan. 5, 2006.

p. 72, **That dependence was clear:** Starbucks, "Starbucks Reports Strong March Revenues," news release, Apr. 6, 2005. Ashley Reed Woodruff, "Starbucks Corp.: Upgrading to Outperform," Bear Stearns, Apr. 15, 2005.

p. 73, **But the next week:** Starbucks, "Starbucks Announces Record Second Quarter Fiscal 2005 Results & Raises Full Year EPS Target," news release, Apr. 27, 2005. Steve Kron, "SBUX: Momentum Shifting Back—Upgrading to Outperform," Goldman Sachs, Apr. 28, 2005.

p. 74, **In recommending that clients:** Benjamin Graham, *The Intelligent Investor* (New York: HarperBusiness Essentials, 1959), pp. 295–301. Warren E. Buffett, *The Essays of Warren Buffett: Lessons for Corporate America,* selected, introduced and arranged by Lawrence A. Cunningham, The Cunningham Group, 2001, pp. 85–89. David Palmer, "Starbucks F2Q-5 EPS and Conference Call Preview," UBS Investment Research, Apr. 25, 2005, p. 6.

p. 76, **It did that by gradually:** Interview with Smith, Jan. 9, 2006. Starbucks, "Starbucks CEO Sees Grounds for Success in International

Markets," news release, Feb. 2, 2000. Starbucks, "Starbucks Reports Strong Third Quarter Results," news release, July 25, 2002. Starbucks, "Starbucks Recaps 2002–2004 Successes and Reiterates Fiscal 2005 Target," news release, Oct. 14, 2004. McDonald's Corp., "Investor Fact Sheet," Jan. 2006. Subway, "Around the World, Restaurant Counts," www.subway.com.

p. 77, **And for those who might:** Day interview. Starbucks, "Asia-Pacific versus U.S.," slide, Oct. 2004 analyst meeting. Starbucks, "Starbucks Outlines International Growth Strategy," news release, Oct. 14, 2004. Starbucks Corp. second quarter earnings conference call, transcript accessed through www.CallStreet.com. "Starbucks Expects China to Become No. 2 Market After US," Dow Jones International News, May 20, 2005. Schultz interview, Jan. 8, 2005.

5. MAY ★ BUYBACKS

p. 81, **The exact date:** Starbucks, "Starbucks Announces Record Second Quarter Fiscal 2005 Results and Raises Full Year EPS Target," news release, Apr. 27, 2005, p. 7. Also Form 10-Q for the quarter ended Apr. 3, 2005, filed with the SEC on May 10, 2005, p. 9. Dow Jones Newswires, "Starbucks Corp, Inst. Equity Holders, 1Q 2005," June 7, 2005.

p. 82, **Stranger still:** Gustavo Grullon and David L. Ikenberry, "What do we know about stock repurchases," *Journal of Applied Corporate Finance* (Spring 2000), p. 47. Also Konan Chan, David Ikenberry, Inmoo Lee, and Yanzhi Wang, "Share Repurchases as a Tool to Mislead Investors: Evidence from Earnings Quality and Stock Performance," (working paper), Sept. 2005, p. 5. Jeremy J. Siegel, *Stocks for the Long Run,* 3rd ed. (New York: McGraw-Hill, 1998), p. 90. Harley-Davidson Inc., "Harley-Davidson Achieves Record Quarterly Revenue and Earnings Per Share," news release, July 13, 2005. Alon Brav, John R. Graham, Campbell R. Harvey, and Roni Michaely, "Payout Policy in the 21st Century," *Journal of Financial Economics,* Sept. 2005, pp. 492, 493, 511.

p. 83, **For that Warren Buffett:** Roger Lowenstein, *Buffett: The Making of an American Capitalist* (New York: Broadway Books, 1995), pp. 185, 193–194. Buffett, *Essays of Warren Buffett,* pp. 67, 135–138. Robert McGough, Suzanne McGee and Cassell Bryan-Low, "Poof! Buyback Binge Now Creates Big Hangover," *The Wall Street Journal,* Dec. 18, 2000, p. C1.

p. 84, **Indeed knowing that investors:** Chan, Ikenberry, Lee, and Wang, p. 3.

p. 84, **The purchases could also:** General Motors Corp., "GM Completes Stock Repurchase Programs Totaling $5 billion, New $4 billion Buyback Program Underway," news release, Mar. 11, 1998, and "GM Reports Record Annual Revenues of $176.6 billion for 1999," news release, Jan. 20, 2000. Scott McCartney, Susan Warren, and Suzanne McGoo, "Flight Plans: Feeling Undervalued, Some Airlines Consider Bumping Stockholders," *The Wall Street Journal,* Mar. 10, 2000, p. A1. Aleksandrs Rozens, "Delta CFO says $3 billion turnaround plan needed for airline's survival," Associated Press, Nov. 28, 2005.

p. 85, **That wasn't a new accusation:** Siegel, pp. 87–92.

p. 85, **In 1982:** Douglas O. Cook, Laurie Krigman, and Chris J. Leach, "An Analysis of SEC Guidelines for Executing Open Market Purchases," *Journal of Business* (April 2003), pp. 289–315.

p. 86, **At the same time:** Interview with Michael J. Mauboussin, Apr. 6, 2006. Interview with David Ikenberry, Apr. 11, 2006. Michael J. Mauboussin, "Clear Thinking about Share Repurchase," Legg Mason Capital Management, Jan. 10, 2006, pp. 1, 4. Standard & Poor's Investment Services data.

p. 87, **Exactly what Starbucks:** Starbucks second quarter news release. Jack Willoughby, "One More Hurdle: America's investment managers are worried about the bull's endurance," *Barron's,* May 2, 2005, accessed from Barron's Online. Starbucks, "Starbucks Announces Strong April Revenues," news release, May 4, 2005. Starbucks, "Starbucks Announces Additional Stock Repurchase Authorization," news release, May 5, 2005. Starbucks, Form 10-Q for the quarter ended Apr. 3, 2005, filed with the SEC May 10, 2005.

p. 88, **Starbucks' public statements:** Interviews with Michael Casey, Oct. 17, 2005, and March 2, 2006. Starbucks, "Starbucks Announces $500 Million Revolving Credit Facility," news release, Aug. 15, 2005.

p. 90, **The sensitivity to price:** Casey interviews. Interview with Kelly Coffey, Goldman Sachs managing director, Equity Capital Markets, Apr. 27, 2006.

p. 90, **That answer was murkier:** Mauboussin interview. Interview with Charlie Munger, vice chairman, Berkshire Hathaway, Nov. 15, 2005. Buffett, *Essays,* p. 136. Interview with Ken Charles Feinberg, Mar. 3, 2006.

6. JUNE ✳ THE INVESTORS

p. 93, **June started on:** Starbucks, "Starbucks Announces Strong May Revenues," news release, June 1, 2005. Hilton Hotels Corp., "Hilton,

Doubletree and Embassy Suites Hotels Sign Deal to Open More Starbucks Stores," news release, June 2, 2005. Starbucks, "Starbucks Demonstrates Commitment to China with an Agreement to Increase Equity Stake in Southern China Operations," news release, June 9, 2005.

p. 94, **There over lunch:** Interviews with Nick Bartolo, May 18, 2005, Oct. 25, 2005, and May 16, 2006, and Mike Utley. TCW, "TCW Concentrated Core Equities," strategy presentation, second quarter 2005. FactSet Research Inc. Interview with Shawn Price, Apr. 28, 2005. Nichola Groom, "Starbucks stock loses steam as sales growth slows," Reuters, Apr. 10, 2005. Morningstar mutual fund data and FactSet Research information on institutional stock holdings.

p. 96, **Even for those institutions:** Tom Lauricella, "Slow and Steady: In Risky Times, Investors Embrace Cautious Dynasty," *The Wall Street Journal,* Nov. 15, 2004, p. A1; Interview with Rob Lovelace, Nov. 2, 2005; Deborah Brewster, "Why Capital is invisible but not invincible," *Financial Times,* Sept. 21, 2004, p. 14; Morningstar, "Analyst Research: American Funds Grth Fund of Amer A," Dec. 20, 2005. Holdings data from FactSet Research. American Funds, "The Growth Fund of America," annual report for the year ended Aug. 31, 2005, pp. 11–14.

p. 98, **Sands Capital:** Eric J. Savitz, "Quarterly Mutual Funds Review—Small is Beautiful," *Barron's,* Oct. 10, 2006, p. L10. Holdings data from FactSet Research.

p. 98, **At TCW:** Bartolo interviews. Interview with Stephen A. Burlingame, May 26, 2006.

p. 100, **In sharp contrast:** Interviews with Theresa Collier, Feb. 9, 2005, Feb. 15, 2005, April 5, 2005, July 22, 2005, Oct. 19, 2005, and Feb. 7, 2006.

p. 102, **But Morningstar wasn't:** Interviews with Carl Sibilski and Pat Dorsey, June 22, 2005, and Sibilski, Feb. 17, 2006. Morningstar analyst notes and reports on Starbucks, Mar. 9, 2005; Apr. 27, 2005, June 15, 2005, July 29, 2005, Aug. 4, 2005, and Nov. 18, 2005.

p. 103, **In Dallas:** Interviews with Don Hodges on Jan. 24, 2005, Mar. 18, 2005, and Aug. 5, 2005, and Eric Marshall, Mar. 18, 2005. Laura Johannes and John Hechinger, "Conflicting Interests: Why a Brokerage Giant Pushes Some Mediocre Mutual Funds," *The Wall Street Journal,* Jan. 9, 2004, p. A1; "Jones Discloses Secret Payments from Fund Firms," *The Wall Street Journal,* Jan. 14, 2005, p. C1, and "SEC Divulges Details of How Edward Jones Pushed Mutual Funds," *The Wall Street Journal,* Dec. 23, 2004, p. C1. Suzanne McGee, "Bustin' Out: A Texas-based 'go-anywhere' fund defies convention—and gets results," *Barron's,* Dec. 29, 2003, p. F4.

p. 106, **Hodges' emotional investment:** Sonya Morris, Hodges Fund research, Morningstar, May 3, 2005.

p. 107, **In Akron, Ohio:** Interviews with Robert Stimpson, June 22, 2005, June 27, 2005, Sept. 29, 2005, Feb. 16, 2006. Oak Associates information from www.oakfunds.com, including Interview with the Portfolio Manager: Rock Oak Core Growth Fund." Christopher Davis, White Oak Select Growth analyst research, Morningstar, Aug. 10, 2005.

p. 109, **Hedge funds have been:** Gregory Zuckerman, "Hedge Funds Grow Popular With Investors," *The Wall Street Journal,* Jan. 3, 2006, p. R12. Zuckerman, "Renaissance's Man: James Simons Does the Math on Fund," *The Wall Street Journal,* July 1, 2005, p. C1. Joseph Nocera, "$100 Billion In the Hands Of a Computer," *The New York Times,* Nov. 19, 2005, p. B1. FactSet Research. Interview with Renaissance spokesman, Nov. 9, 2005.

p. 111, **In a New York office:** Interview with New York short seller, Oct. 5 and Nov. 9, 2005. Interviews with West Coast short seller, Oct. 25, 2005, and Jan. 13, 2006.

7. JULY ✳ THE TRADER

p. 115, **A bachelor party:** Susanne Craig and John Hechinger, "A Wall Street Affair: The Bachelor Party Gets Lots of Attention—Probe Centers on Payments for Fidelity Star's Bash," *The Wall Street Journal,* July 18, 2005, p. A1. Susanne Craig and John Hechinger, "Entertaining Excess: Fishing for Fidelity Business, One Firm Employed Lavish Bait," *The Wall Street Journal,* Aug. 11, 2005, p. A1. "Bids & Offers," *The Wall Street Journal,* July 22, 2005, p. C4. Andrew Caffrey, "Business Brokers say they were expected to woo Fidelity with lavish parties," *The Boston Globe,* July 21, 2005. As of late 2006, Fidelity had not been accused of any wrongdoing.

p. 116, **To a little investor:** Commissions compared from brokerage-firm Web sites. Also David F. Swenson, *Unconventional Success: A Fundamental Approach to Personal Investment* (New York: Free Press, 2005), p. 322.

p. 116, **All those charges:** Securities Industry Association, "Financial Data of NYSE and NASD firms, www.sia.com. Greenwich Associates, "The Legacy of May Day," June 28, 2005. Interview with John Feng, managing director, Greenwich Associates, spring 2006. Andrew Caffrey, "Fidelity reassigns trading chief," *The Boston Globe,* July 12, 2005. Fidelity statistics all come from Statements of Additional Information on each fund: Contrafund for year ended Dec. 31, 2005, in document dated Feb. 28, 2006, p. 13; Magellan, for period ended March 21, 2005, in document dated May 28, 2005, p. 16. Diversified International for year ended Oct. 31, 2005, in document dated Dec. 30, 2005, p. 19; Low-Priced Stock and Growth & Income for year ended July 31, 2005, in document dated Sept. 29, 2005, p. 16.

p. 117, **The stock was still lukewarm:** Matthew J. DiFrisco, "Preview and Analysis of June-Quarter Trends," Thomas Weisel Partners, research report, July 14, 2005, p. 2.

p. 118, **Sharon Zackfia:** William Blair, "Current Better Values List—No. 177," July 12, 2006. Interview with Sharon Zackfia, Sept. 20, 2005.

p. 118, **Keeping a close eye:** Interviews with Chris Rossetti, July 27 and July 28, 2005. Richard Gibson, "PF Chang's Sees Negative 3Q Bistro Comps on 'Soft' Midwest," Dow Jones Newswires, July 27, 2005. Interview with Joe D'Amato, July 27, 2005. Interview with Joe Ricciardi, Knight managing director, broker-dealer trading, and Robby Roberto, July 29, 2005.

p. 124, **The listeners to the call:** Starbucks, "Starbucks Announces Strong Third Quarter Fiscal 2005 Results," news release, July 27, 2005. Starbucks' analyst conference call transcript accessed through www.CallStreet.com. Analyst reports from Sharon Zackfia, William Blair & Co.; John Glass, CIBC World Markets; Dan Geiman, McAdams Wright Ragen; John Ivankoe, JPMorgan, all July 28, 2005.

p. 125, **Trading was at the heart:** Greenwich Associates and John Feng. Interview with Christopher Concannon, Aug. 30, 2005; Interview with Alex Goor, Instinet, July 29, 2005. Knight Trading Group Inc., annual report, 2004, pp. 24–25. Roberto interview.

p. 126, **More change was coming:** Aaron Lucchetti, Susanne Craig, and Dennis K. Berman, "NYSE to Acquire Electronic Trader and Go Public," *The Wall Street Journal,* Apr. 21, 2005, p. A1. Gregory Zuckerman, Aaron Lucchetti, and Dennis K. Berman, "Nasdaq Faces Head-On Assault from NYSE Deal," *The Wall Street Journal,* Apr. 22, 2005, p. A1. Aaron Lucchetti, "Nasdaq Chief Plays Hardball in Instinet Deal," *The Wall Street Journal,* Apr. 25, 2005, p. C1. Interview with Tom Joyce, July 28, 2005.

p. 127, **It turned out that Lime:** Interviews with Michael Richter, Aug. 12, 2005, and Dec. 7, 2005. Interview with Dave Cummings, Tradebot Systems Inc., Aug. 16, 2005. Interview with Brandon Becker, cohead of the securities department at Wilmer Hale, Aug. 26, 2005.

p. 131, **That was clear:** Rossetti interviews. NutriSystem Inc., "Nutri-System, Inc. Announces Record Second Quarter 2005 Revenue Growth," news release, July 27, 2005. Christopher Hinton, "Starbucks

CEO: To Open 30,000 Stores, Including in China," OsterDowJones Commodity Wire, July 28, 2005. E. S. Browning, "Profits Help Lift Nasdaq to Four-Year High," *The Wall Street Journal*, July 29, 2005.

8. AUGUST ★ THE COFFEE MOAT

p. 137, **On August 3:** Starbucks, "Starbucks Announces Strong July Revenues," news release, Aug. 3, 2005. Starbucks, "Launch of Ethos Water Demonstrates Starbucks Leadership Role in Helping Children Around the World Get Clean Water," news release, Aug. 3, 2005. Theresa Howard, "Starbucks takes up cause for safe drinking water," *USA Today*, Aug. 3, 2005, p. B5. Marc Gunther, "Starbucks Stirs up the Water Market: Its new brand of bottled water, Ethos, sells to the rich to help the poor," Fortune.com, Aug. 4, 2005.

p. 138, **On the surface:** Starbucks, Form 10-Q for the quarter ended July 3, 2005, p. 7. Sharon Zackfia, "Starbucks Corporation: Small Acquisition Announced," William Blair & Co. research note, Apr. 12, 2005.

p. 138, **As we heard from investors:** Philip A. Fisher, *Common Stocks and Uncommon Profits and Other Writings* (New York: John Wiley & Sons, 2003), pp. 47–78, 59. Warren E. Buffett, "Chairman's Letter," Berkshire Hathaway Inc., Feb. 28, 1997. Starbucks, "It all starts over a cup of coffee," fiscal 2005 annual report, p. 1.

p. 140, **Trying to quantify:** Cone Inc., "2004 Cone Corporate Citizenship Study: Building Brand Trust." Robert Berner and David Kiley, "Global Brands: *BusinessWeek*/Interbrand rank the companies that best built their images—and made them stick," July 1, 2005, pp. 86–94.

p. 140, **Just as Starbucks:** Interview with Orin Smith, Jan. 9, 2006. Schultz interview, Jan. 8, 2006.

p. 141, **To be a company:** Aja Carmichael, "Pay Grade/Behind the Coffee Counter," *The Wall Street Journal*, Feb. 21, 2006, p. B8.

p. 141, **In the late 1980s:** Schultz and Yang, *Pour Your Heart Into It*, pp. 3–4, 56–57, 102–103, 108–109, 125–130. Schultz interview, Oct. 17, 2005. Starbucks Corp. prospectus, May 15, 1992, p. 24. Jeanne Cummings, "Legislative Grind: Cautiously, Starbucks Put Lobbying on Corporate Menu," *The Wall Street Journal*, Apr. 12, 2005, p. A1.

p. 142, **Starbucks picked up:** Starbucks, "Your Special Blend: A look at Compensation, Benefits, Savings, Stock and other rewards of your partner experience," effective Oct. 1, 2004. Fiscal 2005 Corporate Social Responsibility Annual Report, pp. 68, 17. Matthew Daly, "Starbucks CEO: We spend more on health care than coffee," Associated Press, Sept. 15, 2005. Audrey Lincoff, e-mail response to questions, Sept. 16,

2005. Interview with Jim Donald, Oct. 17, 2005. Carol Hymowitz, "Big Companies Become Big Targets Unless They Guard Images Carefully," *The Wall Street Journal*, Dec. 12, 2005, p. B1.

p. 143, **The Bean Stock:** Starbucks Coffee Company, "Stock Partners in Growth," and "FY05 Bean Stock Grant Awarded," Nov. 17, 2005. Starbucks Corp. Form 10-K for the year ended Oct. 2, 2005, p. 66.

p. 143, **From the earliest days:** Interview with Lon LaFlamme, July 22, 2005.

p. 144, **To keep the experience:** Interviews with Paul Williams, Dec. 21, 2005, and Jan. 10, 2006. Interview with Michelle Gass, June 21, 2005. Interview with John Moore, Dec. 27, 2005. Starbucks, "Starbucks Announces Strong Third Quarter Fiscal 2005 Results," news release, July 27, 2005. Interview with Anne Saunders, June 21, 2005.

p. 145, **The company still spent:** Starbucks Form 10-K, p. 48. Interview with Nancy Kane, Sept. 20, 2005, and e-mail, Apr. 7, 2006. Nichola Groom, "Starbucks treats theater-goers in new promotion," Reuters, Jan. 12, 2005. Marjorie Censer, "A free parking site? It's 'like a miracle,'" *The Princeton Packet*, Dec. 2, 2005. Saunders interview.

p. 146, **The chain got plenty:** "Laugh Lines," *The New York Times*, Nov. 13, 2005, section 4, page 2. "Laugh Lines," *Vancouver Sun*, Oct. 28, 2005, p. D14. David Letterman, *The Late Show with David Letterman*, Nov. 28, 2005. Also "The Wahoo Gazette," www.cbs.com/latenight/lateshow/exclusives/wahoo, Nov. 29, 2005. Craig Ferguson, *The Late, Late Show*, Aug. 1, 2005 and interview with Mitch Graham, spokesman. May Kulthol, comment from Starbucks, via e-mail, May 2, 2006.

p. 147, **Keeping the message:** The company's guiding principles frequently are on the back of company business cards. Day interview. "Starbucks Announces $5 million Education Fund for China," Associated Press, Sept. 19, 2005.

p. 147, **As the world's largest:** Interview with Dub Hay, Starbucks senior vice president, coffee and global procurement, Mar. 1, 2006.

p. 148, **Sometimes the message:** "Starbucks Regrets Charging NYC Rescue Workers for Water," Associated Press, Sept. 25, 2001. "New York City Starbucks charged rescue workers," posting on www.snopes.com, Sept. 29, 2001. Interview with Audrey Lincoff, Aug. 11, 2005. Starbucks, "Beyond the Cup: Corporate Social Responsibility Fiscal 2005 Annual Report," p. 46, and www.starbucks.com/csr.

p. 149, **As the company expanded:** Matthew Mors, "Starbucks Daily Media Recap," internal report, Aug. 25, 2005. Starbucks nutrition information accessed from company Web site, www.starbucks.com., and Starbucks, "You, Starbucks and Nutrition," 2004, pamphlet from company stores. McDonald's nutrition information from www.mcdonalds. com.Starbucks, "Beyond the Cup," p. 46.

p. 150, **Other consumer:** Saunders interview. Blaine Harden, "Java-nomics 101: Today's Coffee is Tomorrow's Debt," *Washington Post,* June 18, 2005. Internal Revenue Service, "TreasuryDirect lets you save by automatic payroll deduction," flyer.

p. 150, **The company also faced:** United States of America before the National Labor Relations Board, Starbucks Corp., Local 660, Industrial Workers of the World, and Charles a/k/a Anthony Polanco, "Order Consolidating Cases, Amended Consolidated Complaint and Notice of Hearing," Nov. 18, 2005. Anthony Ramirez, "Union Steps Up Drive to Organize Starbucks," *The New York Times,* Nov. 26, 2005, p. B5. Steven Gray, "Labor Complaint Hits Starbucks," *The Wall Street Journal,* Nov. 26, 2005, p. A4. Starbucks, "Starbucks and the National Labor Relations Board Enter into Settlement Agreement," news release, March 7, 2006.

p. 151, **The little company:** Interview with Peter Thum and Jonathan Greenblatt, Oct. 17, 2005, and Thum interview, April 28, 2006.

p. 152, **All the while:** Thum and Greenblatt interviews. Schultz interview, Jan. 8, 2006. Interview with Pierre Omidyar spokeswoman, Dec. 9, 2005. Interview with Gerry Lopez, president Starbucks Global Consumer Products, July 21, 2005. Beverage Marketing Corp., "Bottled Water Continues Tradition of Strong Growth in 2005," news release, Apr. 2006. Starbucks, "Starbucks Announces Acquisition of Ethos Water and Commitment to Donate More than $1 Million to Support Clean Water Efforts," news release, Apr. 11, 2005. Starbucks Form 10-K for the year ended Oct. 2, 2005, p. 61.

p. 154, **Rather than create:** "Ethos Water Roadshow" blog, posted on www.ethoswater.com. Jay Leno, from posting on starbucksgossip.type-pad.com, Aug. 5, 2005, and Sanja Gould, Starbucks spokeswoman. Jim Donald, Starbucks Corp. fourth quarter 2005 conference call, Nov. 17, 2005, accessed via www.CallStreet.com.

p. 155, **There was one major hitch:** Starbucks, "Water Quality Issue and Action," Web site posting, Dec. 8, 2005. E-mail from Lara Wyss, Starbucks spokeswoman, Feb. 16, 2006. Interview with Gerry Lopez, Feb. 8, 2006. Thum interview, April 28, 2006. E-mails from Alan Hilowitz, Starbucks spokesman, May 8 and May 21, 2006.

p. 156, **That kind of careful:** Interview with Bruce Milletto, May 5, 2005; Interview with Tom O'Keefe, Jan. 6, 2006. Specialty Coffee Association of America, "Specialty Coffee Retail in the USA, 2004–05," fact sheet.

p. 156, **Some of them even:** "Coffee: In search of great grounds,"

Consumer Reports (Dec. 2004), pp. 47–49. The National Coffee Association of U.S.A., Inc., "National Coffee Drinking Trends, 2005," pp. 50–51. Interview with John Sicher, Editor, *Beverage Digest,* March 6, 2006, and e-mail, April 26, 2006. Specialty Coffee Association fact sheet.

p. 157, **Still none of:** Peet's, www.peets.com. Caribou Coffee, www.Cariboucoffee.com. Monica Soto Ouchi, "Tully's unloads operations in Japan; seeks U.S. growth," *Seattle Times,* Aug. 23, 2005, p. C1.

p. 157, **McDonald's and Dunkin' Donuts:** Janet Adamy, "Brewing Battle: Dunkin' Donuts Tries to Go Upscale, But Not Too Far," *The Wall Street Journal,* Apr. 8, 2006, p. A1.

p. 158, **As with Coca-Cola:** Mark Pendergrast, *For God, Country & Coca-Cola: The Definitive History of the Great American Soft Drink and the Company that Makes It* (New York: Basic Books, 2000), pp. 461–62.

9. SEPTEMBER ★ THE STOCK SPLIT

p. 160, **Starbucks, too, was:** Starbucks, "Starbucks Announces Strong August Revenues," news release, Aug. 31, 2005.

p. 161, **The specific hit:** Susan Buchanan, "Commodities Corner: Hurricane Jolts Java, Too," *Barron's,* Sept. 12, 2005, p. M12. Starbucks, "Beyond the Cup: Corporate Social Responsibility Fiscal 2005 Annual Report," p. 17.

p. 162, **With the stock:** Scott Hillis, "Starbucks sees solid sales, eyes China," Reuters, Sept. 29, 2005. Starbucks, "Starbucks Corporation Announces Fifth 2-1 Stock Split Since Initial Public Offering," news release, Sept. 21, 2005. Starbucks, "Starbucks Announces Additional Stock Purchase Authorization," news release, Sept. 22, 2005. Starbucks. Form 10-K for the year ended Oct. 2, 2005, pp. 41, 62.

p. 163, **The timing:** Fourth quarter 2004 earnings conference call, accessed via CallStreet.com, Nov. 10, 2004, p. 9. Interview with Mary Ekman, Oct. 14, 2005. Casey interview, Feb. 23, 2006.

p. 163, **Why shareholders cared:** Ikenberry interview. Kekst and Company, "Should I Split My Stock," handout to clients. Buffett, *Essays,* pp. 139–141. David Ikenberry and Sundaresh Ramnath, "Underreaction to Self-Selected News Events: The Case of Stock Splits," *Review of Financial Studies* (2002), pp. 491–492.

p. 165, **An intuitive sense:** Interview with Rudy Adams, Oct. 6, 2006, and Diane Ellison, Apr. 18, 2006, of the Greenbills and Greenbills investment club meeting, Jan. 10, 2006.

p. 166, **As the end:** 2005 Form 10-K, p. 64. Starbucks, "Starbucks Announces Record Fourth Quarter and Fiscal Year End 2005 Results," news release, Nov. 17, 2005.

10. OCTOBER ✳ SAME-STORE SALES

p. 167, **The next day:** David Palmer, "September Sales and Earnings Preview," UBS Investment Research, Oct. 3, 2005. Matthew DiFrisco, "Starbucks: Sept. Comp Tops Estimates, Openings Strong," Thomas Weisel Partners, Oct. 5, 2005. John Glass, "Starbucks Corporation: Hot Beverages Warm September Sales," CIBC World Markets, Oct. 5, 2005. Ashley Reed Woodruff, "High Gas Prices? Hurricanes? Not at Starbucks," Bear Stearns, Oct. 6, 2005.

p. 168, **While many numbers:** Interview with Jerry Gallagher, June 14, 2005. Also Meredith Derby, "Chasing Comps," *Women's Wear Daily*, Nov. 15, 2004, p. 20, and Laura Bird and Suzanne McGee, "For Retailers, Monthly Data Lose Value," *The Wall Street Journal*, Mar. 31, 1997, p. C1. Interview with Michael Casey, Jan 5, 2006. Wal-Mart Stores Web site, www.walmartstores.com.

p. 170, **Starbucks began reporting:** Casey interview. Donald interview, Oct. 17, 2005.

In October 2006 Starbucks announced that it would cease reporting monthly same-store sales numbers and report comparable-store growth only quarterly, saying, "We believe that providing the information on a monthly basis encourages a short-term focus and provokes volatility in the company's stock that is not representative of Starbucks' overall and longer-term performance."

p. 171, **Of February's 9 percent growth:** Starbucks news releases, Mar. 2, 2005, April 6, 2005, July 6, 2005, Aug. 3, 2005, and Aug. 31, 2005. Interview with Larry Miller, Oct. 2005. Larry Miller, "MCD: Our Survey Suggests U.S. Sales Could be Up 2.0%–3.0% On Top of a 10.6% Gain a Year Ago," Prudential Equity Group, Oct. 7, 2005.

p. 172, **Occasionally the company's:** Starbucks Corp. third quarter 2004 earnings conference call, transcript accessed through www.CallStreet. com, p. 7. Steven Gray and Amy Merrick, "Latte Letdown: Starbucks Set to Raise Prices," *The Wall Street Journal*, Sept. 2, 2004, p. B1. Lincoff interview, Aug. 11, 2005, and e-mail Sept. 16, 2005. E-mail from Tim Bueneman, Sept. 27, 2004. Richard Gibson, "Starbucks to Raise Beverage Prices Avg of 11 Cents Oct. 6," Dow Jones Newswires, Sept. 27, 2004.

p. 173, **Dan Geiman:** Interview with Dan Geiman, Oct. 19, 2005. Starbucks, news releases: "Starbucks Reports Strong September

Comparable Store Sales Growth of 7%," Oct. 6, 2004. "Starbucks Recaps 2002–2004 Successes and Reiterates Fiscal 2005 Targets," "Starbucks Strong Innovation Pipeline Continues to Surprise and Delight," "Starbucks Lays Out Global Growth Strategy and Expanded Market Opportunity," all Oct. 14, 2004. "Starbucks Begins Fiscal 2005 with Strong October Revenues," Nov. 3, 2004.

p. 174, **In the late 1990s:** Richard Gibson, "Some Meatloaf with the Decaf Latte?" *The Wall Street Journal,* Mar. 16, 1999, p. B1; "Starbucks Corp. Says It Has a Plan To Use Internet for New Category," *The Wall Street Journal,* Apr. 26, 1999, p. B10; "Internet Froth Takes on a New Meaning," *The Wall Street Journal,* May 26, 1999, p. C1; "Starbucks Predicts Profit for Fiscal Year Will Fall 10% Short of Expectations," *The Wall Street Journal,* July 1, 1999, p. A4. Robert Marshall Wells, "Starbucks Stock Take a Big Hit As Outlook Chills," *Seattle Times,* July 1, 1999, p. C1. Richard Gibson, "Starbucks Holders Wake Up, Smell the Coffee and Sell," *The Wall Street Journal,* July 2, 1999, p. B3. Richard Gibson, "Starbucks Cyberspace Mission Returns to Earth After Big Bang on Wall Street," *The Wall Street Journal,* July 23, 1999, p. B4. Robert Marshall Wells, "Starbucks Quiet, But Its Money Talks," *Seattle Times,* July 24, 1999, p. C1. John Cook, "I'll Have a Double-Tall Latte . . . Click! Online Deliverer to Put Drop Boxes in Coffee Shops," *Seattle Post-Intelligencer,* Feb. 15, 2000, p. C1.

p. 175, **Within a few short months:** Starbucks Corp., Form 10-Q for the period Apr. 2, 2000, filed with the SEC, May 17, 2000, p. 6. Starbucks Corp., "Starbucks Reports Fourth Quarter and Fiscal 2000 Results," news release, Nov. 16, 2000.

p. 176, **Orin Smith:** Smith interview, Jan. 9, 2006. Day interview, Feb. 28, 2006. Ames-Karreman interview, Jan. 11, 2006. Starbucks, "The Green Apron Book," Mar. 2004.

p. 177, **Beyond the 2004:** Donald interview. Also Steven Gray, "Coffee on the Double," *The Wall Street Journal,* Apr. 12, 2005, p. B1. Starbucks, "Starbucks Coffee Company Fiscal 2005 Second Quarter Financial Results Prepared Remarks," Apr. 27, 2005, p. 5.

p. 178, **Starbucks wanted:** Paula L. Stepankowsky, "Starbucks Sees Warming Platform in 6,500 Stores By End '08," Dow Jones Newswires, Oct. 5, 2006.

p. 178, **If faster service:** Starbucks, "Starbucks Successful Year in Music Leads to Shift in Paradigm with Introduction of Transformative Approach to Entertainment Industry," Feb. 8, 2006, and "Starbucks Hear Music and Lava Records Set New Precedent in Music; Emerging Band, Antigone Rising, Hits the Charts via 'Hear Music Debut,' "

May 24, 2005. Steven Gray and Ethan Smith, "New Grind: At Star-bucks, a Blend of Coffee and Music Creates a Potent Mix," *The Wall Street Journal,* July 19, 2005, p. A1. Shirley Leung and Jennifer Or-donez, "Musical Taste Maker Emerges for Latte Set," *The Wall Street Journal,* Apr. 29, 2003, p. B1. Starbucks Form 10-K for year ended Oct. 2, 2005, p. 3. "Starbucks Corp., Q3 2005 Earnings Call," accessed from www.CallStreet.com, p. 12.

p. 180, **Sales of sandwiches:** Jim Donald, analyst meeting slide, "Lunch Expansion," Oct. 14, 2004; Form 10-K, p. 3. Also Steven Gray, "Star-bucks Brews Broader Menu—Coffee Chain's Cup Runneth Over with Breakfast, Lunch, Music," *The Wall Street Journal,* Feb. 9, 2005, p. B9.

p. 180, **Right behind:** Starbucks, fourth quarter 2005 earnings conference call, transcript accessed through www.CallStreet.com, pp. 3, 10. David Palmer, "Starbucks Corp.: Takeaways from UBS Sponsored Meeting with Management," UBS Investment Research, Sept. 28, 2005.

p. 181, **Joe Kernen:** Joe Kernen, co-emcee, CNBC–Wall Street Journal Executive Leadership Awards 2005, Nov. 8, 2005. Also "Journal, CNBC Give Awards to Executives," *The Wall Street Journal,* Nov. 9, 2005, p. B4.

p. 182, **Remember Chantico?:** Bruce Horovitz, "Starbucks pours not-better-for-you chocolate drink," *USA Today,* Oct. 14, 2004, p. B1; Don-ald, second quarter remarks, p. 3. Postings on www.starbucksgossip.typepad.com, May 16, 2005, and following. Elizabeth M. Gillespie, "Starbucks pulling Chantico drinking chocolate from menu," Associ-ated Press, Dec. 28, 2005; "In rare flop, Starbucks scraps chocolate drink," Reuters, Feb. 10, 2006.

p. 183, **More successful specialty drinks:** Interviews with Michelle Gass, senior vice president, category management, and Janet Parks, July 21, 2005. Interview with Brad Stevens, Dec. 12, 2005.

p. 184, **How much would all that:** Casey interview, Jan. 5, 2006.

p. 186, **It also changed:** Donald interview. Starbucks, "Starbucks Reports Strong October Revenues," news release, Nov. 3, 2005.

11. NOVEMBER ✳ THE ANALYST

p. 191, **On November 17:** E.S. Browning, "Stocks Rise as Oil Falls, GM Revives, Stirring Fresh Talk of Year-End Rally," *The Wall Street Jour-nal,* Nov. 18, 2005, p. C1. Starbucks, "Starbucks Announces Record Fourth Quarter and Fiscal Year End 2005 Results," news release, Nov. 17, 2005.

p. 192, **More important:** Interviews with Sharon Zackfia, Nov. 18, 2005, Dec. 1–2, 2005, July 24, 2006.

p. 193, **She reviewed:** Zackfia came up with a 28 percent increase for year-end earnings-per-share because her spreadsheet calculates earnings per share out to several decimal points. In this case, she was comparing 60.6 cents a share in fiscal 2005 with 47.3 cents a year ago. Zackfia, "Starbucks Corporation: Strong End of Excellent Fiscal 2005," William Blair research note, Nov. 18, 2005.

p. 194, **Such detail work:** Randall Smith, Susanne Craig, and Deborah Solomon, "Wall Street Firms to Pay $1.4 Billion to End Inquiry," *The Wall Street Journal,* Apr. 29, 2003, p. A1. Ken Brown, "Wrongway Pundits Still Getting Paid," *The Wall Street Journal,* Feb. 23, 2004, p. A1. Susanne Craig and Ken Brown, "Though Pay Is Down, Elite Stock Analysts Are Hot Commodity," *The Wall Street Journal,* Mar. 29, 2004, p. C1.

p. 195, **Trading commissions:** Justin Schack, "Sins of commissions," *Institutional Investor,* Dec. 14, 2005. Greenwich Associates, "U.S. Institutions Tighten Soft-Dollar Spending Policies," news release, May 23, 2005. Arden Dale, "SEC is Close to Clarifying Soft-Dollar Rule," *The Wall Street Journal,* June 26, 2006, p. C7. Susanne Craig, "Can We Talk? Lehman Hopes So," *The Wall Street Journal,* May 4, 2006, p. C1. Interview with Alan Johnson, Johnson Associates, July 31, 2006.

p. 196, **The other radical change:** Landon Thomas Jr., "Wall Street's Harsh New Reality," *The New York Times,* Aug. 17, 2003, p. 1. Feng interview, spring 2006. "Milestone: The 25th Annual Growth Stock Conference," William Blair *Client Focus,* third quarter 2005, p. 13. Gregory Zuckerman and Erik Portanger, "One-on-Ones: Investor Meetings with Executives Surge, Add a Risk of Data Leaks," *The Wall Street Journal,* Aug. 31, 2004, p. A1. Stephen Labaton, "Judge Dismisses Disclosure Suit Brought by S.E.C. Against Siebel," *The New York Times,* Sept. 2, 2005, p. 9.

p. 199, **In addition to wooing:** Zackfia, "Starbucks Corporation: Key Takeaways from Recent Meeting with Management," William Blair research note, Oct. 21, 2005. Interviews with Dan Geiman, Apr. 18 and Oct. 29, 2005. E-mails following management meeting. Geiman, "Starbucks Corp.: Meeting with Management," McAdams Wright Ragen research note, Oct. 6, 2005.

p. 202, **The morning after:** Zackfia interviews. Interviews with Bob Newman, Nov. 17 and Dec. 1, 2005. Zackfia, "TurboChef Technologies, Inc.: Expansion of Starbucks Warming Test Adds Enhanced Visibility on Sales," William Blair research note, Nov. 18, 2005. TurboChef never actually announced the two big contracts in 2005.

p. 206, **Despite its track record:** Brinker analyst list, www.brinker.com. Starbucks list from investor relations section of www.starbucks.com and Ekman interview. Newman interview. Zackfia, "Starbucks Corporation: Around the World in 80 Lattes," William Blair report, Sept. 29, 2004. William Blair "2004 Annual Review," p. 6.

p. 208, **Two weeks later:** Interview with Brad Stevens, Dec. 12, 2005. Starbucks, "Holiday FY06 OOS Campaign Survey," internal memo. E.S. Browning, "Nikkei, Gold Hit Milestones, Dow Nears One," *The Wall Street Journal,* Dec. 2, 2006. "Starbucks Announces Strong November Revenues," news release, Dec. 1, 2005. Zackfia, "Starbucks Corporation: Excellent Start to Holiday Season," William Blair research note, Dec. 1, 2005.

12. DECEMBER ✳ THE EARNINGS

p. 216, **The pressure on:** John R. Graham, Campbell R. Harvey, and Shiva Rajgopal, "The Economic Implications of Corporate Financial Reporting," *Journal of Accounting and Economics* 40 (2005): 1, 12, 14–20.

p. 217, **In notorious cases:** Dionne Searcey, Shawn Young, and Kara Scannell, "Ebbers is Sentenced to 25 Years for $11 Billion WorldCom Fraud," *The Wall Street Journal,* July 14, 2005, p. A1. Jonathan Weil, "Missing Numbers—Behind Wave of Corporate Fraud: A Change in How Auditors Work," *The Wall Street Journal,* Mar. 25, 2004. Gary McWilliams and John Emshwiller, "Trial Begins with a Tale of Two Enrons," *The Wall Street Journal,* Feb. 1, 2006, p. C1.

p. 217, **Similarly in the summer:** Mark Maremont and Rick Brooks, "Report Shows How Krispy Kreme Sweetened Results," *The Wall Street Journal,* Aug. 11, 2005, p. A1. Krispy Kreme, "Krispy Kreme Announces Completion of Special Committee Investigation," news release, Aug. 10, 2006.

p. 218, **The rapt attention:** Robert D. Hershey Jr., "A Flourishing Industry, Predicting What Is and Isn't Flourishing," *The New York Times,* May 17, 1998, p. 7. Zacks overview, www.zacks.com. Interview with Len Zacks, Jan. 2006.

p. 219, **In the 1990s:** Ken Hoover, "Money Managers Returning to Growth," *Investor's Business Daily,* Feb. 9, 2005, p. A8. Harris Collingwood, "The Earnings Cult," *The New York Times Magazine,* June 9,

2002, p. 68. Greenwich Associates, "U.S. Companies Limit Financial Communications," news release, Mar. 1, 2005. Kekst and Company, "To Guide Or Not To Guide," report for clients, Feb. 2006. Gregory Zuckerman, "CEOs Turn Mum About Projecting Earnings," *The Wall Street Journal,* Mar. 1, 2005, p. C1.

p. 220, **Michael Casey:** Casey interview, Oct. 17, 2005. Graham, Harvey, and Rajgopal, pp. 14–16.

p. 221, **Orin Smith:** Smith interviews, Jan. 9, 2006, and Mar. 30, 2006.

p. 223, **Though the company:** Diya Gullapalli, "Outside Audit: Lease Restatements Are Surging," *The Wall Street Journal,* Apr. 20, 2005, p. C4. Starbucks, Form 10-Q for the quarter ended Jan. 2, 2005, pp. 4, 11. Nichola Groom, "Starbucks delays 10-Q to change lease accounting," Reuters, Feb. 11, 2005. Casey interview, Oct. 17, 2005.

p. 225, **By most standards:** Starbucks, Form 10-K for the year ended Oct. 2, 2005, pp. 47–49, 58–59, 61, 63–64, 71. The review of Starbucks' accounting included the following: Interview with Charles Mulford, accounting professor at Georgia Tech, Sept. 15, 2005, and e-mails on Sept. 15, 2005, Dec. 21, 2005, and Dec. 31, 2005. Interviews with West Coast hedge fund manager, Sept. 8, 2005, Oct. 25, 2005, and Jan. 13, 2006, and e-mail Sept. 17, 2005, and Jan. 20, 2006. Interview with Albert Meyer, 2nd Opinion Research, Dec. 28, 2005. Home Depot, first quarter earnings conference call, May 17, 2005, accessed via www.CallStreet.com. Home Depot, Form 10-Q for the quarter ended May 1, 2005, pp. 8, 15.

p. 229, **Curious about:** Casey interviews, Jan. 5, 2006, and Feb. 23, 2006.

13. JANUARY ★ THE ANNUAL REVIEW

p. 234, **Both groups:** Interviews with Nancy Scinto, June 23, 2005, Sept. 7, 2005, Nov. 18, 2005, and Feb. 23, 2006. James B. Arndorfer, "Chicago Trust Group Defects to Voyageur," *Crain's Chicago Business,* Oct. 18, 1999, p. 48. Stock ownership data, FactSet Research, and Thomson Financial.

p. 236, **The stock-picking strategy:** Minutes, Joint Meeting of the Board of Trustees and the Investment Advisory Committee, Employment Retirement System of Texas, June 4, 2004, pp. 5, 7. "Hirings," *Pensions and Investments,* June 14, 2004, p. 20. "Nevada Selects U.S. Equity Managers," *Money Management Letter,* Nov. 5, 2004. "Illinois Teachers calls on 5 equity managers," *Pensions and Investments,* Nov. 15, 2004, p. 30.

p. 237, **By late fall:** The team already had officially reviewed its Starbucks investment for the year, but pulled together current information and walked through the updated information for the purposes of this project. Those at the Nov. 18, 2005, review were Charles F. Henderson, senior managing director and chief investment officer for equities; Jerold L. Stodden, senior portfolio manager; David J. Cox, director of equity investments and senior portfolio manager; Nancy M. Scinto, director of research and senior portfolio manager; Matt Neska, research associate; Steve Rusnak, senior analyst and senior portfolio manager; Rebecca Cook, senior analyst; Nancy Herringer, senior equity trader, and Ryan Larson, equity trader.

p. 245, **Several weeks later:** Valuation Statement, Profit Prophets Investment Club, Dec. 31, 2005. Attending the Jan. 9, 2006, meeting were Elizabeth Peckham, Laura Wharton, Chris Young, Kathy Berd, Laurakay P. Vernon, Jeanette Coate, Jacque Wilder, and Judy Lear.

p. 245, **The club formed:** Interviews with Judy Lear, Apr. 16, 2005, Oct. 19, 2005, Feb. 28, 2006.

p. 246, **On a rainy Monday night:** Interview with Kenneth S. Janke Sr., Sept. 29, 2005. During 2005 the organization began using the name "BetterInvesting." Calmetta Y. Coleman, "Beardstown Ladies Add a Disclaimer to That Warm Tale," *The Wall Street Journal*, Feb. 27, 1998, p. A1. Calmetta Y. Coleman, "Beardstown Ladies 'Fess Up to Big Goof," *The Wall Street Journal*, Mar. 18, 1998, p. C1. Christopher Lukach, BetterInvesting investment club statistics, via e-mail, Sept. 28, 2005.

p. 247, **With the steep decline:** Cynthia Kyle, "100 Top Companies: Our Annual Survey," *BetterInvesting* magazine, Apr. 2005, pp. 33–38.

p. 247, **Maury Elvekrog:** Maury Elvekrog, "Engineering a Portfolio Turnaround," May 2005, pp. 13–16; "Early Success Can Be Deceiving," Sept. 2005, pp. 16–18; "Avoiding Humdrum Results," March 2006, pp. 14–16, all in *BetterInvesting*. Interview with Maury Elvekrog, Feb. 14, 2006. Interview with Joan Porter, Feb. 16, 2005.

p. 248, **Lots of other clubs:** Kyle, p. 36. Janke interview.

p. 249, **For the Profit Prophets:** Bonnie Biafore, *Stock Selection Handbook* (Madison Heights, Mich.: National Association of Investors, 2003), pp. 3–7, 19.

EPILOGUE: ✳ ANOTHER NEW YEAR

p. 255, **This new year:** Starbucks, "Starbucks Announces Record First Quarter Fiscal 2006 Results, Strong January 2006 Revenues, Raises Earnings Targets," news release, Feb. 1, 2006. Starbucks, first quarter 2006 earnings conference call, Feb. 1, 2006, accessed via www.

CallStreet.com., pp. 2–3, 5–6, 9. Schultz interview, Jan. 11, 2006. Steven Gray and Kate Kelly, "Starbucks Plans to Make Debut in Movie Business," *The Wall Street Journal,* Jan. 12, 2006, p. A1.

p. 259, **The next day:** E.S. Browning, "Despite Oil Drop, Dow Falls 101.97 as Investors Fret," *The Wall Street Journal,* Feb. 3, 2006, p. C1.

p. 259, **Over twelve months:** Starbucks, combined from Form 10-K for the year ended Oct. 2, 2005, p. 64, and Form 10-Q for the quarter ended Jan. 1, 2006, p. 23.

p. 260, **I made plans:** Sibilski interview, Feb. 17, 2006. Carl Sibilski, "Starbucks," Morningstar, Dec. 27, 2005, and Dec. 30, 2005. Mike Trigg, "How to Spot a Great Growth Stock," Morningstar, Feb. 3, 2006.

p. 261, **As before investment:** Stimpson interview, Feb. 16, 2006. Morningstar, "Total Returns: Rock Oak Core Growth," July 31, 2006.

p. 262, **At the same time:** Scinto interview, Feb. 23, 2006. Voyageur Asset Management Inc., Large Cap Growth Equity Fourth Quarter 2005 summary, accessed from www.Voyageur.net. Mylene Mangalindan, "Amazon's Earnings Tumble 43%," *The Wall Street Journal,* Feb. 3, 2006, p. A3.

p. 264, **While the pros:** Starbucks volunteer training session, Feb. 7, 2006.

p. 265, **All the planning:** Jim Donald on the shareholder needing medical treatment, Bear, Stearns Retail, Restaurants & Consumer Conference, Mar. 9, 2006, transcript accessed via www.CallStreet.com, p. 3. Also, Starbucks, "Starbucks Unprecedented Performance Continues into 2006," and "Starbucks Coffee Company Increases International Store Count by More than 20 Percent Year Over Year," news releases, both Feb. 8, 2006. Monica Soto Ouchi, "Everyone goes home happy from the Starbucks-palooza," *Seattle Times,* Feb. 9, 2006, p. D1. Kristen Millares Bolt, "Star of Starbucks' show remains rapid growth," *Seattle Post-Intelligencer,* Feb. 9, 2006, p. D1.

p. 269, **Beyond Tony Bennett:** After this manuscript was completed, the company raised its long-term target to 20,000 stores in the United States and 20,000 internationally. Starbucks, "Starbucks Coffee Company Outlines Core Strategies to Continue Delivering Long-Term Shareholder Value in Sixth Biennial Analyst Conference," news release, Oct. 5, 2006.

p. 270, **Theresa Collier:** Collier interview, Feb. 7, 2006.

p. 272, **On the afternoon of:** Rodgers interview, Feb. 8, 2006.

Selected Bibliography

Bedbury, Scott, with Stephen Fenichell. *A New Brand World: 8 Principles for Achieving Brand Leadership in the 21st Century.* New York: Penguin Books, 2002.

Bernstein, Peter L. *Capital Ideas: The Improbable Origins of Wall Street.* New York: The Free Press, 1992.

Briloff, Abraham J. *More Debits than Credits: The Burnt Investor's Guide to Financial Statements.* New York: Harper & Row, 1976.

Buffett, Mary, and David Clark. *Buffettology: The Previously Unexplained Techniques That Have Made Warren Buffett the World's Most Famous Investor.* New York: Fireside, 1997.

Buffett, Warren E. *The Essays of Warren Buffett: Lessons for Corporate America.* Selected, arranged, and introduced by Lawrence A. Cunningham, The Cunningham Group, 1st rev. ed., 2001.

Dorsey, Pat. *The Five Rules for Successful Stock Investing: Morningstar's Guide to Building Wealth and Winning in the Market.* Hoboken, NJ: John Wiley & Sons, 2004.

Egerton, Henry C. *Handling Protest at Annual Meetings.* New York: The Conference Board, Inc., 1971.

Emerson, Frank D., and Franklin C. Latcham. *Shareholder Democracy: A Broader Outlook for Corporations.* Cleveland: The Press of Case Western Reserve University, 1954.

Fisher, Philip A. *Common Stocks and Uncommon Profits and Other Writings.* Hoboken, NJ: John Wiley & Sons, 2003.

Gilbert, Lewis D. *Dividends and Democracy.* Larchmont, NY: American Research Council, 1956.

Graham, Benjamin. *The Intelligent Investor: A Book of Practical Counsel.* New York: HarperBusiness Essentials, 2003.

Koehn, Nancy F. *Brand New: How Entrepreneurs Earned Consumers' Trust from Wedgewood to Dell.* Boston: Harvard Business School Press, 2001.

Livingston, J. A. *The American Stockholder,* Philadelphia: J. B. Lippincott Company, 1958.

Lowenstein, Roger. *Buffett: The Making of an American Capitalist.* New York: Broadway Books, 1995.

————. *Origins of the Crash: The Great Bubble and Its Undoing.* New York: Penguin Books, 2004.

Malkiel, Burton. *A Random Walk Down Wall Street: The Time-Tested Strategy for Successful Investing.* New York: W. W. Norton & Company, 2003.

Moore, John. *Tribal Knowledge: Business Wisdom Brewed from the Grounds of Starbucks' Corporate Culture.* Chicago: Kaplan Publishing, 2006.

Oldenburg, Ray. *The Great Good Place: Cafes, Coffee Shops, Bookstores, Bars, Hair Salons and other Hangouts at the Heart of a Community.* New York: Marlowe & Co., 1999.

Pendergrast, Mark. *For God, Country and Coca-Cola: The Definitive History of the Great American Soft Drink and the Company That Makes It.* New York: Basic Books, 2000.

————. *Uncommon Grounds: The History of Coffee and How It Transformed Our World.* New York: Basic Books, 1999.

Rubinfeld, Arthur, with Collins Hemingway. *Built for Growth: Expanding Your Business Around the Corner or Across the Globe.* Upper Saddle River, NJ: Wharton School Publishing, 2005.

Schultz, Howard, and Dori Jones Yang. *Pour Your Heart Into It: How Starbucks Built a Company One Cup at a Time.* New York: Hyperion, 1997.

Siegel, Jeremy J. *Stocks for the Long Run: The Definitive Guide to Financial Market Returns and Long-Term Investment Strategies.* New York: McGraw-Hill, 2002.

Smith, Orin C. "Transforming Whole Beans to 'Coffee Experience,' " in *Investing Under Fire: Winning Strategies from the Masters for Bulls, Bears, and the Bewildered,* edited by Alan R. Ackerman. Princeton, NJ: Bloomberg Press, 2003.

Swenson, David F. *Pioneering Portfolio Management: An Unconventional Approach to Institutional Investment.* New York: The Free Press, 2000.

————. *Unconventional Success: A Fundamental Approach to Personal Investment.* New York: Free Press, 2005.

Wright, Robert E. *The Wealth of Nations Rediscovered: Integration and Expansion in American Financial Markets, 1780–1850.* Cambridge, England: Cambridge University Press, 2002.

Acknowledgments

An undertaking like this can become a reality only with the help of those who are willing to take the time to grant interviews, offer their expertise, and provide direction. I am incredibly grateful for the support and cooperation I received from many, many people, especially those who shared the goal of bringing the stock market to life.

I chose Starbucks, not the other way around, and it's never comfortable for a person or an entity to be put under the microscope. After some initial reluctance, Starbucks officials agreed to grant interviews, initially approaching the project with all the joy of a patient headed to a colonoscopy. But once onboard, those who agreed to interviews were always gracious and friendly.

In addition to scheduled interviews, Howard Schultz took time from a busy weekend to spend part of a Sunday sharing his vision for the company and answering a stream of questions. Michael Casey patiently walked through accounting issues, sales data, details about buybacks, and a range of other financial queries over several sessions, always offering specific and straightforward answers. Orin Smith also sat down for several hours to thoughtfully share company history and perspective. I especially appreciate their time, candor, and patience.

The folks in the global communications and media relations group were always upbeat, even when they were rejecting some of my many requests. Sanja Gould, T. May Kulthol, Lara Wyss, and Audrey Lincoff bore the brunt of the many phone calls, e-mails, and follow-up questions, and sat through many of the formal interviews, though Valerie Hwang, Alan Hilowitz, Chris Gorley, Christy Salcido, and Kristine Hung also had their share of the fun.

I am immensely appreciative of these current and former Starbucks employees, directors, early investors, and other key players in the company's success who generously gave their insights and recollections in interviews and discussions that often ran a couple of hours: Jennifer Ames-Karreman, Jerry Baldwin, Howard Behar, Peter Breck, Kevin Carothers, Major Cohen, Martin Coles, Christine Day, Terry Diamond, David DiPrieto, Mary Ekman, Michael Epsteen, Craig Foley, Michelle Gass, Jonathan Greenblatt, Scott Greenburg, Dub Hay, Nancy Kane, Lon LaFlamme, Olden Lee, Dan Levitan, Gerardo Lopez, Yves Mizrahi, John Moore, Janet Parks, Dawn Pinaud, Arnie Prentice, Jack Rodgers, Arthur Rubinfeld, Herman Sarkowsky, Doug Satzman, Anne Saunders, Jamie Shennan, Launi Skinner, May Snowden, Brad Stevens, Scott Svenson, Sandra Taylor, Peter Thum, Peter Tremblay, and Paul Williams.

A number of intelligent and thoughtful individual investors were very helpful. In particular, Theresa Collier, Charles and Marjorie Jenner, Judy Lear, Laurakay Vernon, the Profit Prophets, Lily Yamada, Rudy Adams, Diane Ellison, and the Greenbills investment club spent a great deal of time sharing their experiences, philosophies, and personal information.

The investment, accounting, and finance professionals and academics who offered their vision and methods were absolutely invaluable. I am especially grateful to Nancy Scinto and Ryan Larson at Voyageur; Don Hodges, Preston Silvey, and Eric Marshall of the Hodges Fund; Nick Bartolo, Steve Burlingame, and Mike Utley at TCW; Pat Dorsey and Carl Sibilski at Morningstar; Robert Stimpson of Oak; Rob Lovelace and Chuck Freadhoff at American Funds; Chuck Mulford, Jerry Gallagher and Neal Aronson; Charlie Munger of Berkshire Hathaway; Chris Lukach, Ken Janke, and Maury Elvekrog from BetterInvesting; Ralph Acampora, Neil

Baron, Richard Baum, Kelly Coffey, Ken Charles Feinberg, Joe Hargett, Campbell Harvey, David Ikenberry, Michael Mauboussin, Shawn Price, Jack Rothstein, and Len Zacks.

The trading section would never have come to life without the immeasurable help of Margaret Wyrwas and her colleagues at Knight, especially Tom Joyce, Chris Rossetti, and Joe D'Amato, who let me see the trading floor exactly as it was. At Knight, Robby Roberto, Joe Ricciardi, Leonard Amoruso, Jenkins Marshall, James Smyth, Alexander Wang, Joseph Mazzella, and Frank Grampone also made time for interviews. Michael Richter, Alex Goor, Christopher Concannon, Dave Cummings, John Feng, and Brandon Becker patiently walked me through their vast understanding of this complex and fascinating part of the market.

Similarly, the insight into the work of analysts couldn't have happened without the thoughtful participation of Sharon Zackfia, Bob Newman, and Tony Zimmer at William Blair. Many analysts agreed to multiple interviews over the course of the year, including Zackfia, Andrew Barish, Dan Geiman, John Glass, Larry Miller, David Palmer, and Ashley Reed Woodruff. Matt DiFrisco, Mark Kalinowski, and Nicole Miller were also helpful.

Understanding the coffee business and retail real estate wouldn't have been possible without the additional aid of Michael Coles, Cynthia Chang, Brett Smith, Nicholas Cho, and Tom O'Keefe, as well as Bruce Milletto, George Howell, Aaron Kiel, Mike Ferguson, Todd Walls, and Dave Ward.

A special thanks goes to Jeff Brotman, Richard Galanti, Gary Kelly, Larry Rand, and Carol Cone, busy executives who took time out for interviews that filled in gaps and provided crucial background information. Entire sections of this book wouldn't have happened without the aid of Terry, Charlotte, Jim, Donna, Richard, Mike, and Mark—all investment titans who didn't want to be quoted but who devoted significant effort in making this story better and more informative.

Larry Ingrassia conceived the idea of following a year in the life of a stock and was nice enough to leave it behind when he moved on to a fabulous new job. Rose Ellen D'Angelo of the *Journal's* book group relayed the idea and let me run with it, providing much needed assistance at crucial moments. Ken Wells, a prince of an editor and a person, was unwavering in his enthusiasm and support, especially during some difficult days. My former *Journal* colleagues Larry Rout, Ann Zimmerman, and Dave Kansas offered indispensable feedback; Brooks Barnes, Ken Brown, Kevin Helliker, Aaron Lucchetti, Randy Smith, and Jonathan Weil gave much needed assists. Dick Gibson, the Dow Jones Newswires' outstanding restaurant reporter, shared some of his vast Starbucks knowledge, and Steven Gray and Janet Adamy, the *Journal's* excellent Starbucks beat reporters, and their bureau chief Bryan Gruley, couldn't have been more collegial about the turf invasion.

At Crown, John Mahaney was a dream editor whose humor, calm demeanor, and penetrating insights shaped the story and took the sting out of a challenging project. His assistant Lindsay Orman, copy editor Mary Flower, and senior production editor Cindy Berman provided the necessary magic to make a drafty manuscript into a beautiful book.

I'd be remiss if I didn't also thank "my" baristas, Priscilla in downtown Dallas and Heather in Lake Highlands, both longtime Starbucks employees who have always done their jobs with tremendous energy and exuberance.

Finally, I am deeply indebted to and immensely grateful for the support and love of my family, especially as days and nights and weekends all melted into one endless workday. My daughters, Abby and Jenny, patiently put up with months of travel and months more of writing and revision that cut into family vacations, high school celebrations, and prime family time and required us to test far more Starbucks' products than any human should. And triple-venti thank-yous to Scott, my sounding board, idea man, morning coffee maker, first reader, co-worker, partner in crime, husband, and best friend, who understands both the pain and the pure joy that comes with high expectations.

Index

ABOUT THE AUTHOR

KAREN BLUMENTHAL has been a financial journalist for more than twenty-five years, including two decades as a reporter, editor, and Dallas bureau chief at *The Wall Street Journal*. She has written about a wide range of financial and corporate subjects and has appeared on *ABC World News Tonight*, the *Today Show*, and the *PBS Nightly Business Report*. *Kiplinger's* magazine named *Grande Expectations* one of the five best investing reads of 2007. Karen is also the author of two award-winning books for young people and the upcoming *The Wall Street Journal. Guide to Starting Your Financial Life*. While she occasionally splurges on a nonfat, mocha latte, her Starbucks' beverage of choice is a basic, tall drip coffee.

Printed in the United States
by Baker & Taylor Publisher Services